W0231566

The Filmmaker's Pocket Reference

Blain Brown

Focal Press
Boston London

Focal Press is an imprint of Butterworth–Heinemann.

Copyright © 1994 by Blain Brown.

All rights reserved.

No part of this publication may be reproduced, stored in a retrieval system, or transmitted, in any form or by any means, electronic, mechanical, photocopying, recording, or otherwise, without the prior written permission of the publisher.

Recognizing the importance of preserving what has been written, it is the policy of Butterworth–Heinemann to have the books it publishes printed on acid-free paper, and we exert our best efforts to that end.

Library of Congress Cataloging-in-Publication Data

Brown, Blain.
The filmmaker's pocket reference / Blain Brown.
p. cm.
Includes index.
ISBN 0-240-80058-3
1. Cinematography—Handbooks, manuals, etc.
I. Title.
TR850.B76 1994 93-43461
778.5—dc20

British Library Cataloguing-in-Publication Data
A catalogue record for this book is available from the British Library.

Butterworth-Heinemann
313 Washington Street
Newton, MA 02158

Contents

Figures

Tables

Introduction

Film and video production becomes more technically involved every day. With the advent of new technology, more advanced equipment, the film-video interface, and more involved post-production techniques, the production technician is faced with situations and equipment that require a knowledge of specific data and methodology.

To be fully prepared to deal with every situation, the filmmaker would need to carry an entire reference library: film data sheets, lens charts, photometric data, HMI sync charts, ampacity lists, etc. At best, this is an inconvenience, and at worst, all but impossible. Production is a highly mobile operation; a premium is always placed on lightening the load.

The Filmmaker's Pocket Reference consolidates key data and methods relevant to the work of the cinematographer, videographer, lighting director, gaffer, electrician, grip, camera assistant, set builder, and rigger. Relevant information is also included for production managers, location managers, and production assistants, particularly in regard to their relationship with the technical departments.

SECTION 1

Camera

Table 1.1 Film Camera Data

35mm Cameras

Aaton 8-35

Silent	Yes
Shutter Angle (°)	180
Power (V)	16 DC
Lens Mount	Aaton bayonet
Size of Magazine (ft.)	200, 400
Weight (lb.)	11 (200')
Note	Designed for hand-held work

Arriflex 535

Silent	Yes
Shutter Angle (°)	11-180
Speed (fps)	3-50
Power (V)	24 DC
Lens Mount	PL
Registration	2-pin
Size of Magazine (ft.)	400, 1000

Arriflex BL IV

Silent	Yes
Shutter Angle (°)	144, 172.8, 180
Speed (fps)	6-40
Power (V)	12 DC
Lens Mount	PL
Registration	2-pin
Size of Magazine (ft.)	400, 1000
Weight (lb.)	32
Note	Interchangeable aperture plates

Arriflex BL III

Silent	Yes
Shutter Angle (°)	144, 172.8, 180
Speed (fps)	6-40
Power (V)	12 DC
Lens Mount	PL
Registration	2-pin
Size of Magazine (ft.)	400, 1000
Weight (lb.)	28.5
Note	Interchangeable aperture plates

Arriflex BL I, II

Silent	Yes
Shutter Angle (°)	180
Speed (fps)	6-50
Power (V)	12 DC
Lens Mount	Arri B-mount

Table 1.1 Film Camera Data *(continued)*

Registration	2-pin
Size of Magazine (ft.)	400, 1000
Weight (lb.)	28
Arriflex III	
Silent	No
Shutter Angle (°)	135, 144, 172.8, 180
Speed (fps)	6-120
Power (V)	12 DC
Lens Mount	PL
Registration	1-pin
Size of Magazine (ft.)	200, 400, 1000
Weight (lb.)	17 (400')
Note	Will run in reverse and stop frame
Arriflex IIC	
Silent	No
Shutter Angle (°)	165[1]
Speed (fps)	8-35
Power (V)	16, 24, 32
Lens Mount	Arri B-mount
Size of Magazine (ft.)	200, 400
Weight (lb.)	12
Note	Optimum HMI sync with 165° shutter at 24 fps = 51.7 Hz
Arriflex IIC High Speed	
Silent	No
Shutter Angle (°)	165
Speed (fps)	8-80
Power (V)	32 DC
Lens Mount	Arri B-mount
Size of Magazine (ft.)	200, 400
Weight (lb.)	12
Arriflex IIIC	
Silent	No
Shutter Angle (°)	0-165
Speed (fps)	6-100
Power (V)	12 DC
Lens Mount	PL
Size of Magazine (ft.)	200, 400
Weight (lb.)	14
Eyemo	
Silent	No
Shutter Angle (°)	150
Speed (fps)	64 (max.)
Power	Windup
Lens Mount	C-mount
Size of Magazine (ft.)	100, 400
Note	Standard "crash" camera; often available modified for crystal sync.
Cinema Products CP 35	
Silent	Yes
Shutter Angle (°)	5-180
Speed (fps)	4-32
Power (V)	30 DC

Table 1.1 Film Camera Data *(continued)*

Lens Mount	BNCR
Registration	2-pin
Size of Magazine (ft.)	1000
Note	Mitchell NC-based camera
Cinema Products CP FX35	
Silent	No
Shutter Angle (°)	11.25, 27.5, 45, 90, 144, 172.8, 180
Speed (fps)	5-150
Power (V)	12 DC
Lens Mount	BNCR
Registration	2-pin
Size of Magazine (ft.)	400, 1000
Weight (lb.)	34
Mitchell NC and BNC	
Silent	Yes (BNC)
Shutter Angle (°)	0-175[2]
Speed (fps)	0-32
Power (V)	12 DC, 110/220 AC
Lens Mount	BNCR
Registration	2-pin
Size of Magazine (ft.)	400, 1000
Weight (lb.)	70
Note	Reverse, stop motion, dissolves, etc.
Mitchell High Speed	
Silent	No
Shutter Angle (°)	0-175
Speed (fps)	0-120
Power (V)	12 DC, 110/220 AC
Lens Mount	BNCR
Registration	2-pin
Size of Magazine (ft.)	400, 1000
Weight (lb.)	70
Mitchell S-35R	
Silent	Blimped for sound filming.
Shutter Angle (°)	0-170
Speed (fps)	12-128[3]
Power (V)	24/36 DC, 115 AC
Lens Mount	3-prong twist
Registration	2-pin
Size of Magazine (ft.)	400, 1000
Weight (lb.)	39 (400')
Note	High-speed requires 36 V DC or 115 V AC
Moviecam	
Silent	Yes
Shutter Angle (°)	45-180, 90, 144, 172.8
Speed (fps)	1-50
Power (V)	24 DC
Lens Mount	PL or BNCR
Registration	2-pin
Size of Magazine (ft.)	500, 1000
Moviecam Compact	
Silent	Yes
Shutter Angle (°)	45, 90, 120, 144, 172.8, 180
Speed (fps)	4-36

Table 1.1 Film Camera Data *(continued)*

Power (V)	24 DC
Lens Mount	PL or BNCR
Registration	2-pin
Size of Magazine (ft.)	500, 1000
Note	Reverse 12-32 fps
Panaflex (Gold and Platinum)	
Silent	Yes
Shutter Angle (°)	50-200
Speed (fps)	6-32
Power (V)	24 DC
Lens Mount	Panavision
Registration	2-pin
Size of Magazine (ft.)	400, 1000
Weight (lb.)	34 (400')
Note:	Panaflex-X has fixed viewfinder and is not hand-holdable.
Panastar	
Silent	Yes
Shutter Angle (°)	40-180
Speed (fps)	4-120 (crystal)[4]
Power (V)	24 DC
Lens Mount	Panavision
Registration	2-pin
Size of Magazine (ft.)	500, 1000
Note	Reverse running
Ultracam	
Silent	Yes
Shutter Angle (°)	45-175[5]
Speed (fps)	8-32[6]
Power (V)	24 DC
Lens Mount	BNC
Registration	2-pin
Size of Magazine (ft.)	500, 1000
Weight (lb.)	31
Photosonics 4B	
Silent	No
Shutter Angle (°)	72
Speed (fps)	416-2082
Power (V)	380 AC, 3-phase
Lens Mount	BNCR
Size of Magazine (ft.)	1000
Weight (lb.)	125
Note	Requires Photosonics technician as AC
Photosonics 4ER	
Silent	No
Shutter Angle (°)	5-120
Speed (fps)	6-360
Power (V)	220/240 AC, 1-phase
Lens Mount	Photosonics
Registration	4-pin
Size of Magazine (ft.)	1000
Weight (lb.)	125
Note	Requires Photosonics technician as AC

Table 1.1 Film Camera Data *(continued)*

Image 300

Silent	No
Shutter Angle (°)	120
Speed (fps)	24-300
Power (V)	220/240 AC, 1-phase
Lens Mount	Photosonics or BNCR
Registration	2-pin
Size of Magazine (ft.)	1000
Weight (lb.)	100

16mm Cameras

Aaton

Silent	Yes
Shutter Angle (°)	180[7]
Speed (fps)	6-28[8]
Power (V)	12 DC
Lens Mount	Aaton bayonet, Arri PL or Panavision
Size of Magazine (ft.)	100, 400
Weight (lb.)	14
Note	Convertible to Super 16

Arriflex 16S

Silent	No
Shutter Angle (°)	180
Speed (fps)	5-55
Power (V)	12 DC
Lens Mount	Arri bayonet
Registration	1-pin
Size of Magazine (ft.)	100, 200, 400[9]
Weight (lb.)	9.25

Arriflex 16 BL

Silent	Yes
Shutter Angle (°)	180
Speed (fps)	10-40
Power (V)	12 DC
Lens Mount	Arri bayonet
Registration	1-pin
Size of Magazine (ft.)	200, 400, 1200
Weight (lb.)	9.25
Note	Forward and reverse running

Arriflex 16 SR

Silent	Yes
Shutter Angle (°)	180[10]
Speed (fps)	5-75
Power (V)	12 DC
Lens Mount	Arri bayonet
Registration	1-pin
Size of Magazine (ft.)	400
Weight (lb.)	11

Arriflex 16 SR HS

Silent	Yes
Shutter Angle (°)	178
Speed (fps)	5-150
Power (V)	12 DC

Table 1.1 Film Camera Data *(continued)*

Lens Mount	Arri bayonet
Registration	1-pin
Size of Magazine (ft.)	400
Weight (lb.)	11
Note	Requires special high-speed magazines
Arriflex SR III	
Silent	Yes
Shutter Angle (°)	90, 135, 144, 172.8, 180
Speed (fps)	24, 25, 29.97, 30 crystal programable, variable crystal from 5 to 75 fps
Power (V)	24
Lens Mount	PL
Registration	Pin registered compensating link
Size of Magazine (ft.)	400
Weight (lb.)	12
Note	Both standard 16mm and Super 16. Swingover reflex viewfinder operates from either side. Integral 80 bit timecode.
Arriflex SR III Highspeed	
Silent	Yes
Shutter Angle (°)	90, 135, 144, 172.8, 180
Speed (fps)	24, 25, 29.97, 30 crystal programable, variable crystal from 10 to 150 fps
Power (V)	24
Lens Mount	PL
Registration	Pin registered compensating link
Size of Magazine (ft.)	400
Weight (lb.)	12
Note	Both standard 16mm and Super 16. Swingover reflex viewfinder operates from either side. Integral 80 bit timecode.
GSAP	
Silent	No
Shutter Angle (°)	120
Speed (fps)	24 or 50
Power (V)	24 DC
Lens Mount	C-mount or Arri B
Size of Magazine (ft.)	50 (cartridge)
Filmo	
Silent	No
Shutter Angle (°)	204 or 216
Speed (fps)	64 (max.)
Power	Windup
Lens Mount	C-mount
Size of Magazine (ft.)	100 (daylight load)
Note	16mm version of Eyemo
CP 16	
Silent	Yes
Shutter Angle (°)	180
Speed (fps)	12-36[11]
Power (V)	20 DC
Lens Mount	CP-mount
Size of Magazine (ft.)	400, 1200
Weight (lb.)	17

Table 1.1 Film Camera Data *(continued)*

GSMO	
Silent	No
Shutter Angle (°)	180
Speed (fps)	12-64[12]
Power (V)	20 DC
Lens Mount	CP-mount
Size of Magazine (ft.)	100, 200, 400
Weight (lb.)	10
Panaflex 16	
Silent	Yes
Shutter Angle (°)	50-200
Speed (fps)	4-36 crystal
Power (V)	24 DC
Lens Mount	Panavision
Registration	2-pin
Size of Magazine (ft.)	400, 1200
Weight (lb.)	38
Note	Reverse 4-50 fps
Photosonics	
Silent	No
Shutter Angle (°)	160[13]
Speed (fps)	24-500[14]
Power (V)	28 DC, 115 AC
Lens Mount	C-mount
Registration	2-pin
Size of Magazine (ft.)	200, 400, 1200
Weight (lb.)	18
Note	Film must be daylight load, double perf
Eclair NPR	
Silent	Yes
Shutter Angle (°)	5-180
Speed (fps)	4-40
Power (V)	12 DC
Lens Mount	CA- and C-mount
Registration	1-pin
Size of Magazine (ft.)	400
Weight (lb.)	22
Eclair ACL	
Silent	Yes
Shutter Angle (°)	175
Speed (fps)	8-75[15]
Power (V)	12 DC
Lens Mount	C-mount
Size of Magazine (ft.)	200, 400
Weight (lb.)	13

Notes:

1. Variable shutter (BV) available: 0°-160°
2. Shutter variable while camera is running
3. Many different motors available
4. All speeds both forward and reverse. One frame increments plus 29.97.
5. Variable in 45° increments: 45°, 90°, 135°, 175°, must be set while camera is running
6. 8, 12, 16, 18, 20, 24, 25, 28, 29.97 fps
7. 172.5° and 175° shutters available

8. 6, 12, 18, 20, 24, 25, 28, 29.97
9. 100' Daylite spool loaded internally
10. Super 16 model with 172.8° available
11. Discrete crystal controlled steps: 12, 16, 24, 25, 32
12. Discrete crystal controlled steps: 12, 16, 24, 25, 32, 48, 64
13. Interchangeable shutters: 7.5°, 15°, 22.5°, 30°, 45°, 60°, 90°, 120°, variable 7.5°-160°
14. IPD models: 16-400 fps
15. 8, 12, 50, 75 fps

PANNING SPEED

Panning too quickly across static subjects of average contrast produces a strobing effect. Table 1.2 shows acceptable panning speeds for various lens and frame rate combinations. As a rule of thumb, with static subjects, a 180° shutter, and a frame rate of 24 frames per second (fps), if the subject takes 5 seconds or more to travel from one edge of the frame to the other as you pan, the scene will not strobe.

SHOOTING WITH HMIs

Shooting with HMIs—as well as compact indium discharge (CID), fluorescent, and other AC-powered nontungsten lights—always presents the danger of flicker. Flicker appears on film as a rhythmic change in exposure. It is caused by uneven exposure from frame to frame as a result of a mismatch in the output waveform of the light and the frame rate of the camera. Flicker can be serious enough to render the product of an entire shooting unusable.

Flicker is a potential problem when using any source powered by alternating current (AC), but the result is negligible with tungsten filament lamps because the tungsten continues to glow even when the current momentarily drops to zero. There is some loss of output, but it is minimal, usually only about 10% to 20%.

With enclosed-arc lamps, such as HMIs as well as compact source iodine (CSI) and CID lamps, the variation is greater. For an HMI with a standard reactance ballast, the minimum output may be as low as 17% of the total output. At first glance, it might seem as though you could simply average the maximum and minimum output (58%) and take this as the total average output of the light. In a crude sort of way this is exactly what happens. In film, however, there is another complication: The shutter is opening and closing at a rate that may be different from the rate at which the light output is fluctuating. When the shutter

Table 1.2 Panning Speeds for 180° Shutter and Static Scene

Frame Rate	Lens										
(fps)	20mm	28mm	35mm	40mm	50mm	75mm	85mm	100mm	150mm	180mm	300mm
8	27	45	55	60	**1.5**	**2**	**2.5**	**3**	**4**	**5**	**7**
12	18	30	36	42	54	70	**1.5**	**2**	**2.5**	**3.5**	**5**
16	13	23	27	32	41	55	70	**1.5**	**2**	**2.5**	**3.5**
20	11	18	22	25	27	43	60	70	**1.5**	**2**	**3**
24	9	15	18	21	23	36	50	60	80	**1.5**	**2.5**
32	7	11	14	16	20	27	38	45	60	75	2
48	4.5	7.5	9	11	13	18	25	30	40	55	75
60	3.5	6	7	8	11	14	20	24	32	40	60
75	3	5	6	7	9	12	17	19	26	35	50
90	2.4	4	5	6	7	10	14	16	21	29	40
120	1.8	3	4	4	5	7	10	12	16	22	30

Note: This table gives the time required for a 90° pan at various frame rates and with various lenses. Values shown in bold type are times in minutes; other values are given in seconds.

and the light output vary in relation to one another, each film frame "sees" different amounts of the cycle. The result is unequal exposure. This problem can occur in three ways:

1. The frame rate of the camera varies.
2. The frequency of the electrical supply varies.
3. The frame rate of the shutter creates a mismatch in the synchronization of the shutter and the light output.

The danger of HMI flicker is always greatest when there are no other nonflicker sources—such as tungsten, direct current (DC) arcs, daylight, etc.—and when all HMIs are run on the same electrical phase. The risk is reduced by combining other sources or by powering the HMIs on all three electrical phases. None of these options completely eliminates the risk of at least a small amount of noticeable exposure variation, however.

To prevent flicker, four conditions are absolutely essential:

1. constant frequency in the AC power supply
2. constant framing rate in the camera
3. compatible shutter angle
4. compatible frame rate

In practice, the first two conditions are met either by using crystal controls on the generator and camera or by running one or both of them from the local AC mains, which in most countries are considered reliable in frequency. Compatible shutter angles and frame rates can be determined by consulting Tables 1.3 to 1.5. A fifth condition, the relationship of AC frequency to shutter angle, is generally crucial only in high-speed cinematography and is usually not a factor in most types of filming.

At a camera speed of 24 fps, if a stable power supply is ensured, the shutter angle can be varied from 90° to 200° with relatively little risk. Theoretically, the ideal shutter angle with a 60-hertz (Hz) power supply is 144° because this results in an exposure time of $^1/_{60}$ second and thus matches the frequency of the power supply. In practice, there is little risk in using a 180° shutter if the camera is crystal-controlled and the power supply is regulated. At 180°, the camera exposes two and a half pulses per frame, rather than exactly two pulses per frame with 144°, and so exposure can theoretically vary by as much as 9%. When shooting at 24 fps with a 50-Hz power supply, the ideal shutter angle is 172.8°.

Table 1.3 lists the safe frame rates for shooting at any shutter angle and at specific shutter angles with either 50- or 60-Hz electrical supplies. A simplified series for 60-Hz power is shown in Table 1.4. An easy way to arrive at a safe

Table 1.3A HMI Filming Speeds: Safe Frame Rates (in Frames per Second) for Any Shutter Angle

60 Hertz	50 Hertz	60 Hertz	50 Hertz
120	100	6.666	5.555
60	50	6.315	5.263
40	33.333	6	5
30	25	5.714	7.461
24	20	5.454	4.545
20	16.666	5.217	4.347
17.143	14.285	5	4.166
15	12.5	4.8	4
13.333	11.111	4	3.333
12	10	3.75	3.125
10.909	9.09	3	2.5
10	8.333	2.5	2
9.231	7.692	2	1.25
8.571	7.142	1.875	1
8	6.666	1.5	
7.5	6.25	1	
7.508	5.882		

Courtesy Cinematography Electronics

Table 1.3B HMI Filming Speeds: Safe Frame Rates for Specific Shutter Angles

60 Hertz		50 Hertz	
Shutter Angle (°)	Frame Rate (fps)	Shutter Angle (°)	Frame Rate (fps)
215	71.667	215	59.722
210	70	210	58.333
200	66.667	200	55.556
195	65	195	54.167
190	63.333	190	52.778
172.8	57.6	172.8	48
170	56.667	170	47.222
165	55	165	45.833
160	53.333	160	44.444
150	50	150	41.667
144	48	144	40
140	46.667	140	38.889
135	45	135	37.5
130	43.333	130	36.111
110	36.667	110	30.556
105	35	105	29.167
100	33.333	100	27.778
80	26.667	86.4	24
75	25	80	22.222

Courtesy Cinematography Electronics

Table 1.4 Simplified HMI Filming Speeds at 60 Hertz with Any Shutter Angle

120
60
40
30
24
20
15
12
10
8
6
5
4
2
1

Table 1.5 Simplified HMI Filming Speeds at 50 Hertz with Any Shutter Angle

100
50
25
20
10
5
4
2
1

frame rate for 60-Hz power is to divide 120 by a whole number. For example, $120 \div 4 = 30$, which is a safe filming speed. For 50-Hz power systems, divide 100 by a whole number, as shown in Table 1.5.

The Power Supply

Any variation in the frequency of the power supply results in an exposure fluctuation of approximately two-fifths f-stop. The time required for one cycle of fluctuation to occur depends on by how much the power supply varies. Table 1.6 shows the fluctuation cycles for several power supply variations, and Table 1.7 gives the shutter angles for various HMI frequencies.

When working with a generator, it is essential that it be crystal-controlled. Governor controls are never sufficient for the accuracy demanded. Even with a crystal-controlled

Table 1.6 Effect of Power Supply Variation on HMIs

Power Supply (Hz)	Fluctuation Cycle (sec.)
60 ± 0.0025	200
60 ± 0.005	100
60 ± 0.01	50
60 ± 0.02	25
60 ± 0.05	10

Courtesy Crawford Generators

Table 1.7 Shutter Angles for HMI Filming

Shutter Angle (°)	HMI Frequency (Hz)	Notes
144	60	Optimum for 60 Hz, 24 fps
165	52.4	
170	50.8	
172.8	50	Optimum for 50 Hz, 24 fps
175	49.4	
180	48	Optimum for 50 Hz, 25 fps
200	43.2	

generator, a frequency meter should be used and constantly monitored. As a general rule, a variation of plus or minus one-quarter of a cycle is considered acceptable.

Flicker-Free HMIs

The newest generation of HMIs uses flicker-free ballasts, which minimize the danger of exposure fluctuation. Flicker-free units use electronic ballasts instead of the older iron-core reactance ballasts. They utilize two basic principles: (1) square-wave output and (2) high frequency. Square-wave ballasts operate by modifying the waveform of the power supply. They "square" it so that the output is angular, instead of the normal sinusoidal pattern. The rising and falling sections of the wave occupy a much smaller portion of the total. As a result, the light output is "off" for a much shorter time. This method is used in most battery-powered HMI sunguns, and thus flicker is seldom a problem with them.

The other method of eliminating flicker is increased frequency. With 200 or 250 cycles per second there is less likelihood of a mismatch from frame to frame. The major disadvantage of this method is an increase in the noise level of the light. Some flicker-free units are switchable from normal to flicker-free operation. Some electrical considerations apply to flicker-free ballasts. See "HMI Safety" in Section 5.

FILMING PRACTICAL MONITORS

Because a video monitor presents a scanned image, most spot meters do not give accurate readings. They tend to underestimate the luminance, often by a stop or more. Calibrate your own meter with tests.

Working monitors or televisions in a scene exhibit a roll bar unless precautions are taken to prevent it. The solution depends on the nature of the monitor and the requirements of the scene being filmed.

Source video falls into one of three categories:

1. NTSC, PAL, or SECAM video from broadcast television, cable, or prerecorded videotape on the set
2. a computer monitor, graphics workstation, video game, or other nonstandard CRT display
3 specially prepared 24-fps video signal

The final output can be one of four types:

1. film shot to be transferred directly to videotape, either with or without sync sound
2. film shot for theatrical projection at 24 fps with sync sound
3. film shot for theatrical projection without sync sound
4. film that will be edited as a film work print, using conventional post-production methods, and then transferred to video. Although film editors and video transfer houses can accommodate film shot at nonstandard frame rates (even with lip-sync dialogue), the inconvenience may prove undesirable in certain circumstances.

NTSC video (the American broadcast standard for all television and video recording) is based on a 3.58-megahertz (MHz) subcarrier, which results in a frame rate of 29.97 fps. Thus, each video field is "on" for approximately 1/60 second (actually, it is 1/59.94). The frame rate of a motion picture camera with a 180° shutter is 1/48 second. The discrepancy between these two frame rates results in the roll bar effect.

Unfortunately, it is impossible to lock a roll bar off the screen at the standard 24-fps camera speed. There are several methods available to achieve the desired result.

Transfer of Film Directly to Video

This is the simplest method with which to work. Use crystal control to run the camera at 29.97 fps at 180° shutter. This method works only with a shutter angle of 180° or more. It works for both MOS and sync-sound filming.

Theatrical Projection

For theatrical projection, which must be shot at sound sync speed (24 fps in the United States), use a 144° shutter and a crystal-controlled camera at 23.976 fps. This works because a 144° shutter equals 1/60 second exposure, which approximates the video exposure time. The roll bar will still be visible, but it can be minimized and locked in place on the screen. In your exposure calculations, you must compensate for the one-third stop loss that occurs when closing down to 144°.

Of course, this method is only possible when using cameras that have adjustable shutters. Always inform rental house personnel when you will be filming practical monitors so that they can ensure that all equipment is compatible.

Theatrical Projection for Sync Sound

If the filming is without sync sound, shooting can occur at 29.97 fps with 180° shutter or at 23.976 with 144° shutter. At 29.97 fps, the action will appear to be noticeably slowed when projected at 24 fps; if this is not acceptable, the 23.976-fps method should be used. If the film is to be transferred to video, either method may be used, but be sure to slate the film clearly and log the variation onto the camera reports so that the video transfer house will know how to deal with it.

Video Conversion

An alternative eliminates all problems associated with this type of filming. Many video houses and location video operators are capable of transferring video source material to 24-fps video, which may then be filmed at normal camera speeds without the roll bar. This method must be used in conjunction with a camera capable of supplying a framing pulse as output.

Filming Nonstandard CRTs

CRTs other than standard video, such as computer screens or video games, have widely varying frame rates. It is often necessary to determine the frame rate from the manufacturer's specifications, with a frequency checker, or by observing the image through the viewfinder or gate while varying the frame rate of the camera with a crystal speed control. The most reliable method is to use a portion of the video signal to drive the camera. This is accomplished with a synchronizer unit.

Shooting Video of Computer Monitors

Shooting video of computer monitors can be just as difficult as filming them. Because computer monitor frame rates usually differ from standard NTSC video, the screen will seem to flicker, which may be unacceptable for some applications. In practice, it may be necessary to alter the scan rate of the computer monitor to conform to video standard.

Synchronizers are available that alter the scan rate of some monitors. For MS-DOS computers, software patches can be used to adjust the scan rates. As a last resort, it is possible to replace the video tube in the monitor with a similar tube that has long-persistence phosphors. If the decay rate of the phosphor is longer than the scan rate, the flicker is eliminated, but some smearing of the image may result.

Determining Filming Speed

When shooting computer monitors, two pieces of information are essential: the shutter ratio of the camera and the filming scan rate of the monitor.

Shutter Ratio

Shutter ratio is the relationship between the shutter angle, also known as the *exposure angle*, of the camera and the reflex viewing mirror. For example, in a camera such as the Arri BL II, both the shutter and the mirror are 180°. This makes the shutter ratio 1 (180 ÷ 180 = 1). If the shutter is 144° and the mirror is 180°, the ratio is 144 ÷ 180 = 0.8.

When the shutter ratio is 1, the image in the eyepiece exactly matches what reaches the film. When the shutter ratio is not 1, a slight mismatch occurs between what is visible in the eyepiece and what exposes the film. Because the eyepiece sees the image slightly longer (180° versus 144° in this example), the eyepiece sees some areas of the monitor as overexposed because they are scanned twice while the mirror is in position. Because of the reduced shutter, the film exposure is correct.

Filming Scan Rate

The filming scan rate is one-half the rate at which the computer scans. A monitor with a scan rate of 59.94 has a filming scan rate of 29.97. Most computers have a filming scan rate of 27 Hz to 32 Hz.

Filming Speed

Filming speed (in frames per second) is determined by multiplying the shutter ratio by the filming scan rate:

filming speed (fps) = shutter ratio × filming scan rate

If the shutter ratio is 1, then the filming speed is the same as the filming scan rate:

shutter angle	=	180°
mirror angle	=	180°
shutter ratio	=	180° ÷ 180 = 1
filming scan rate	=	31.25

Therefore,

filming speed = 1 × 31.25 = 31.25

For a shutter ratio other than 1, the filming speed is not the same as the filming scan rate:

shutter angle	=	144°
mirror angle	=	180°
shutter ratio	=	144 ÷ 180 = 0.8
filming scan rate	=	31.25

Therefore,

$$\text{filming speed} = 0.8 \times 31.25 = 25$$

If the scan rate of the monitor is not known and no measuring equipment is available to check it, it will be necessary to find the correct filming speed by trial and error. Start at 30 fps, and adjust the speed control by one-frame increments until the scan line is slowed down. Then adjust by 0.1-frame increments, and so on, to further reduce rolling until the bar is stationary. Differences of 0.001 fps may take a minute to show movement. Obviously, this part of the process is done without film.

Once the speed has been determined, you can load film, start the camera, and observe the roll bar. Pushing the phase button rolls the bar off the screen. This process must be repeated every time the camera is started.

50-Hz Video

With a camera running at 25 fps and a 180° shutter, there should be no problem with roll bar. If the roll bar is visible, it will be necessary to shift it as follows:

1. Use a phase shifter.
2. Rock the on/off switch until the roll bar disappears.
3. Switch quickly from 25 fps to 24 fps to shift the phase.

Working with Specific Equipment

Panavision

Panavision makes two different devices:

1. Field-to-Frame Synchronizer. This device slaves the camera motor to a composite video source—it will not work with a radio frequency (RF) signal—and automatically phases the roll bar off the screen when the phasing button is depressed. The red light turns to green when the phasing is complete. The Field-to-Frame Synchronizer is designed to work when there is a difference between the camera speed and the video frame rate. It is therefore necessary to set the camera speed control to a slightly different frame rate, such as 29.3 fps. The frame rate should be slower than the video rate but very close to it.

2. Video/Film Synchronizer (VFS). This device also uses the composite video signal to drive the camera. In conjunction with a 144° shutter on the camera, the VFS drives the

camera motor at 23.976 fps. The unit also has a line position adjustment, which allows the operator to change the position of the roll bar on the screen, this must be done with the camera running. The green light indicates that sync has been achieved.

Other Cameras

Cinematography Electronics manufactures three units that are suitable to syncing cameras to video:

1. HMI and TV Crystal Control. This unit offers crystal control at the following speeds: 7.5, 15, 23.976, 24, 29.97, 30, 40, 60, and 120 fps. The roll bar is phased by flipping the switch from "TV" to "24" and back while observing the monitor through the camera viewfinder. For sound recording, a sync cable may be run from the unit to the recorder.

2. Precision Speed Control. This unit is not limited to a preset range of speeds and is thus useful in a wider range of situations, such as with computer monitors. It offers crystal-locked speed control to three decimal places and a range from 1 to 50 fps. It is compatible with Arriflex BL III and IV, 35-3, and SR cameras. It has a phase button to adjust the position of the roll bar. To use it with nonstandard or unknown video frame rates, observe the monitor through the viewfinder with the camera running, and adjust the camera speed until the roll bar freezes. Then use the phase button to adjust its position.

The Cine Check, another device from Cinematography Electronics, reads and displays the frame rate of a video monitor. It is, however, a four-digit display and usually serves as only a rough guide.

3. Film Video Synchronizing Control. This unit includes a signal pickup that is attached to the side of the video monitor to sense its frame rate. Its speed range is 8 to 65 fps, and it is compatible with the Arriflex BL III and IV, 35-3, SR cameras, Panavision cameras, and Aaton cameras. It includes automatic phasing.

Five functions must be set before using the Film/Video Synchronizing Control:

1. Function select switch
   - The projector/camera position is for 1:1 filming conditions to lock the camera to a projected image or to lock two camera shutters together.
   - The computer/video position is for filming standard NTSC video, PAL monitors, or computer terminals.
   - The two-field–comp/video position is for filming double video or computer fields, when required.

The film speed will be one-half of what is achieved in the computer/video (one-field) position, but it will have twice the resolution and brightness on film.

2. Phase thumbwheel knob. This knob is used to adjust the phase relationship between the camera shutter and the source. After initial phasing, the same phase relationship is achieved each time the camera is started.
3. 144/180 shutter switch. This switch must be set to match the camera shutter angle. The unit will automatically adjust the camera speed to compensate for the change. To maintain automatic phasing, the power and the source input must not be interrupted.
4. 75-ohm switch. This switch terminates the BNC coax input. "On" switches the 75-ohm load in. "Off" switches the 75-ohm load off. The 75-ohm termination only affects the video monitor.
5. 26/60 audio 25/50 switch. This switch controls the pilotone frequency at the audio connector. When in the 24/60 position, the output is proportional to the ratio of 24:60 (1:2.5) or 25:50 (1:2). Output voltage is 2 volts, peak to peak.

Filming speed is determined automatically by the combination of scan rate or speed of source and the setting of the 144/180 shutter switch. When the camera is turned on, the red "search" LED lights. As synchronization is achieved, the "search" LED goes out and the green "sync" LED lights, indicating that the camera and source are locked.

Moviecam Super is an integral part of the Moviecam system. The variable-speed module allows for a full range of crystal speed control.

WORKING IN COLD WEATHER

Filming in extremely cold weather can be difficult. Some film cameras may need to be weatherized by removing or replacing the lubricating oils, which could fail to function at low temperatures.

Film becomes quite brittle in cold temperatures and low humidity, and it is recommended that film be run through the camera as soon as feasible after removal from the manufacturer's packaging. Estar-base films are less susceptible to cold conditions than are other film types. Loaded magazines should be kept as warm as possible. Try to avoid leaving film in magazines for long periods. Film that is allowed to dry out for too long is subject to breakage at loop points and to static marking on the film due to electrostatic buildup during operation.

Apparent film speed may be reduced by low temperatures, and tests are recommended. As a rule of thumb, an increase in exposure of one full T-stop may be necessary when temperatures drop down to –50°F.

The exposed metal of cameras, lenses, magazines, and tripods must never come into contact with bare skin because it will freeze to the skin surface immediately. Cover any metal parts that may come near the face or hands.

The movement of equipment from one temperature extreme to another should be accomplished gradually. Do not take a warm camera outdoors in one step if snow is blowing, and conversely, do not take a cold camera immediately indoors for shooting, as condensation will result. If cameras are to be used outdoors on successive days, it may be necessary to leave the equipment in a protected area at no more than 32°F. An alternate method is to place the camera in an airtight and moisture-proof bag while outdoors and then bring it into the warm area. This will cause condensation to occur on the bag and not primarily on the camera.

Batteries become inefficient and may fail to operate in very low temperatures. Contact with cold surfaces can cause batteries to discharge rapidly.

WORKING IN THE TROPICS

The heat and high humidity of tropical locations can foster the growth of microorganisms inside lenses, on film stock, filters, and so on. Sealing the equipment in plastic bags inside their cases or using moisture-tight cases will help. In either case, desiccants, which absorb moisture, should be placed inside with the equipment.

Film stock and, to a lesser extent, videotape are susceptible to deterioration under high-heat and high-humidity conditions. Whenever possible, use portable coolers to refrigerators in conjunction with adequate amounts of desiccant. Desiccants must be replaced or recharged periodically. Some can be recharged by heating; consult the manufacturer's instructions. Dehumidifiers may also be useful.

Raw stock should be left unopened in the original packaging until needed. Once opened, stock should be used quickly. Opened packages should be returned to the cooler or refrigerators as soon as possible, preferably in a sealed can with a desiccant inside. Film should be processed as soon as possible after exposure to prevent latent image shifts, which can occur in exposed stock. Color film stock should be stored at temperatures below 55°F. Be sure to observe the correct warm-up times before opening the package, particularly in high humidity.

In equipment storage rooms, a lower relative humidity can be obtained by maintaining a temperature slightly higher than the ambient temperature. Proper air circulation should be maintained.

All pieces of equipment should be kept as clean as possible. Brief exposure to direct sunlight and air helps prevent fungus growth.

WORKING UNDERWATER

Underwater housings are available for most cameras, both film and video. They are generally rated for the maximum safe working depth. Splash boxes, which are open on top but watertight and have a clear glass window, can be used for shooting at or just below the water surface or as a safety measure when the camera is very near to water. Underwater light meters are also available, as are underwater housings for some meters.

In most cases, except for very clear water and limited depths, underwater filming occurs at low-light levels, and high-speed film and fast lenses are preferable. Because it is seldom practical to shoot from far away, wider lenses tend to be used underwater more often than long ones. Water has a higher refractive index than air (1.33), and objects appear 25% closer. This increases the apparent focal length of a lens and also affects focal distance. It has no effect on reflex focusing or judging distance by eye, but if a tape measure is used, the measured distance should be reduced by 25%. Tables 1.8 to 1.10 give some typical underwater lens equivalents. Because movements tend to be slower underwater, many photographers undercrank film cameras, generally to 22 fps.

Water, even fresh water, acts as a filter, absorbing the red wavelengths first, then the orange, and so on down the spectrum, until all frequencies are absorbed. Water thus becomes progressively bluer as depth increases, and there is no light at all below a certain depth, which varies according to the clarity of the water. A warming filter may be desirable to compensate for color balance and to act as a haze filter.

Several underwater lighting units are available; most of them are small battery-operated sungun units. Observe the manufacturer's rated maximum depth carefully, as exceeding it may lead to an implosion and a short circuit. Underwater PARs are available in both tungsten (100-watt PAR 64 and 650-watt PAR 36) and HMI (1200-watt) models. The 650-watt PARs can be powered by batteries, running two units for up to an hour. Tungsten-halogen PAR 64s and PAR 36s are also available in watertight housings. The

Table 1.8 35mm Lens Equivalents for Underwater Work

Focal Length (mm)		Angle of View (°)	
Above Water	Under-water	Above Water	Under-water
12	16	80	60
16	21	65	49
24	32	45	34
35	47	32	24
50	67	25	19
80	106	15	11

Table 1.9 16mm Lens Equivalents for Underwater Work

Focal Length (mm)		Angle of View (°)	
Above Water	Under-water	Above Water	Under-water
12	16	45	34
16	21	20	15
24	32	12	9
35	47	17	13
55	73	10	8
80	106	7	5

Table 1.10 2/3-Inch Video Lens Equivalents for Underwater Work

Focal Length (mm)		Angle of View (°)	
Above Water	Under-water	Above Water	Under-water
12	16	40	30
16	21	30	23
24	32	20	15
35	47	115	86
55	73	9	7
80	106	6.5	5

PAR 36 can be configured for use with an underwater battery pack that can run two lights for an hour. In the tungsten units, the bulbs can be changed to alter the beam from wide flood to narrow spot and for daylight or tungsten balance. Smaller openface and fresnel units are also made, some with dichroic filters for daylight balance. The HMIs run on a long cable with the ballast above water. Units are available that can operate at depths of up to 220 feet.

When the light source is very close to the lens and reflection from underwater particles creates a haze effect, it is generally best to move the light source away from the lens. Ordinary nonoptical glass—such as might be found in swimming pool viewing ports, glass-bottom boats, and so on—tends to be green, and some filtration may be necessary. When shooting through glass, it is important to eliminate all reflections of the camera or objects behind the camera either by keeping the lens very close to the glass or by blacking out the camera, operators, and other objects.

OTHER CAMERA NOTES

- Most cameras have 3/8" x 16 or 1/4" x 20 tapped holes for mounting.
- Never put lens cleaning fluid directly on the lens. Put it on the lens tissue instead.
- Always close at least one latch on a case.
- Never run a camera without manually advancing it a few frames.
- Long lenses require support.
- Ship zooms with focus set at infinity.
- Gelatin filters move the focus back by one-third of their thickness. Typical gelatin filters are 0.0015 inches (0.04 millimeters) in thickness. This will most affect wide-angle lenses at wide apertures.
- Camera battery connections are listed in Table 1.11.

Table 1.11 Camera Battery Connections

Standard Cannon 4-pin XLR battery connections on 12 V DC batteries:

- Pin 1: –12 V DC power supply to camera
- Pin 2: Pilotone and sync marker
- Pin 3: Pilotone and sync marker
- Pin 4: +12 V DC power supply to camera

Arriflex Cannon 5-pin XLR battery connections:

- Pin 1: –12 V DC power supply to camera
- Pin 2: +8 V (Arri S)
- Pin 3: +12 V (BL, SR, 35-3)
- Pin 4: +16 V (2B, 2C)
- Pin 5: Quick-charge temperature-sensing

Theatrical release formats

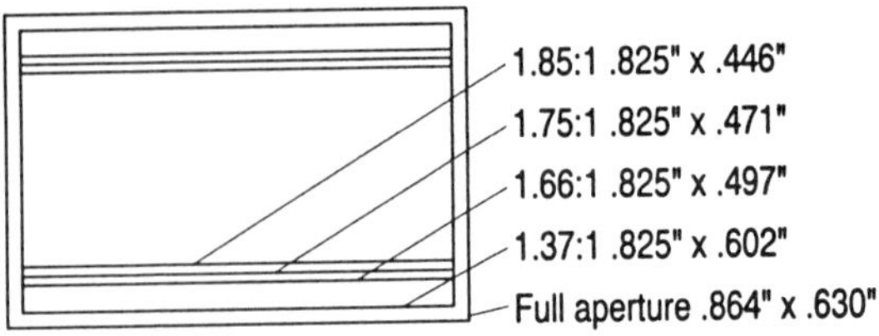

Television apertures

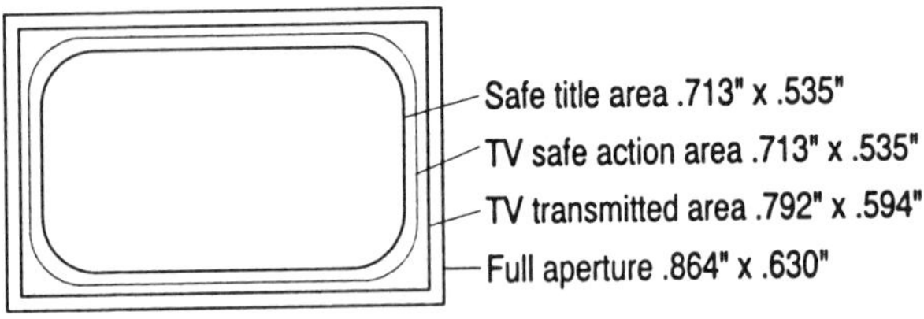

Figure 1.1 35mm apertures

16mm apertures

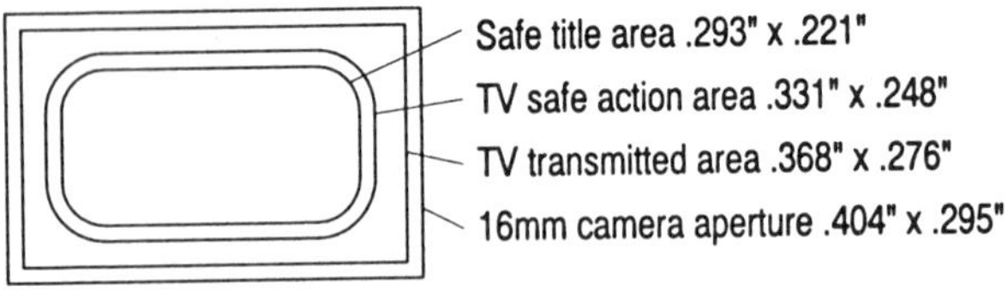

16mm finder markings

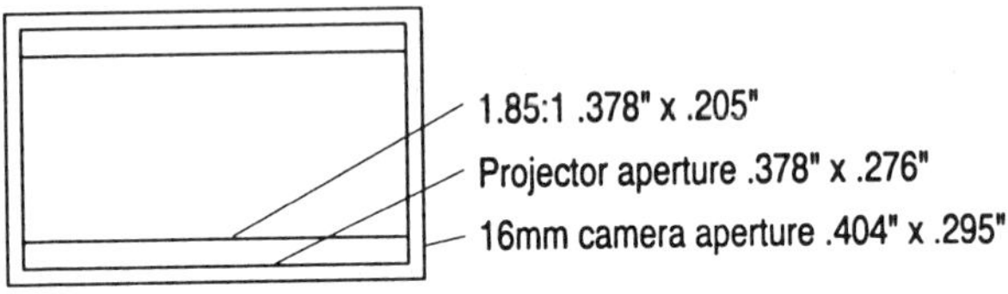

Super 16

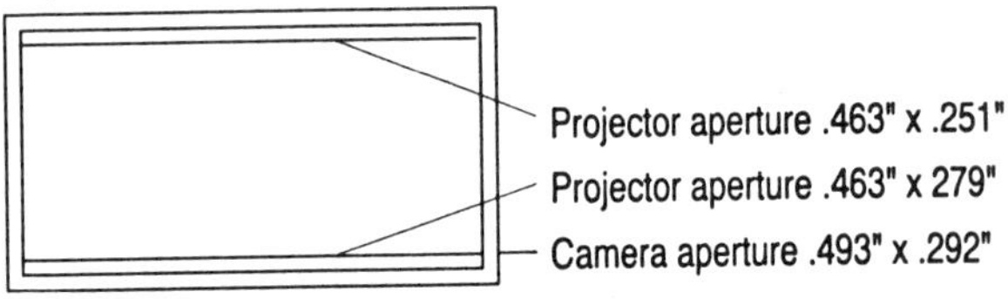

Figure 1.2 16mm apertures

SECTION 2

Optics

F-STOP

The f-stop, or f-number, of a lens is the ratio of the focal length of the lens to the diameter of the entrance pupil. The entrance pupil is approximately equal to the diaphragm. This is a purely mathematical calculation that does not account for the varying efficiencies of different lens designs. T-stop (true stop) is a measurement of actual light transmission as measured on an optical bench. F-stops are used in depth of field and hyperfocal calculations, and T-stops are used in setting exposure.

When setting the aperture on a lens, never go backward. Most apertures have a certain amount of backlash for which you must compensate. If it is necessary to go to a larger stop, open up the lens all the way, and then reset the stop.

OPTICS FORMULAS

Figure 2.1 illustrates the basic elements of optics.

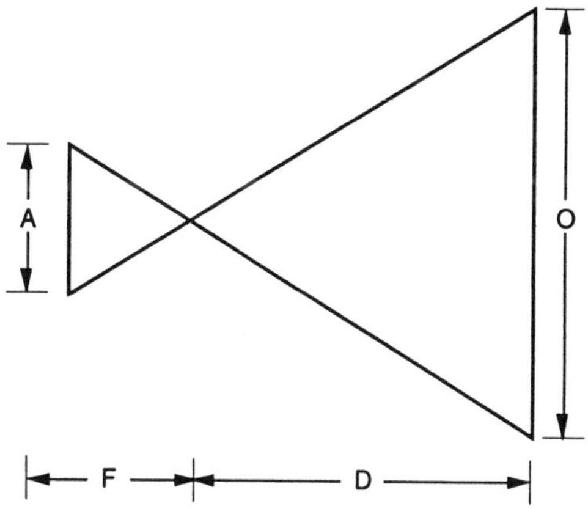

O = object size
D = distance
F = focal length
A = aperture size

Figure 2.1 Basic optical diagram

The fundamental optics formula is as follows:

$$\frac{O}{A} = \frac{D}{F}$$

$$\frac{\text{object size}}{\text{aperture size}} = \frac{\text{distance}}{\text{focal length}}$$

There are several variations on this basic formula:

$$D = \frac{O \times F}{A}$$

$$\text{distance} = \frac{\text{object size} \times \text{focal length}}{\text{aperture size}}$$

$$O = \frac{D \times A}{F}$$

$$\text{object size} = \frac{\text{distance} \times \text{aperture size}}{\text{focal length}}$$

$$F = \frac{D \times A}{O}$$

$$\text{focal length} = \frac{\text{distance} \times \text{aperture size}}{\text{object size}}$$

$$A = \frac{F \times O}{D}$$

$$\text{aperture size} = \frac{\text{focal length} \times \text{object size}}{\text{distance}}$$

In anamorphic photography, the aperture width is equal to twice the aperture size (2A).

HYPERFOCAL DISTANCE

For every focal length and f-stop there is a particular focus distance that is special: the hyperfocal distance. This is the closest focus distance at which both objects at infinity and closer objects are in focus. When a lens is set at the hyperfocal distance, everything from one-half of the hyperfocal distance to infinity is in focus. The formula for hyperfocal distance is as follows:

$$H = \frac{F^2}{f \times Cc}$$

$$\text{hyperfocal distance} = \frac{(\text{focal length})^2}{\text{f-stop x circle of confusion}}$$

The circle of confusion is the size of the image at the focal plane of a point source of light. The larger the image, the more unfocused the image is. The circle of confusion (Cc) is a way of defining how focused an image must be to be acceptably sharp. The following values of Cc are generally used in calculations of depth of field and hyperfocal distance:

16mm cameras:	Cc = 0.0006 inch
35mm cameras:	Cc = 0.001 inch

DEPTH OF FIELD

Depth of field is a plane of focus, perpendicular to the optical axis, in which objects are focused to acceptable sharpness. The near and far planes of sharpness are calculated as follows:

$$ND = \frac{H \times S}{H + (S-F)}$$

near distance =

$$\frac{\text{hyperfocal distance x distance from camera to object}}{\text{hyperfocal distance + (distance from camera to object – focal length)}}$$

$$FD = \frac{H \times S}{H - (S-F)}$$

far distance =

$$\frac{\text{hyperfocal distance x distance from camera to object}}{\text{hyperfocal distance – (distance from camera to object – focal length)}}$$

The depth of field for 35mm film and lenses of various focal lengths is given in Tables 2.1 to 2.18. The depth of field for 16mm film is given in Tables 2.19 to 2.31. Note that the values given for depth of field are ranges.

Table 2.1 35mm Depth of Field: 10mm Lens

F-stop	Hyperfocal Distance (ft.)	Focus Distance 6"	8"	10"	1'	1'6"	2'	2'6"	3'	3'6"	4'	5'	6'	8'	10'	15'
1.4	9.2	0'5.69"	0'7.5"	0'9.1"	0'10.8"	1'3.5"	1'7.7"	1'3.5"	2'3.2"	2'6"	2'9"	3'3"	3'8"	4'3"	4'10"	5'9"
		0'6.34"	0'8.67"	0'10.9"	1'1.5"	1'9.5"	2'6.6"	1'9.5"	4'5.3"	5'8"	7'1"	10'11"	17'2"	60'2"	∞	∞
2	6.5	0'5.57"	0'7.28"	0'8.8"	0'10.4"	1'2.6"	1'6.3"	1'2.6"	2'0.6"	2'3"	2'6"	2'10"	3'1"	3'7"	3'11"	4'6"
		0'6.5"	0'8.97"	0'11.4"	1'2.2"	1'11.4"	2'10.8"	1'11.4"	5'7.2"	7'8"	10'6"	22'2"	84'6"	34'6"	19'9"	12'8"
2.8	4.6	0'5.4"	0'7"	0'8.4"	0'9.9"	1'1.6"	1'4.7"	1'1.6"	1'9.8"	1'12"	2'2"	2'5"	2'7"	2'11"	3'2"	3'6"
		0'6.7"	0'9.4"	1'0.1"	1'3.3"	2'2.7"	3'6.4"	2'2.7"	8'7"	14'6"	30'1"	∞	∞	∞	∞	∞
4	3.2	0'5.2"	0'6.7"	0'7.9"	0'9.2"	1'0.3"	1'2.8"	1'0.3"	1'6.7"	1'8"	1'9"	1'12"	2'1"	2'4"	2'5"	2'8"
		0'7.1"	0'10.1"	1'1.4"	1'5.4"	2'9.6"	5'3.1"	2'9.6"	42'3.2"	∞	∞	∞	∞	∞	∞	∞
5.6	2.3	0'4.9"	0'6.2"	0'7.3"	0'8.4"	0'10.9"	1'0.9"	0'10.9"	1'3.6"	1'5"	1'6"	1'7"	1'8"	1'9"	1'10"	1'12"
		0'7.7"	0'11.3"	1'3.6"	1'9.2"	4'3.5"	15'0.6"	4'3.5"	∞	∞	∞	∞	∞	∞	∞	∞
8	1.6	0'4.6"	0'5.7"	0'6.6"	0'7.4"	0'9.3"	0'10.7"	0'9.3"	1'0.6"	1'1"	1'2"	1'3"	1'3"	1'4"	1'5"	1'5"
		0'8.7"	1'1.7"	1'8.5"	2'7.5"	21'1.6"	9'7.5"	21'1.6"	∞	∞	∞	∞	∞	∞	∞	∞
11	1.2	0'4.2"	0'5.1"	0'5.8"	0'6.5"	0'7.9"	0'8.9"	0'6.3"	0'10.1"	0'11"	0'11"	0'11"	0'12"	1'0"	1'1"	1'1"
		0'10.4"	1'6.7"	2'10"	6'8.9"	∞	∞	∞	∞	∞	∞	∞	∞	∞	∞	∞
16	0.8	0'3.7"	0'4.4"	0'4.9"	0'5.4"	0'6.3"	0'6.9"	0'6.3"	0'7.6"	0'8"	0'8"	0'8"	0'9"	0'9"	0'9"	0'9"
		1'3.8"	3'11.3"	∞	∞	∞	∞	∞	∞	∞	∞	∞	∞	∞	∞	∞
22	0.6	0'3.2"	0'3.8"	0'4.1"	0'4.4"	0'5.1"	0'5.4"	0'5.1"	0'5.9"	0'6"	0'6"	0'6"	0'6"	0'7"	0'7"	0'7"
		3'4.4"	∞	∞	∞	∞	∞	∞	∞	∞	∞	∞	∞	∞	∞	∞
32	0.4	0'2.7"	0'3"	0'3.3"	0'3.5"	0'3.8"	0'4"	0'3.8"	0'4.3"	0'4"	0'4"	0'4"	0'5"	0'5"	0'5"	0'5"
		∞	∞	∞	∞	∞	∞	∞	∞	∞	∞	∞	∞	∞	∞	∞

Note: Circle of confusion = 0.001.

Table 2.2 35mm Depth of Field: 14mm Lens

F-stop	Hyperfocal Distance (ft.)	Focus Distance														
		6"	8"	10"	1'	1'6"	2'	2'6"	3'	3'6"	4'	5'	6'	8'	10'	15'
1.4	18.1	0'5.84"	0'7.75"	0'9.5"	0'11.4"	1'4.6"	1'9.6"	2'2.4"	2'6.9"	2'11"	3'3"	3'11"	4'6"	5'7"	6'5"	8'2"
		0'6.17"	0'8.35"	0'10.4"	1'0.7"	1'7.6"	2'3"	2'10.8"	3'7.2"	4'4"	5'2"	6'11"	8'12"	14'4"	22'4"	87'12"
2	12.7	0'5.77"	0'7.64"	0'9.3"	0'11.1"	1'4.1"	1'8.7"	2'1.1"	2'5.1"	2'9"	3'0"	3'7"	4'1"	4'11"	5'7"	6'10"
		0'6.25"	0'8.49"	0'10.7"	1'1"	1'8.4"	2'4.5"	3'1.4"	3'11.2"	4'10"	5'10"	8'3"	11'5"	21'9"	47'7"	∞
2.8	9.0	0'5.7"	0'7.5"	0'9.1"	0'10.8"	1'3.4"	1'7.7"	1'11.5"	2'3"	2'6"	2'9"	3'3"	3'7"	4'3"	4'9"	5'8"
		0'6.4"	0'8.7"	0'11"	1'1.5"	1'9.6"	2'6.8"	3'5.5"	4'5.9"	5'9"	7'2"	11'2"	17'10"	69'5"	∞	∞
4	6.3	0'5.6"	0'7.3"	0'8.8"	0'10.4"	1'2.6"	1'6.2"	1'9.5"	2'0.4"	2'3"	2'5"	2'10"	3'1"	3'6"	3'11"	4'5"
		0'6.5"	0'9"	0'11.5"	1'2.3"	1'11.6"	2'11.1"	4'1.6"	5'8.4"	7'10"	10'10"	23'10"	115'4"	∞	∞	∞
5.6	4.5	0'5.4"	0'7"	0'8.4"	0'9.8"	1'1.5"	1'4.6"	1'7.3"	1'9.6"	1'12"	2'1"	2'4"	2'7"	2'11"	3'1"	3'6"
		0'6.7"	0'9.4"	1'0.2"	1'3.4"	2'2.9"	3'7"	5'7.1"	8'11"	15'6"	34'9"	∞	∞	∞	∞	∞
8	3.2	0'5.2"	0'6.6"	0'7.9"	0'9.1"	1'0.2"	1'2.7"	1'4.8"	1'6.5"	1'8"	1'9"	1'11"	2'1"	2'3"	2'5"	2'7"
		0'7.1"	0'10.2"	1'1.5"	1'5.5"	2'10.2"	5'5.2"	11'10.9"	57'8.2"	∞	∞	∞	∞	∞	∞	∞
11	2.3	0'4.9"	0'6.2"	0'7.3"	0'8.4"	0'10.9"	1'0.8"	0'11.6"	1'3.6"	1'5"	1'6"	1'7"	1'8"	1'9"	1'10"	1'12"
		0'7.7"	0'11.3"	1'3.6"	1'9.2"	4'3.7"	15'3.2"	∞	∞	∞	∞	∞	∞	∞	∞	∞
16	1.6	0'4.6"	0'5.6"	0'6.5"	0'7.4"	0'9.2"	0'10.6"	0'11.6"	1'0.4"	1'1"	1'2"	1'2"	1'3"	1'4"	1'4"	1'5"
		0'8.8"	1'1.9"	1'8.9"	2'8.6"	28'10.1"	∞	∞	∞	∞	∞	∞	∞	∞	∞	∞
22	1.2	0'4.2"	0'5.1"	0'5.8"	0'6.4"	0'7.8"	0'8.8"	0'9.5"	0'10"	0'10"	0'11"	0'11"	0'12"	1'0"	1'0"	1'1"
		0'10.6"	1'7.2"	2'11.7"	7'7.6"	∞	∞	∞	∞	∞	∞	∞	∞	∞	∞	∞
32	0.8	0'3.7"	0'4.4"	0'4.9"	0'5.3"	0'6.2"	0'6.8"	0'7.2"	0'7.5"	0'8"	0'8"	0'8"	0'8"	0'9"	0'9"	0'9"
		1'4.3"	4'4.5"	∞	∞	∞	∞	∞	∞	∞	∞	∞	∞	∞	∞	∞

Note: Circle of confusion = 0.001.

Table 2.3 35mm Depth of Field: 16mm Lens

F-stop	Hyperfocal Distance (ft.)	Focus Distance														
		6"	8"	10"	1'	1'6"	2'	2'6"	3'	3'6"	4'	5'	6'	8'	10'	15'
1.4	23.6'	0'5.88"	0'7.82"	0'9.6"	0'11.5"	1'4.9"	1'10.1"	2'3.1"	2'7.9"	3'1"	3'5"	4'2"	4'9"	6'0"	7'0"	9'2"
		0'6.13"	0'8.27"	0'10.3"	1'0.5"	1'7.2"	2'2.2"	2'9.6"	3'5.2"	4'1"	4'10"	6'4"	8'1"	12'1"	17'4"	41'1"
2	16.5'	0'5.82"	0'7.73"	0'9.5"	0'11.3"	1'4.5"	1'9.4"	2'2.1"	2'6.5"	2'11"	3'3"	3'10"	4'5"	5'5"	6'3"	7'10"
		0'6.19"	0'8.38"	0'10.5"	1'0.8"	1'7.8"	2'3.3"	2'11.3"	3'8"	4'5"	5'3"	7'2"	9'5"	15'6"	25'4"	161'9"
2.8	11.8'	0'5.8"	0'7.6"	0'9.3"	0'11.1"	1'4"	1'8.5"	2'0.8"	2'4.7"	2'8"	3'0"	3'6"	13'0"	4'9"	5'5"	6'7"
		0'6.3"	0'8.5"	0'10.7"	1'1.1"	1'8.6"	2'4.9"	3'2.1"	4'0.3"	5'0"	6'1"	8'8"	12'2"	24'10"	65'3"	∞
4	8.3'	0'5.7"	0'7.4"	0'9.1"	0'10.7"	1'3.2"	1'7.3"	1'11"	2'2.4"	2'6"	2'8"	3'1"	3'6"	4'1"	4'6"	5'4"
		0'6.4"	0'8.7"	0'11.1"	1'1.7"	1'10"	2'7.7"	3'7"	4'8.5"	6'1"	7'9"	12'8"	21'11"	248'0"	∞	∞
5.6	5.9'	0'5.5"	0'7.2"	0'8.7"	0'10.3"	1'2.4"	1'5.9"	1'9.1"	2'0"	2'2"	2'5"	2'8"	3'0"	3'5"	3'9"	4'3"
		0'6.6"	0'9.1"	0'11.6"	1'2.4"	2'0.1"	3'0.3"	4'4"	6'1.2"	8'7"	12'5"	32'8"	∞	∞	∞	∞
8	4.1'	0'5.4"	0'6.9"	0'8.3"	0'9.7"	1'1.2"	1'4.2"	1'6.7"	1'8.9"	1'11"	2'0"	2'3"	2'5"	2'9"	2'11"	3'3"
		0'6.8"	0'9.6"	1'0.5"	1'3.8"	2'4.3"	3'10.5"	6'3.9"	10'11.3"	22'10"	124'0"	∞	∞	∞	∞	∞
11	3.0'	0'5.1"	0'6.6"	0'7.8"	0'9"	1'0"	1'2.4"	1'1.6"	1'6"	1'7"	1'9"	1'11"	2'0"	2'2"	2'4"	2'6"
		0'7.2"	0'10.3"	1'1.8"	1'6"	2'11.9"	5'11.7"	14'10.2"	1485'4.5"	∞	∞	∞	∞	∞	∞	∞
16	2.1'	0'4.8"	0'6.1"	0'7.1"	0'8.1"	0'10"	1'0.2"	1'1.6"	1'2.7"	1'4"	1'4"	1'6"	1'6"	1'8"	1'9"	1'10"
		0'7.9"	0'11.9"	1'4.6"	1'11.2"	5'5.6"	62'0"	∞	∞	∞	∞	∞	∞	∞	∞	∞
22	1.5'	0'4.5"	0'5.6"	0'6.4"	0'7.2"	0'9"	0'10.3"	0'11.3"	1'0"	1'1"	1'1"	1'2"	1'2"	1'3"	1'4"	1'4"
		0'9"	1'2.5"	1'10.2"	2'11.9"	742'8"	∞	∞	∞	∞	∞	∞	∞	∞	∞	∞
32	1.0'	0'4"	0'4.9"	0'5.5"	0'6.1"	0'7.3"	0'8.2"	0'8.8"	0'9.2"	0'10"	0'10"	0'10"	0'11"	0'11"	0'11"	1'0"
		0'11.6"	1'10.9"	4'2.6"	31'0"	∞	∞	∞	∞	∞	∞	∞	∞	∞	∞	∞

Note: Circle of confusion = 0.001.

Table 2.4 35mm Depth of Field: 20mm Lens

F-stop	Hyperfocal Distance (ft.)	Focus Distance 6"	8"	10"	1'	1'6"	2'	2'6"	3'	3'6"	4'	5'	6'	8'	10'	15'
1.4	36.9	0'5.92"	0'7.9"	0'9.7"	0'11.7"	1'5.3"	1'10.8"	2'4.1"	2'9.3"	3'2"	3'7"	4'5"	5'2"	6'7"	7'10"	10'8"
		0'6.08"	0'8.19"	0'10.2"	1'0.3"	1'6.8"	2'1.4"	2'8.2"	3'3.2"	3'10"	4'6"	5'9"	7'2"	10'3"	13'9"	25'3"
2	25.8	0'5.89"	0'7.84"	0'9.6"	0'11.6"	1'5"	1'10.3"	2'3.4"	2'8.3"	3'1"	3'6"	4'2"	4'10"	6'1"	7'3"	9'6"
		0'6.12"	0'8.25"	0'10.3"	1'0.5"	1'7.1"	2'2"	2'9.2"	3'4.7"	4'1"	4'9"	6'2"	7'10"	11'7"	16'4"	35'9"
2.8	18.5	0'5.8"	0'7.8"	0'9.5"	0'11.4"	1'4.6"	1'9.7"	2'2.4"	2'7"	2'11"	3'3"	3'11"	4'6"	5'7"	6'6"	8'3"
		0'6.2"	0'8.3"	0'10.4"	1'0.7"	1'7.6"	2'2.9"	2'10.7"	3'7"	4'4"	5'1"	6'10"	8'11"	14'1"	21'10"	80'2"
4	12.9	0'5.8"	0'7.6"	0'9.4"	0'11.1"	1'4.1"	1'8.8"	2'1.1"	2'5.2"	2'9"	3'1"	3'7"	4'1"	4'11"	5'8"	6'11"
		0'6.2"	0'8.5"	0'10.6"	1'1"	1'8.4"	2'4.4"	3'1.2"	3'10.9"	4'10"	5'10"	8'2"	11'2"	21'0"	44'3"	∞
5.6	9.2	0'5.7"	0'7.5"	0'9.1"	0'10.8"	1'3.5"	1'7.7"	1'11.6"	2'3.2"	2'6"	2'9"	3'3"	3'8"	4'3"	4'10"	5'9"
		0'6.3"	0'8.7"	0'10.9"	1'1.5"	1'9.5"	2'6.6"	3'5.2"	4'5.3"	5'8"	7'1"	10'11"	17'2"	60'2"	∞	∞
8	6.5	0'5.6"	0'7.3"	0'8.8"	0'10.4"	1'2.6"	1'6.3"	1'9.6"	2'0.6"	2'3"	2'6"	2'10"	3'1"	3'7"	3'11"	4'6"
		0'6.5"	0'9"	0'11.4"	1'2.2"	1'11.4"	2'10.8"	4'0.9"	5'7.2"	7'8"	10'6"	22'2"	84'6"	∞	∞	∞
11	4.7	0'5.4"	0'7"	0'8.5"	0'9.9"	1'1.6"	1'4.8"	1'4.9"	1'10"	2'0"	2'2"	2'5"	2'8"	2'12"	3'2"	3'7"
		0'6.7"	0'9.4"	1'0.1"	1'3.2"	2'2.4"	3'5.8"	5'4.1"	8'3.6"	13'9"	26'11"	∞	∞	∞	∞	∞
16	3.2	0'5.2"	0'6.7"	0'7.9"	0'9.2"	1'0.3"	1'2.8"	1'4.9"	1'6.7"	1'8"	1'9"	1'12"	2'1"	2'4"	2'5"	2'8"
		0'7.1"	0'10.1"	1'1.4"	1'5.4"	2'9.6"	5'3.1"	11'0.9"	42'3.2"	∞	∞	∞	∞	∞	∞	∞
22	2.3	0'4.9"	0'6.3"	0'7.4"	0'8.4"	0'11"	1'1"	1'2.5"	1'3.8"	1'5"	1'6"	1'7"	1'8"	1'10"	1'11"	2'0"
		0'7.6"	0'11.2"	1'3.4"	1'8.9"	4'1.8"	13'5.7"	∞	∞	∞	∞	∞	∞	∞	∞	∞
32	1.6	0'4.6"	0'5.7"	0'6.6"	0'7.4"	0'9.3"	0'10.7"	0'11.8"	1'0.6"	1'1"	1'2"	1'3"	1'3"	1'4"	1'5"	1'5"
		0'8.7"	1'1.7"	1'8.5"	2'7.5"	21'1.6"	∞	∞	∞	∞	∞	∞	∞	∞	∞	∞

Note: Circle of confusion = 0.001.

Table 2.5 35mm Depth of Field: 25mm Lens

F-stop	Hyperfocal Distance (ft.)	Focal Distance														
		6"	8"	10"	1'	1'6"	2'	2'6"	3'	3'6"	4'	6'	8'	10'	15'	20'
1.4	57.2'	0'5.95"	0'7.95"	0'9.8"	0'11.8"	1'5.5"	1'11.2"	2'4.7"	2'10"	3'4"	3'9"	5'5"	7'0"	8'6"	11'11"	14'10"
		0'6.05"	0'8.14"	0'10.1"	1'0.2"	1'6.5"	2'0.9"	2'7.4"	3'2"	3'9"	4'4"	6'8"	9'4"	12'1"	20'4"	30'9"
2	40.0'	0'5.93"	0'7.91"	0'9.8"	0'11.7"	1'5.3"	1'10.9"	2'4.2"	2'9"	3'3"	3'8"	5'3"	6'8"	8'0"	10'11"	13'4"
		0'6.08"	0'8.18"	0'10.2"	1'0.3"	1'6.7"	2'1.3"	2'8"	3'3"	3'10"	4'5"	7'1"	10'0"	13'4"	24'0"	40'0"
2.8	28.6'	0'5.9"	0'7.9"	0'9.7"	0'11.6"	1'5.1"	1'10.4"	2'3.6"	2'9"	3'1"	3'6"	5'0"	6'3"	7'5"	9'10"	11'9"
		0'6.1"	0'8.2"	0'10.3"	1'0.4"	1'7"	2'1.8"	2'8.9"	3'4"	4'0"	4'8"	7'7"	11'1"	15'5"	31'7"	66'7"
4	20.0'	0'5.9"	0'7.8"	0'9.6"	0'11.4"	1'4.7"	1'9.8"	2'2.7"	2'7"	3'0"	3'4"	4'7"	5'9"	6'8"	8'7"	10'0"
		0'6.2"	0'8.3"	0'10.4"	1'0.6"	1'7.5"	2'2.7"	2'10.3"	3'6"	4'3"	5'0"	8'7"	13'4"	20'0"	59'11"	∞
5.6	14.3'	0'5.8"	0'7.7"	0'9.4"	0'11.2"	1'4.3"	1'9.1"	2'1.5"	2'6"	2'10"	3'2"	4'3"	5'2"	5'11"	7'4"	8'4"
		0'6.2"	0'8.4"	0'10.6"	1'0.9"	1'8.1"	2'3.9"	3'0.4"	3'10"	4'8"	5'7"	10'4"	18'2"	33'4"	∞	∞
8	10.0'	0'5.7"	0'7.5"	0'9.2"	0'10.9"	1'3.7"	1'8"	2'0"	2'4"	2'7"	2'10"	3'9"	4'5"	5'0"	6'0"	6'8"
		0'6.3"	0'8.6"	0'10.9"	1'1.3"	1'9.2"	2'6"	3'4"	4'3"	5'5"	6'8"	15'0"	39'11"	∞	∞	∞
11	7.3'	0'5.6"	0'7.4"	0'8.9"	0'10.5"	1'2.9"	1'6.8"	1'8"	2'1"	2'4"	2'7"	3'3"	3'10"	4'3"	4'11"	5'4"
		0'6.4"	0'8.9"	0'11.2"	1'1.9"	1'10.7"	2'9.1"	3'10"	5'1"	6'9"	8'11"	34'3"	∞	∞	∞	∞
16	5.0'	0'5.5"	0'7.1"	0'8.5"	0'10"	1'1.8"	1'5.1"	1'8"	1'11"	2'1"	2'3"	2'9"	3'1"	3'4"	3'9"	4'0"
		0'6.7"	0'9.3"	0'11.9"	1'3"	2'1.7"	3'4"	5'0"	7'6"	11'8"	20'0"	∞	∞	∞	∞	∞
22	3.6'	0'5.3"	0'6.8"	0'8.1"	0'9.4"	1'0.7"	1'3.5"	1'6"	1'8"	1'9"	1'11"	2'3"	2'6"	2'8"	2'11"	3'1"
		0'7"	0'9.9"	1'0.9"	1'4.5"	2'6.6"	4'5.3"	8'0"	17'1"	92'4"	∞	∞	∞	∞	∞	∞
32	2.5'	0'5"	0'6.3"	0'7.5"	0'8.6"	0'11.3"	1'1.3"	1'3"	1'4"	1'6"	1'6"	1'9"	1'11"	2'0"	2'2"	2'3"
		0'7.5"	0'11"	1'2.9"	1'8"	3'9"	10'0"	∞	∞	∞	∞	∞	∞	∞	∞	∞

Note: Circle of confusion = 0.001.

Table 2.6 35mm Depth of Field: 35mm Lens

F-stop	Hyperfocal Distance (ft.)	Focus Distance														
		10"	1'	1'6"	2'	2'6"	3'	3'6"	4'	6'	8'	10'	15'	20'	25'	40'
1.4	113.0'	0'9.89"	0'11.9"	1'5.8"	1'11.6"	2'5.4"	2'11.1"	3'4.7"	3'10"	5'8"	7'6"	9'2"	13'3"	17'0"	20'6"	29'7"
		0'10.03"	1'0.1"	1'6.2"	2'0.4"	2'6.7"	3'1"	3'7.3"	4'2"	6'4"	8'7"	11'0"	17'4"	24'4"	32'1"	61'11"
2	79.1'	0'9.86"	0'11.9"	1'5.7"	1'11.4"	2'5.1"	2'10.7"	3'4.2"	3'10"	5'7"	7'3"	8'11"	12'7"	16'0"	19'0"	26'7"
		0'10.07"	1'0.2"	1'6.3"	2'0.6"	2'7"	3'1.4"	3'7.9"	4'3"	6'6"	8'11"	11'5"	18'6"	26'9"	36'7"	80'11"
2.8	56.5'	0'9.8"	0'11.8"	1'5.5"	1'11.2"	2'4.7"	2'10.2"	3'3.6"	3'9"	5'5"	7'0"	8'6"	11'10"	14'9"	17'4"	23'5"
		0'10.1"	1'0.2"	1'6.5"	2'0.9"	2'7.4"	3'2"	3'8.8"	4'4"	6'9"	9'4"	12'2"	20'5"	30'11"	44'10"	136'11"
4	39.6'	0'9.8"	0'11.7"	1'5.3"	1'10.8"	2'4.2"	2'9.5"	3'2.6"	3'8"	5'3"	6'8"	8'0"	10'11"	13'3"	15'4"	19'11"
		0'10.2"	1'0.3"	1'6.7"	2'1.3"	2'8"	3'3"	3'10.1"	4'5"	7'1"	10'0"	13'5"	24'2"	40'5"	67'11"	∞
5.6	28.3'	0'9.7"	0'11.6"	1'5.1"	1'10.4"	2'3.6"	2'8.5"	3'1.4"	3'6"	4'11"	6'3"	7'5"	9'10"	11'9"	13'3"	16'7"
		0'10.3"	1'0.4"	1'7"	2'1.8"	2'8.9"	3'4.3"	3'11.9"	4'8"	7'7"	11'2"	15'6"	32'0"	68'5"	217'0"	∞
8	19.8'	0'9.6"	0'11.4"	1'4.7"	1'9.8"	2'2.6"	2'7.3"	2'11.7"	3'4"	4'7"	5'8"	6'8"	8'6"	9'11"	11'1"	13'3"
		0'10.4"	1'0.6"	1'7.5"	2'2.7"	2'10.3"	3'6.4"	4'3"	5'0"	8'7"	13'5"	20'3"	62'1"	∞	∞	∞
11	14.4'	0'9.4"	0'11.2"	1'4.3"	1'9.1"	2'1.6"	2'3.6"	2'9.8"	3'2"	4'3"	5'2"	5'11"	7'4"	8'4"	9'2"	10'7"
		0'10.6"	1'0.9"	1'8.1"	2'3.9"	3'0.3"	3'9.5"	4'7.5"	5'6"	10'4"	18'0"	32'10"	∞	∞	∞	∞
16	9.9'	0'9.2"	0'10.9"	1'3.6"	1'8"	1'11.9"	2'3.6"	2'7"	2'10"	3'9"	4'5"	5'0"	6'0"	6'7"	7'1"	7'11"
		0'10.9"	1'1.3"	1'9.2"	2'6.1"	3'4.1"	4'3.7"	5'5"	6'9"	15'3"	41'10"	∞	∞	∞	∞	∞
22	7.2'	0'8.9"	0'10.5"	1'2.9"	1'6.8"	1'10.3"	2'1.4"	2'4.3"	2'7"	3'3"	3'9"	4'2"	4'10"	5'3"	5'7"	6'1"
		0'11.3"	1'1.9"	1'10.7"	2'9.2"	3'10"	5'1.8"	6'9.8"	9'0"	36'2"	∞	∞	∞	∞	∞	∞
32	4.9'	0'8.5"	0'10"	1'1.8"	1'5.1"	1'7.9"	1'10.4"	2'0.6"	2'3"	2'9"	3'1"	3'4"	3'9"	4'0"	4'2"	4'5"
		1'0"	1'3"	2'1.8"	3'4.3"	5'0.7"	7'7.5"	12'0"	20'11"	∞	∞	∞	∞	∞	∞	∞

Note: Circle of confusion = 0.001.

Table 2.7 35mm Depth of Field: 50mm Lens

F-stop	Hyperfocal Distance (ft.)	Focus Distance 10"	1'	1'6"	2'	2'6"	3'	3'6"	4'	6'	8'	10'	15'	25'	50'	75'
1.4	230.7	0'9.92"	0'11.95"	1'5.9"	1'11.8"	2'5.7"	2'11.5"	3'5.4"	3'11.2"	5'10"	7'9"	9'7"	14'1"	22'7"	41'1"	56'7"
		0'10"	1'0.05"	1'6.1"	2'0.2"	2'6.3"	3'0.5"	3'6.6"	4'0.8"	6'2"	8'3"	10'5"	16'1"	28'0"	63'10"	111'2"
2	161.5	0'9.91"	0'11.93"	1'5.8"	1'11.7"	2'5.5"	2'11.3"	3'5.1"	3'10.8"	5'9"	7'7"	9'5"	13'9"	21'8"	38'2"	51'3"
		0'10.01"	1'0.07"	1'6.2"	2'0.3"	2'6.5"	3'0.7"	3'6.9"	4'1.2"	6'3"	8'5"	10'8"	16'6"	29'7"	72'5"	140'1"
2.8	115.3	0'9.9"	0'11.9"	1'5.8"	1'11.6"	2'5.4"	2'11.1"	3'4.8"	3'10.4"	5'8"	7'6"	9'2"	13'3"	20'7"	34'11"	45'5"
		0'10"	1'0.1"	1'6.2"	2'0.4"	2'6.7"	3'1"	3'7.3"	4'1.7"	6'4"	8'7"	10'11"	17'3"	31'11"	88'3"	214'6"
4	80.7	0'9.9"	0'11.9"	1'5.7"	1'11.4"	2'5.1"	2'10.7"	3'4.3"	3'9.7"	5'7"	7'3"	8'11"	12'8"	19'1"	30'11"	38'11"
		0'10.1"	1'0.2"	1'6.3"	2'0.6"	2'7"	3'1.4"	3'7.9"	4'2.5"	6'6"	8'11"	11'5"	18'5"	36'3"	131'4"	1056'9"
5.6	57.7	0'9.8"	0'11.8"	1'5.5"	1'11.2"	2'4.8"	2'10.2"	3'3.6"	3'8.9"	5'5"	7'0"	8'6"	11'11"	17'5"	26'9"	32'7"
		0'10.1"	1'0.2"	1'6.5"	2'0.9"	2'7.4"	3'2"	3'8.7"	4'3.6"	6'8"	9'3"	12'1"	20'3"	44'2"	376'2"	∞
8	40.4	0'9.8"	0'11.7"	1'5.4"	1'10.9"	2'4.3"	2'9.5"	3'2.6"	3'7.7"	5'3"	6'8"	8'0"	10'11"	15'5"	22'4"	26'3"
		0'10.2"	1'0.3"	1'6.7"	2'1.3"	2'8"	3'2.9"	3'10"	4'5.3"	7'1"	10'0"	13'4"	23'10"	65'8"	∞	∞
11	29.4	0'9.7"	0'11.6"	1'5.1"	1'10.5"	2'3.6"	2'8.7"	2'11.8"	3'6.2"	4'12"	6'3"	7'6"	9'11"	13'6"	18'6"	21'1"
		0'10.2"	1'0.4"	1'7"	2'1.8"	2'8.8"	3'4.1"	3'11.7"	4'7.6"	7'6"	11'0"	15'2"	30'8"	168'6"	∞	∞
16	20.2	0'9.6"	0'11.4"	1'4.8"	1'9.8"	2'2.7"	2'7.3"	2'11.8"	3'4.1"	4'8"	5'9"	6'8"	8'7"	11'2"	14'5"	15'11"
		0'10.4"	1'0.6"	1'7.4"	2'2.6"	2'10.2"	3'6.3"	4'2.8"	4'11.9"	8'6"	13'3"	19'10"	58'5"	∞	∞	∞
22	14.7	0'9.4"	0'11.2"	1'4.3"	1'9.1"	2'1.6"	2'5.9"	2'9.9"	3'1.7"	4'3"	5'2"	5'11"	7'5"	9'3"	11'4"	12'3"
		0'10.6"	1'0.9"	1'8"	2'3.8"	3'0.2"	3'9.2"	4'7.2"	5'6"	10'2"	17'7"	31'5"	∞	∞	∞	∞
32	10.1	0'9.2"	0'10.9"	1'3.7"	1'8"	2'0"	2'3.8"	2'7.2"	2'10.4"	3'9"	4'6"	5'0"	6'0"	7'2"	8'5"	8'11"
		0'10.9"	1'1.3"	1'9.1"	2'5.9"	3'3.9"	4'3.2"	5'4.3"	6'7.5"	14'10"	38'7"	∞	∞	∞	∞	∞

Note: Circle of confusion = 0.001.

Table 2.8 35mm Depth of Field: 75mm Lens

F-stop	Hyperfocal Distance (ft.)	Focus Distance 2"	2'6"	3'	4'	5'	6'	7'	9'	10'	15'	20'	25'	40'	50'	100'
1.4	519.0	1'11.91"	2'5.86"	2'11.8"	3'11.6"	4'11.4"	5'11.2"	6'10.9"	8'10.2"	9'10"	14'7"	19'3"	23'10"	37'2"	45'7"	83'10"
		2'0.09"	2'6.15"	3'0.2"	4'0.4"	5'0.6"	6'0.8"	7'1.1"	9'1.9"	10'2"	15'5"	20'10"	26'3"	43'4"	55'4"	123'10"
2	363.3	1'11.87"	2'5.79"	2'11.7"	3'11.5"	4'11.2"	5'10.8"	6'10.4"	8'9.4"	9'9"	14'5"	18'11"	23'5"	36'0"	43'11"	78'5"
		2'0.13"	2'6.21"	3'0.3"	4'0.5"	5'0.8"	6'1.2"	7'1.7"	9'2.7"	10'3"	15'8"	21'2"	26'10"	44'11"	58'0"	138'0"
2.8	259.5	1'11.8"	2'5.7"	2'11.6"	3'11.3"	4'10.9"	5'10.4"	6'9.8"	8'8.4"	9'8"	14'2"	18'7"	22'10"	34'8"	41'11"	72'2"
		2'0.2"	2'6.3"	3'0.4"	4'0.8"	5'1.2"	6'1.7"	7'2.3"	9'3.9"	10'5"	15'11"	21'8"	27'8"	47'3"	61'11"	162'8"
4	181.6	1'11.7"	2'5.6"	2'11.4"	3'11"	4'10.4"	5'9.7"	6'8.9"	8'6.9"	9'6"	13'10"	18'0"	22'0"	32'9"	39'2"	64'6"
		2'0.3"	2'6.4"	3'0.6"	4'1.1"	5'1.7"	6'2.5"	7'3.4"	9'5.6"	10'7"	16'4"	22'6"	29'0"	51'4"	68'12"	222'6"
5.6	129.7	1'11.6"	2'5.4"	2'11.2"	3'10.6"	4'9.8"	5'8.8"	6'7.7"	8'5"	9'3"	13'5"	17'4"	21'0"	30'7"	36'1"	56'6"
		2'0.4"	2'6.6"	3'0.9"	4'1.5"	5'2.4"	6'3.5"	7'4.8"	9'8.1"	10'10"	17'0"	23'8"	31'0"	57'10"	81'4"	436'2"
8	90.8'	1'11.5"	2'5.2"	2'10.8"	3'10"	4'8.9"	5'7.5"	6'6"	8'2.3"	9'0"	12'10"	16'5"	19'7"	27'9"	32'3"	47'7"
		2'0.5"	2'6.8"	3'1.2"	4'2.2"	5'3.5"	6'5.1"	7'7"	9'11.9"	11'3"	18'0"	25'8"	34'6"	71'6"	111'3"	∞
11	66.1	1'11.3"	2'4.9"	2'10.4"	3'9.3"	4'7.8"	5'6"	6'0.8"	7'11"	8'8"	12'3"	15'4"	18'2"	24'11"	28'5"	39'9"
		2'0.7"	2'7.2"	3'1.7"	4'3.1"	5'4.9"	6'7.2"	7'10"	10'5"	11'9"	19'5"	28'8"	40'3"	101'5"	205'9"	∞
16	45.4	1'11"	2'4.4"	2'9.8"	3'8.1"	4'6"	5'3.6"	6'0.8"	7'6.1"	8'2"	11'3"	13'11"	16'1"	21'3"	23'10"	31'3"
		2'1.1"	2'7.7"	3'2.5"	4'4.6"	5'7.4"	6'11"	8'3.3"	11'2.7"	12'10"	22'5"	35'9"	55'7"	335'9"	∞	∞
22	33.0	1'10.6"	2'3.9"	2'9"	3'6.8"	4'4.1"	5'0.9"	5'9.3"	7'0.9"	7'8"	10'4"	12'5"	14'3"	18'1"	19'11"	24'10"
		2'1.5"	2'8.5"	3'3.6"	4'6.6"	5'10.7"	7'4"	8'10.6"	12'4.5"	14'4"	27'6"	50'9"	102'10"	∞	∞	∞
32	22.7	1'10.1"	2'3"	2'7.8"	3'4.8"	4'1.2"	4'9"	5'4.2"	6'5.3"	6'11"	9'0"	10'8"	11'11"	14'6"	15'7"	18'6"
		2'2.3"	2'9.7"	3'5.5"	4'10.3"	6'4.9"	8'1.9"	10'1.4"	14'10.9"	17'10"	44'2"	167'10"	∞	∞	∞	∞

Note: Circle of confusion = 0.001.

Table 2.9 35mm Depth of Field: 85mm Lens

F-stop	Hyperfocal Distance (ft.)	Focus Distance 2'	2'6"	3'	4'	5'	6'	7'	9'	10'	15'	20'	25'	40'	50'	100'
1.4	666.6	1'11.9"	2'5.9"	2'11.8"	3'11.7"	4'11.6"	5'11.4"	6'11.1"	8'11"	9'10"	14'8"	19'5"	24'1"	37'9"	46'6"	86'11"
		2'0.1"	2'6.1"	3'0.2"	4'0.3"	5'0.5"	6'0.7"	7'0.9"	9'1"	10'2"	15'4"	20'7"	26'0"	42'7"	54'1"	117'8"
2	466.6	1'11.9"	2'5.84"	2'11.8"	3'11.6"	4'11.4"	5'11.1"	6'11"	8'10"	9'9"	14'6"	19'2"	23'9"	36'10"	45'2"	82'4"
		2'0.1"	2'6.16"	3'0.2"	4'0.4"	5'0.6"	6'0.9"	7'1"	9'2"	10'3"	15'6"	20'11"	26'5"	43'9"	56'0"	127'3"
2.8	333.3	1'11.9"	2'5.8"	2'11.7"	3'11.4"	4'11.1"	5'10.7"	6'10"	8'9"	9'9"	14'4"	18'10"	23'3"	35'9"	43'6"	76'11"
		2'0.1"	2'6.2"	3'0.3"	4'0.6"	5'0.9"	6'1.3"	7'2"	9'3"	10'4"	15'8"	21'3"	27'0"	45'5"	58'10"	142'10"
4	233.3	1'11.8"	2'5.7"	2'11.5"	3'11.2"	4'10.7"	5'10.2"	6'10"	8'8"	9'7"	14'1"	18'5"	22'7"	34'2"	41'2"	70'0"
		2'0.2"	2'6.3"	3'0.5"	4'0.8"	5'1.3"	6'1.9"	7'3"	9'4"	10'5"	16'0"	21'11"	28'0"	48'3"	63'8"	175'0"
5.6	166.6	1'11.7"	2'5.6"	2'11.4"	3'10.9"	4'10"	5'9"	6'9"	8'6"	9'5"	13'9"	17'10"	21'9"	32'3"	38'6"	62'6"
		2'0.3"	2'6.5"	3'0.7"	4'1.2"	5'2"	6'3"	7'4"	9'6"	10'8"	16'6"	22'9"	29'5"	52'8"	71'5"	250'0"
8	116.7	1'11.6"	2'5.4"	2'11.1"	3'10.4"	4'10"	5'8"	6'7"	8'4"	9'3"	13'3"	17'1"	20'7"	29'9"	35'0"	53'10"
		2'0.4"	2'6.7"	3'1"	4'1.7"	5'3"	6'4"	7'5"	9'9"	10'11"	17'3"	24'2"	31'10"	60'10"	87'6"	∞
11	84.8	1'11.4"	2'5.1"	2'10.8"	3'9.8"	4'9"	5'7"	6'3"	8'2"	8'11"	12'9"	16'2"	19'4"	27'2"	31'6"	45'11"
		2'0.6"	2'6.9"	3'1.3"	4'2.4"	5'4"	6'5"	7'8"	10'1"	11'4"	18'3"	26'2"	35'5"	75'8"	121'9"	∞
16	58.3	1'11.2"	2'4.8"	2'10.2"	3'8.9"	4'7"	5'5"	6'3"	7'10"	8'6"	11'11"	14'11"	17'6"	23'9"	26'11"	36'10"
		2'0.9"	2'7.3"	3'2"	4'3.5"	5'6"	6'8"	7'11"	10'8"	12'1"	20'2"	30'5"	43'9"	127'4"	∞	∞
22	42.4	1'10.9"	2'4.3"	2'9.6"	3'7.9"	4'6"	5'3"	6'0"	7'5"	8'1"	11'1"	13'7"	15'9"	20'7"	22'11"	29'9"
		2'1.2"	2'7.9"	3'2.7"	4'5"	5'8"	6'12"	8'5"	11'5"	13'1"	23'2"	37'10"	60'11"	∞	∞	∞
32	29.2	1'10.5"	2'3.6"	2'8.6"	3'6.2"	4'3"	4'12"	5'8"	6'11"	7'5"	9'11"	11'10"	13'6"	16'10"	18'5"	22'7"
		2'1.8"	2'8.8"	3'4.1"	4'7.6"	6'0"	7'7"	9'3"	13'0"	15'3"	30'11"	63'8"	∞	∞	∞	∞

Note: Circle of confusion = 0.001.

Table 2.10 35mm Depth of Field: 100mm Lens

F-stop	Hyperfocal Distance (ft.)	Focus Distance													
		4'	5'	6'	7'	8'	9'	10'	12'	15'	20'	25'	30'	50'	100'	200'
1.4	922.6	3'11.8"	4'11.7"	5'11.5"	6'11"	7'11"	8'11"	9'11"	11'10"	14'9"	19'7"	24'4"	29'1"	47'5"	90'3"	164'4"
		4'0.2"	5'0.3"	6'0.5"	7'1"	8'1"	9'1"	10'1"	12'2"	15'3"	20'5"	25'8"	31'0"	52'10"	112'2"	255'4"
2	645.8	3'11.7"	4'11.5"	5'11.3"	6'11"	7'11"	8'11"	9'10"	11'9"	14'8"	19'5"	24'1"	28'8"	46'5"	86'7"	152'9"
		4'0.3"	5'0.5"	6'0.7"	7'1"	8'1"	9'2"	10'2"	12'3"	15'4"	20'8"	26'0"	31'6"	54'2"	118'4"	289'9"
2.8	461.3	3'11.6"	4'11.4"	5'11.1"	6'11"	7'10"	8'10"	9'9"	11'8"	14'6"	19'2"	23'9"	28'2"	45'1"	82'2"	139'6"
		4'0.4"	5'0.7"	6'0.9"	7'1"	8'2"	9'2"	10'3"	12'4"	15'6"	20'11"	26'5"	32'1"	56'1"	127'8"	353'1"
4	322.9	3'11.4"	4'11.1"	5'10.7"	6'10"	7'10"	8'9"	9'8"	11'7"	14'4"	18'10"	23'2"	27'5"	43'4"	76'4"	123'6"
		4'0.6"	5'0.9"	6'1.4"	7'2"	8'2"	9'3"	10'4"	12'6"	15'9"	21'4"	27'1"	33'1"	59'2"	144'10"	525'5"
5.6	230.7	3'11.2"	4'10.7"	5'10.2"	6'10"	7'9"	8'8"	9'7"	11'5"	14'1"	18'5"	22'7"	26'7"	41'1"	69'9"	107'1"
		4'0.8"	5'1.3"	6'1.9"	7'3"	8'3"	9'4"	10'5"	12'8"	16'1"	21'11"	28'0"	34'6"	63'10"	176'6"	1504'10"
8	161.5	3'10.8"	4'10.2"	5'9.4"	6'9"	7'7"	8'6"	9'5"	11'2"	13'9"	17'10"	21'8"	25'4"	38'2"	61'9"	89'4"
		4'1.2"	5'1.9"	6'2.8"	7'4"	8'5"	9'6"	10'8"	13'0"	16'6"	22'10"	29'7"	36'10"	72'5"	262'9"	∞
11	117.4	3'10.4"	4'9.5"	5'8.5"	6'7"	7'6"	8'1"	9'3"	10'11"	13'4"	17'1"	20'7"	23'11"	35'1"	54'0"	74'0"
		4'1.7"	5'2.7"	6'3.9"	7'5"	8'7"	9'9"	10'11"	13'4"	17'2"	24'1"	31'9"	40'4"	87'1"	673'11"	∞
16	80.7	3'9.7"	4'8.5"	5'7"	6'5"	7'3"	8'1"	8'11"	10'5"	12'8"	16'0"	19'1"	21'10"	30'11"	44'8"	57'6"
		4'2.5"	5'4"	6'5.8"	7'8"	8'11"	10'2"	11'5"	14'1"	18'5"	26'7"	36'3"	47'9"	131'4"	∞	∞
22	58.7	3'8.9"	4'7.3"	5'5.3"	6'3"	7'0"	7'10"	8'7"	10'0"	11'11"	14'11"	17'6"	19'10"	27'0"	37'0"	45'5"
		4'3.5"	5'5.6"	6'8.2"	7'11"	9'3"	10'8"	12'1"	15'1"	20'2"	30'4"	43'6"	61'4"	336'11"	∞	∞
32	40.4	3'7.7"	4'5.4"	5'2.7"	6'0"	6'8"	7'4"	8'0"	9'3"	10'11"	13'4"	15'5"	17'3"	22'4"	28'9"	33'7"
		4'5.3"	5'8.5"	7'0.6"	8'6"	10'0"	11'7"	13'4"	17'1"	23'10"	39'8"	65'8"	116'10"	∞	∞	∞

Note: Circle of confusion = 0.001.

Table 2.11 35mm Depth of Field: 135mm Lens

F-stop	Hyperfocal Distance (ft.)	Focus Distance 2'	3'	4'	5'	6'	7'	8'	9'	10'	12'	15'	25'	50'	100'	200'
1.4	1681.5	1'11.97"	2'11.9"	3'11.9"	4'11.8"	5'11.7"	6'11.7"	7'11.5"	8'11"	9'11"	11'11"	14'10"	24'8"	48'7"	94'5"	178'9"
		2'0.03"	3'0.1"	4'0.1"	5'0.2"	6'0.3"	7'0.4"	8'0.5"	9'1"	10'1"	12'1"	15'2"	25'5"	51'6"	106'4"	227'0"
2	1177.0	1'11.96"	2'11.9"	3'11.8"	4'11.7"	5'11.6"	6'11.5"	7'11.4"	8'11"	9'11"	11'11"	14'10"	24'6"	48'0"	92'2"	170'11"
		2'0.04"	3'0.1"	4'0.2"	5'0.3"	6'0.4"	7'0.5"	8'0.7"	9'1"	10'1"	12'1"	15'2"	25'7"	52'3"	109'3"	240'11"
2.8	840.7	1'11.9"	2'11.9"	3'11.8"	4'11.6"	5'11.5"	6'11.3"	7'11.1"	8'11"	9'11"	11'10"	14'9"	24'3"	47'2"	89'4"	161'7"
		2'0.1"	3'0.1"	4'0.2"	5'0.4"	6'0.5"	7'0.7"	8'0.9"	9'1"	10'1"	12'2"	15'3"	25'9"	53'2"	113'6"	262'5"
4	588.5	1'11.9"	2'11.8"	3'11.7"	4'11.5"	5'11.3"	6'11"	7'10.7"	8'10"	9'10"	11'9"	14'8"	24'0"	46'1"	85'6"	149'3"
		2'0.1"	3'0.2"	4'0.3"	5'0.5"	6'0.7"	7'1"	8'1.3"	9'2"	10'2"	12'3"	15'5"	26'1"	54'8"	120'6"	302'11"
5.6	420.4	1'11.9"	2'11.7"	3'11.5"	4'11.3"	5'11"	6'10.6"	7'10.2"	8'10"	9'9"	11'8"	14'6"	23'7"	44'8"	80'9"	135'6"
		2'0.1"	3'0.3"	4'0.5"	5'0.7"	6'1"	7'1.4"	8'1.9"	9'2"	10'3"	12'4"	15'7"	26'7"	56'9"	131'3"	381'6"
8	294.3	1'11.8"	2'11.6"	3'11.4"	4'11"	5'10.6"	6'10"	7'9.5"	8'9"	9'8"	11'6"	14'3"	23'1"	42'9"	74'8"	119'1"
		2'0.2"	3'0.4"	4'0.7"	5'1"	6'1.5"	7'2"	8'2.7"	9'3"	10'4"	12'6"	15'10"	27'4"	60'3"	151'6"	624'4"
11	214.0	1'11.8"	2'11.5"	3'11.1"	4'10.6"	5'10"	6'8.2"	7'8.5"	8'8"	9'7"	11'4"	14'0"	22'5"	40'6"	68'2"	103'5"
		2'0.2"	3'0.5"	4'0.9"	5'1.4"	6'2.1"	7'2.8"	8'3.7"	9'5"	10'6"	12'9"	16'2"	28'4"	65'3"	187'9"	3055'10"
16	147.1	1'11.7"	2'11.3"	3'10.7"	4'10"	5'9.2"	6'8.2"	7'7"	8'6"	9'4"	11'1"	13'7"	21'4"	37'4"	59'6"	84'9"
		2'0.3"	3'0.7"	4'1.3"	5'2.1"	6'3.1"	7'4.2"	8'5.5"	9'7"	10'9"	13'1"	16'8"	30'1"	75'9"	312'2"	∞
22	107.0	1'11.6"	2'11"	3'10.3"	4'9.3"	5'8.2"	6'6.8"	7'5.3"	8'4"	9'2"	10'9"	13'2"	20'3"	34'1"	51'8"	69'8"
		2'0.5"	3'1"	4'1.9"	5'2.9"	6'4.3"	7'5.9"	8'7.8"	9'10"	11'0"	13'6"	17'5"	32'7"	93'10"	1527'11"	∞
32	73.6	1'11.4"	2'10.6"	3'9.5"	4'8.2"	5'6.6"	6'4.7"	7'2.6"	8'0"	8'10"	10'4"	12'6"	18'8"	29'9"	42'5"	53'9"
		2'0.7"	3'1.5"	4'2.8"	5'4.4"	6'6.4"	7'8.8"	8'11.7"	10'3"	11'7"	14'4"	18'10"	37'10"	156'1"	∞	∞

Note: Circle of confusion = 0.001.

Table 2.12 35mm Depth of Field: 200mm Lens

F-stop	Hyperfocal Distance (ft.)	Focus Distance 5'	6'	7'	8'	9'	10'	12'	15'	20'	25'	30'	50'	100'	200'	300'
1.4	3690.5	4'11.92"	5'11.9"	6'11.8"	7'11.8"	8'11.7"	9'11.7"	11'11.5"	14'11"	19'11"	24'10"	29'9"	49'4"	97'4"	189'9"	277'5"
		5'0.08"	6'0.1"	7'0.2"	8'0.2"	9'0.3"	10'0.3"	12'0.5"	15'1"	20'1"	25'2"	30'3"	50'8"	102'9"	211'6"	326'7"
2	2583.3	4'11.88"	5'11.8"	6'11.8"	7'11.7"	8'11.6"	9'11.5"	11'11.3"	14'11"	19'10"	24'9"	29'8"	49'1"	96'3"	185'8"	268'9"
		5'0.12"	6'0.2"	7'0.2"	8'0.3"	9'0.4"	10'0.5"	12'0.7"	15'1"	20'2"	25'3"	30'4"	51'0"	104'0"	216'9"	339'5"
2.8	1845.2	4'11.8"	5'11.8"	6'11.7"	7'11.6"	8'11.5"	9'11.4"	11'11.1"	14'11"	19'9"	24'8"	29'6"	48'8"	94'10"	180'5"	258'1"
		5'0.2"	6'0.2"	7'0.3"	8'0.4"	9'0.5"	10'0.7"	12'0.9"	15'1"	20'3"	25'4"	30'6"	51'5"	105'9"	224'4"	358'3"
4	1291.7	4'11.8"	5'11.7"	6'11.5"	7'11.4"	8'11.3"	9'11.1"	11'10.7"	14'10"	19'8"	24'6"	29'4"	48'2"	92'10"	173'2"	243'5"
		5'0.2"	6'0.3"	7'0.5"	8'0.6"	9'0.8"	10'0.9"	12'1.4"	15'2"	20'4"	25'6"	30'9"	52'0"	108'5"	236'8"	390'9"
5.6	922.6	4'11.7"	5'11.5"	6'11.4"	7'11.2"	8'11"	9'10.7"	11'10.2"	14'9"	19'7"	24'4"	29'1"	47'5"	90'3"	164'4"	226'5"
		5'0.3"	6'0.5"	7'0.6"	8'0.8"	9'1.1"	10'1.3"	12'1.9"	15'3"	20'5"	25'8"	31'0"	52'10"	112'2"	255'4"	444'7"
8	645.8	4'11.5"	5'11.3"	6'11.1"	7'10.8"	8'10.5"	9'10.2"	11'9.4"	14'8"	19'5"	24'1"	28'8"	46'5"	86'7"	152'9"	204'10"
		5'0.5"	6'0.7"	7'0.9"	8'1.2"	9'1.5"	10'1.9"	12'2.7"	15'4"	20'8"	26'0"	31'6"	54'2"	118'4"	289'9"	560'3"
11	469.7	4'11.4"	5'11.1"	6'10.8"	7'10.4"	8'10"	9'8.4"	11'8.4"	14'6"	19'2"	23'9"	28'2"	45'2"	82'5"	140'3"	183'1"
		5'0.6"	6'0.9"	7'1.3"	8'1.7"	9'2.1"	10'2.6"	12'3.8"	15'6"	20'11"	26'5"	32'1"	55'11"	127'1"	348'4"	830'4"
16	322.9	4'11.1"	5'10.7"	6'10.2"	7'9.7"	8'9.1"	9'8.4"	11'6.8"	14'4"	18'10"	23'2"	27'5"	43'4"	76'4"	123'6"	155'6"
		5'0.9"	6'1.4"	7'1.9"	8'2.4"	9'3.1"	10'3.8"	12'5.6"	15'9"	21'4"	27'1"	33'1"	59'2"	144'10"	525'5"	4227'1"
22	234.8	4'10.7"	5'10.2"	6'9.6"	7'8.8"	8'8"	9'7.1"	11'5"	14'1"	18'5"	22'7"	26'7"	41'3"	70'2"	108'0"	131'9"
		5'1.3"	6'1.9"	7'2.6"	8'3.4"	9'4.3"	10'5.3"	12'7.8"	16'0"	21'10"	28'0"	34'5"	63'6"	174'2"	1347'10"	∞
32	161.5	4'10.2"	5'9.4"	6'8.5"	7'7.5"	8'6.3"	9'5"	11'2"	13'9"	17'10"	21'8"	25'4"	38'2"	61'9"	89'4"	104'12"
		5'1.9"	6'2.8"	7'3.8"	8'5"	9'6.4"	10'7.9"	12'11.6"	16'6"	22'10"	29'7"	36'10"	72'5"	262'9"	∞	∞

Note: Circle of confusion = 0.001.

Table 2.13 35mm Depth of Field: 250mm Lens

F-stop	Hyperfocal Distance (ft.)	Focus Distance 5'	6'	7'	8'	9'	10'	12'	15'	20'	25'	30'	50'	100'	200'	300'
1.4	5766.4	4'11.95"	5'11.9"	6'11.9"	7'11.9"	8'11.8"	9'11.8"	11'11.7"	15'0"	19'11"	24'11"	29'10"	49'7"	98'4"	193'4"	285'2"
		5'0.05"	6'0.1"	7'0.1"	8'0.1"	9'0.2"	10'0.2"	12'0.3"	15'0"	20'1"	25'1"	30'2"	50'5"	101'9"	207'2"	316'6"
2	4036.5	4'11.93"	5'11.9"	6'11.9"	7'11.8"	8'11.8"	9'11.7"	11'11.6"	14'11"	19'11"	24'10"	29'9"	49'5"	97'7"	190'7"	279'3"
		5'0.07"	6'0.1"	7'0.1"	8'0.2"	9'0.2"	10'0.3"	12'0.4"	15'1"	20'1"	25'2"	30'3"	50'8"	102'6"	210'5"	324'1"
2.8	2883.2	4'11.9"	5'11.9"	6'11.8"	7'11.7"	8'11.7"	9'11.6"	11'11.4"	14'11"	19'10"	24'9"	29'8"	49'2"	96'8"	187'0"	271'9"
		5'0.1"	6'0.2"	7'0.2"	8'0.3"	9'0.3"	10'0.4"	12'0.6"	15'1"	20'2"	25'3"	30'4"	50'11"	103'7"	214'11"	334'10"
4	2018.2	4'11.9"	5'11.8"	6'11.7"	7'11.6"	8'11.5"	9'11.4"	11'11.1"	14'11"	19'10"	24'8"	29'7"	48'9"	95'3"	182'0"	261'2"
		5'0.1"	6'0.2"	7'0.3"	8'0.4"	9'0.5"	10'0.6"	12'0.9"	15'1"	20'2"	25'4"	30'5"	51'3"	105'3"	222'0"	352'5"
5.6	1441.6	4'11.8"	5'11.7"	6'11.6"	7'11.5"	8'11.3"	9'11.2"	11'10.8"	14'10"	19'9"	24'7"	29'5"	48'4"	93'6"	175'8"	248'4"
		5'0.2"	6'0.3"	7'0.4"	8'0.5"	9'0.7"	10'0.8"	12'1.2"	15'2"	20'3"	25'5"	30'8"	51'10"	107'5"	232'3"	378'10"
8	1009.1	4'11.7"	5'11.6"	6'11.4"	7'11.2"	8'11"	9'10.8"	11'10.3"	14'9"	19'7"	24'5"	29'2"	47'8"	91'0"	166'11"	231'3"
		5'0.3"	6'0.4"	7'0.6"	8'0.8"	9'1"	10'1.2"	12'1.7"	15'3"	20'5"	25'8"	30'11"	52'7"	111'0"	249'5"	426'11"
11	733.9	4'11.6"	5'11.4"	6'11.2"	7'11"	8'10.7"	9'9.7"	11'9.7"	14'8"	19'6"	24'2"	28'10"	46'10"	88'0"	157'2"	212'11"
		5'0.4"	6'0.6"	7'0.8"	8'1.1"	9'1.3"	10'1.7"	12'2.4"	15'4"	20'7"	25'11"	31'3"	53'8"	115'9"	274'11"	507'5"
16	504.6	4'11.4"	5'11.2"	6'10.9"	7'10.5"	8'10.1"	9'9.7"	11'8.7"	14'7"	19'3"	23'10"	28'4"	45'6"	83'6"	143'3"	188'2"
		5'0.6"	6'0.9"	7'1.2"	8'1.5"	9'2"	10'2.4"	12'3.5"	15'6"	20'10"	26'4"	31'11"	55'6"	124'9"	331'4"	740'0"
22	367.0	4'11.2"	5'10.8"	6'10.4"	7'10"	8'9.4"	9'8.8"	11'7.4"	14'5"	19'0"	23'5"	27'9"	44'0"	78'7"	129'5"	165'1"
		5'0.8"	6'1.2"	7'1.6"	8'2.1"	9'2.7"	10'3.4"	12'4.9"	15'8"	21'2"	26'10"	32'8"	57'11"	137'6"	439'7"	∞
32	252.3	4'10.8"	5'10.3"	6'9.7"	7'9"	8'8.3"	9'7.4"	11'5.5"	14'2"	18'6"	22'9"	26'10"	41'9"	71'7"	111'7"	137'0"
		5'1.2"	6'1.8"	7'2.4"	8'3.1"	9'4"	10'5"	12'7.2"	15'11"	21'9"	27'9"	34'1"	62'4"	165'8"	∞	∞

Note: Circle of confusion = 0.001.

Table 2.14 35mm Depth of Field: 300mm Lens

F-stop	Hyperfocal Distance (ft.)	Focus Distance														
		8'	9'	10'	12'	15'	20'	25'	30'	40'	50'	60'	75'	100'	200'	300'
1.4	8303.6	7'11.91"	8'11.9"	9'11.9"	11'11.8"	14'11.7"	19'11.4"	24'11.1"	29'11"	39'10"	49'8"	59'7"	74'4"	98'10"	195'4"	289'6"
		8'0.09"	9'0.1"	10'0.1"	12'0.2"	15'0.3"	20'0.6"	25'0.9"	30'1"	40'2"	50'4"	60'5"	75'8"	101'3"	204'11"	311'3"
2	5812.5	7'11.87"	8'11.8"	9'11.8"	11'11.7"	14'11.5"	19'11.2"	24'10.7"	29'10"	39'9"	49'7"	59'5"	74'1"	98'4"	193'4"	285'3"
		8'0.13"	9'0.2"	10'0.2"	12'0.3"	15'0.5"	20'0.8"	25'1.3"	30'2"	40'3"	50'5"	60'8"	76'0"	101'9"	207'2"	316'4"
2.8	4151.8	7'11.8"	8'11.8"	9'11.7"	11'11.6"	14'11.4"	19'10.8"	24'10.2"	29'9"	39'7"	49'5"	59'2"	73'8"	97'8"	190'10"	279'9"
		8'0.2"	9'0.2"	10'0.3"	12'0.4"	15'0.7"	20'1.2"	25'1.8"	30'3"	40'5"	50'7"	60'11"	76'5"	102'6"	210'1"	323'4"
4	2906.3	7'11.7"	8'11.7"	9'11.6"	11'11.4"	14'11.1"	19'10.4"	24'9.4"	29'8"	39'5"	49'2"	58'9"	73'1"	96'8"	187'1"	271'11"
		8'0.3"	9'0.3"	10'0.4"	12'0.6"	15'0.9"	20'1.7"	25'2.6"	30'4"	40'7"	50'11"	61'3"	77'0"	103'7"	214'9"	334'6"
5.6	2075.9	7'11.6"	8'11.5"	9'11.4"	11'11.2"	14'10.7"	19'9.7"	24'8.4"	29'7"	39'3"	48'10"	58'4"	72'5"	95'5"	182'5"	262'1"
		8'0.4"	9'0.5"	10'0.6"	12'0.8"	15'1.3"	20'2.3"	25'3.7"	30'5"	40'9"	51'3"	61'9"	77'10"	105'1"	221'4"	350'8"
8	1453.1	7'11.5"	8'11.3"	9'11.2"	11'10.8"	14'10.2"	19'8.7"	24'6.9"	29'5"	38'11"	48'4"	57'7"	71'4"	93'7"	175'10"	248'8"
		8'0.5"	9'0.7"	10'0.8"	12'1.2"	15'1.9"	20'3.3"	25'5.3"	30'8"	41'2"	51'9"	62'7"	79'1"	107'5"	231'11"	378'1"
11	1056.8	7'11.3"	8'11.1"	9'10.9"	11'10.4"	14'9.5"	19'5.6"	24'5.1"	29'2"	38'6"	47'9"	56'9"	70'0"	91'4"	168'2"	233'8"
		8'0.7"	9'0.9"	10'1.1"	12'1.7"	15'2.6"	20'4.6"	25'7.3"	30'11"	41'7"	52'6"	63'7"	80'9"	110'5"	246'8"	418'11"
16	726.6	7'11"	8'10.7"	9'10.4"	11'9.7"	14'8.4"	19'5.6"	24'2"	28'10"	37'11"	46'9"	55'5"	68'0"	87'11"	156'10"	212'4"
		8'1.1"	9'1.4"	10'1.7"	12'2.4"	15'3.8"	20'6.8"	25'10.7"	31'4"	42'4"	53'8"	65'5"	83'8"	116'0"	276'0"	511'0"
22	528.4	7'10.6"	8'10.2"	9'9.8"	11'8.8"	14'7"	19'3.2"	23'10.4"	28'5"	37'2"	45'8"	53'11"	65'8"	84'1"	145'1"	191'4"
		8'1.5"	9'1.9"	10'2.3"	12'3.3"	15'5.3"	20'9.4"	26'2.9"	31'10"	43'3"	55'3"	67'8"	87'5"	123'4"	321'10"	∞
32	363.3	7'9.9"	8'9.4"	9'8.8"	11'7.4"	14'4.9"	18'11.5"	23'4.7"	27'9"	36'0"	43'11"	51'6"	62'2"	78'5"	129'0"	164'4"
		8'2.2"	9'2.7"	10'3.4"	12'4.9"	15'7.8"	21'2"	26'10.2"	32'8"	44'11"	58'0"	71'10"	94'6"	138'0"	∞	∞

Note: Circle of confusion = 0.001.

Table 2.15 35mm Depth of Field: 600mm Lens

F-stop	Hyperfocal Distance (ft.)	Focus Distance 25'	30'	35'	40'	50'	60'	75'	100'	150'	200'	300'	400'	500'	1000'	1500'
1.4	33214.4'	24' 11.8"	30' 0"	34' 11.6"	39' 11"	49' 11"	59' 11"	74' 10"	99' 8"	149' 4"	198' 10"	297' 4"	395' 3"	492' 7"	970' 9"	1435' 2"
		25' 0.2"	30' 0.3"	35' 0"	40' 1"	50' 1"	60' 1"	75' 2"	100' 4"	150' 8"	201' 3"	302' 9"	404' 11"	507' 8"	1031' 1"	1570' 11"
2	23250.1'	24' 11.7"	29' 11.5"	34' 11"	39' 11"	49' 11"	59' 10"	74' 9"	99' 7"	149' 0"	198' 4"	296' 2"	393' 3"	489' 6"	958' 9"	1409' 1"
		25' 0.3"	30' 0.5"	35' 1"	40' 1"	50' 1"	60' 2"	75' 3"	100' 5"	151' 0"	201' 9"	303' 11"	407' 0"	511' 0"	1044' 11"	1603' 5"
2.8	16607.2'	24' 11.5"	29' 11"	34' 11"	39' 11"	49' 10"	59' 9"	74' 8"	99' 5"	148' 8"	197' 7"	294' 8"	390' 7"	485' 5"	943' 2"	1375' 9"
		25' 0.5"	30' 1"	35' 1"	40' 1"	50' 2"	60' 3"	75' 4"	100' 7"	151' 4"	202' 5"	305' 6"	409' 10"	515' 6"	1064' 1"	1648' 11"
4	11625.0'	24' 11.4"	29' 11"	34' 11"	39' 10"	49' 9"	59' 8"	74' 6"	99' 2"	148' 1"	196' 7"	292' 5"	386' 8"	479' 5"	920' 10"	1328' 7"
		25' 0.6"	30' 1"	35' 1"	40' 2"	50' 3"	60' 4"	75' 6"	100' 10"	152' 0"	203' 6"	307' 11"	414' 3"	522' 6"	1094' 1"	1722' 3"
5.6	8303.6'	24' 11.1"	29' 11"	34' 10"	39' 10"	49' 8"	59' 7"	74' 4"	98' 10"	147' 4"	195' 4"	289' 6"	381' 7"	471' 7"	892' 6"	1270' 6"
		25' 0.9"	30' 1"	35' 2"	40' 2"	50' 4"	60' 5"	75' 8"	101' 3"	152' 9"	204' 11"	311' 3"	420' 3"	532' 0"	1136' 11"	1830' 8"
8	5812.5'	24' 10.7"	29' 10"	34' 9"	39' 9"	49' 7"	59' 5"	74' 1"	98' 4"	146' 3"	193' 4"	285' 3"	374' 3"	460' 5"	853' 3"	1192' 4"
		25' 1.3"	30' 2"	35' 3"	40' 3"	50' 5"	60' 8"	76' 0"	101' 9"	154' 0"	207' 2"	316' 4"	429' 7"	547' 1"	1207' 9"	2021' 9"
11	4227.3'	24' 10.2"	29' 9"	34' 9"	39' 8"	49' 5"	58' 9"	73' 8"	97' 8"	144' 10"	190' 12"	280' 1"	365' 5"	447' 1"	808' 8"	1107' 2"
		25' 1.8"	30' 3"	35' 4"	40' 5"	50' 7"	60' 10"	76' 4"	102' 5"	155' 6"	209' 11"	322' 11"	441' 10"	567' 1"	1309' 10"	2325' 0"
16	2906.3'	24' 9.4"	29' 8"	34' 7"	39' 5"	49' 2"	58' 9"	73' 1"	96' 8"	142' 8"	187' 1"	271' 11"	351' 7"	426' 7"	744' 0"	989' 4"
		25' 2.6"	30' 4"	35' 5"	40' 7"	50' 11"	61' 3"	77' 0"	103' 7"	158' 2"	214' 9"	334' 6"	463' 10"	603' 11"	1524' 7"	3100' 0"
22	2113.6'	24' 8.5"	29' 7"	34' 5"	39' 3"	48' 10"	58' 4"	72' 5"	95' 6"	140' 1"	182' 9"	262' 9"	336' 4"	404' 4"	678' 10"	877' 4"
		25' 3.6"	30' 5"	35' 7"	40' 9"	51' 3"	61' 9"	77' 9"	105' 0"	161' 5"	220' 11"	349' 7"	493' 4"	654' 11"	1897' 11"	5166' 7"
32	1453.1'	24' 7"	29' 5"	34' 2"	38' 11"	48' 4"	57' 7"	71' 4"	93' 7"	136' 0"	175' 10"	248' 8"	313' 8"	372' 0"	592' 4"	738' 1"
		25' 5.3"	30' 8"	35' 10"	41' 2"	51' 9"	62' 7"	79' 1"	107' 5"	167' 3"	231' 11"	378' 1"	551' 11"	762' 4"	3206' 10"	∞

Note: Circle of confusion = 0.001.

Table 2.16 35mm Depth of Field: 800mm Lens

F-stop	Hyperfocal Distance	Focus Distance														
		40'	50'	60'	75'	100'	150'	200'	250'	300'	400'	500'	600'	750'	1000'	1500'
1.4	59047.8'	39'11.7"	49'11"	59'11"	74'11"	99'10"	149'7"	199'4"	248'11"	298'6"	397'4"	495'10"	594'0"	740'7"	983'4"	1462'10"
		40'0.3"	50'1"	60'1"	75'1"	100'2"	150'5"	200'8"	251'1"	301'6"	402'9"	504'3"	606'2"	759'8"	1017'3"	1539'1"
2	41333.5'	39'11.5"	49'11"	59'11"	74'10"	99'9"	149'5"	199'0"	248'6"	297'10"	396'2"	494'0"	591'5"	736'8"	976'5"	1447'6"
		40'0.5"	50'1"	60'1"	75'2"	100'3"	150'7"	201'0"	251'6"	302'2"	403'11"	506'1"	608'10"	763'10"	1024'10"	1556'6"
2.8	29523.9'	39'11.4"	49'11"	59'11"	74'10"	99'8"	149'3"	198'8"	247'11"	297'0"	394'8"	491'8"	588'1"	731'5"	967'3"	1427'6"
		40'1"	50'1"	60'1"	75'2"	100'4"	150'9"	201'4"	252'2"	303'1"	405'6"	508'7"	612'5"	769'7"	1035'1"	1580'3"
4	20666.7'	39'11"	49'11"	59'10"	74'9"	99'6"	148'11"	198'1"	247'0"	295'8"	392'5"	488'2"	583'1"	723'9"	953'10"	1398'6"
		40'1"	50'1"	60'2"	75'3"	100'6"	151'1"	201'11"	253'1"	304'5"	407'11"	512'5"	617'11"	778'3"	1050'10"	1617'5"
5.6	14762.0'	39'11"	49'10"	59'9"	74'7"	99'4"	148'6"	197'4"	245'10"	294'0"	389'5"	483'7"	576'7"	713'9"	936'7"	1361'8"
		40'1"	50'2"	60'3"	75'5"	100'8"	151'6"	202'9"	254'4"	306'3"	411'2"	517'6"	625'5"	790'2"	1072'8"	1669'8"
8	10333.4'	39'10"	49'9"	59'8"	74'6"	99'0"	147'10"	196'2"	244'1"	291'6"	385'1"	476'11"	567'1"	699'3"	911'9"	1309'10"
		40'2"	50'3"	60'4"	75'7"	101'0"	152'3"	203'11"	256'2"	309'0"	416'1"	525'5"	637'0"	808'8"	1107'2"	1754'9"
11	7515.2'	39'9"	49'8"	59'6"	74'3"	98'8"	145'9"	194'10"	241'11"	288'6"	379'9"	468'10"	555'8"	681'11"	882'7"	1250'5"
		40'3"	50'4"	60'6"	75'9"	101'4"	153'1"	205'6"	258'7"	312'6"	422'6"	535'8"	652'1"	833'2"	1153'6"	1874'1"
16	5166.7'	39'8"	49'6"	59'4"	73'11"	98'1"	145'9"	192'7"	238'6"	283'6"	371'3"	455'11"	537'7"	654'11"	837'10"	1162'6"
		40'4"	50'6"	60'8"	76'1"	102'0"	154'6"	208'1"	262'9"	318'6"	433'7"	553'7"	678'10"	877'4"	1240'0"	2113'8"
22	3757.6'	39'7"	49'4"	59'1"	73'6"	97'5"	144'3"	189'11"	234'5"	277'10"	361'6"	441'3"	517'5"	625'3"	789'10"	1072'1"
		40'5"	50'8"	61'0"	76'6"	102'9"	156'3"	211'3"	267'10"	326'0"	447'8"	576'9"	714'0"	937'0"	1362'8"	2496'8"
32	2583.3'	39'5"	49'1"	58'8"	72'11"	96'3"	141'9"	185'8"	227'11"	268'9"	346'4"	418'11"	486'11"	581'3"	720'11"	949'0"
		40'8"	51'0"	61'5"	77'3"	104'0"	159'3"	216'9"	276'9"	339'5"	473'3"	620'0"	781'6"	1056'10"	1631'7"	3576'11"

Note: Circle of confusion = 0.001.

Table 2.17 35mm Depth of Field: 1000mm Lens

F-stop	Hyperfocal Distance (ft.)	Focus Distance 60'	70'	80'	90'	100'	125'	150'	200'	250'	300'	400'	500'	750'	1000'	1500'
2.8	46131.1'	59'11"	69'11"	79'10"	89'10"	99'9"	124'8"	149'6"	199'2"	248'8"	298'1"	396'7"	494'8"	738'0"	978'9"	1452'9"
		60'1"	70'1"	80'2"	90'2"	100'3"	125'4"	150'6"	200'10"	251'4"	302'0"	403'6"	505'6"	762'5"	1022'2"	1550'5"
4	32291.8'	59'11"	69'10"	79'10"	89'9"	99'8"	124'6"	149'4"	198'9"	248'1"	297'3"	395'1"	492'5"	733'0"	970'0"	1433'5"
		60'1"	70'2"	80'2"	90'3"	100'4"	125'6"	150'8"	201'3"	251'11"	302'10"	405'0"	507'10"	767'10"	1031'11"	1573'1"
5.6	23065.6'	59'10"	69'9"	79'9"	89'8"	99'7"	124'4"	149'0"	198'3"	247'4"	296'2"	393'2"	489'5"	726'5"	958'5"	1408'5"
		60'2"	70'3"	80'3"	90'4"	100'5"	125'8"	151'0"	201'9"	252'9"	303'11"	407'1"	511'1"	775'2"	1045'4"	1604'4"
8	16145.9'	59'9"	69'8"	79'7"	89'6"	99'5"	124'0"	148'7"	197'7"	246'2"	294'6"	390'4"	485'0"	716'8"	941'8"	1372'6"
		60'3"	70'4"	80'5"	90'6"	100'7"	126'0"	151'5"	202'6"	253'11"	305'8"	410'2"	516'0"	786'6"	1066'0"	1653'8"
11	11742.5'	59'8"	69'7"	79'6"	89'4"	99'2"	123'8"	148'1"	196'8"	244'9"	292'6"	386'10"	479'7"	705'0"	921'6"	1330'1"
		60'4"	70'5"	80'7"	90'8"	100'10"	126'4"	151'11"	203'6"	255'5"	307'10"	414'1"	522'3"	801'2"	1093'1"	1719'8"
16	8072.9'	59'7"	69'5"	79'3"	89'0"	98'9"	123'1"	147'3"	195'2"	242'6"	289'3"	381'1"	470'10"	686'3"	889'9"	1265'0"
		60'5"	70'7"	80'10"	91'0"	101'3"	127'0"	152'10"	205'1"	258'0"	311'7"	420'10"	533'0"	826'10"	1141'5"	1842'4"
22	5871.2'	59'5"	69'2"	78'11"	88'8"	98'4"	122'5"	144'8"	193'5"	239'9"	285'5"	374'6"	460'9"	665'1"	854'6"	1194'9"
		60'7"	70'10"	81'1"	91'5"	101'9"	127'9"	153'11"	207'1"	261'1"	316'2"	429'3"	546'7"	859'10"	1205'3"	2014'9"
32	4036.5'	59'1"	68'10"	78'5"	88'0"	97'7"	121'3"	144'8"	190'7"	235'5"	279'3"	363'11"	444'11"	632'6"	801'5"	1093'7"
		60'11"	71'3"	81'7"	92'1"	102'6"	129'0"	155'9"	210'5"	266'6"	324'1"	444'0"	570'8"	921'2"	1329'4"	2387'1"
45	2870.4'	58'9"	68'4"	77'10"	87'3"	96'8"	119'9"	142'7"	187'0"	230'0"	271'7"	351'1"	425'10"	594'8"	741'8"	985'2"
		61'3"	71'9"	82'4"	92'11"	103'7"	130'8"	158'3"	215'0"	273'10"	335'0"	464'9"	605'6"	1015'3"	1534'8"	3141'11"
64	2018.2'	58'3"	67'8"	76'11"	86'2"	95'3"	117'9"	139'7"	182'0"	222'5"	261'2"	333'10"	400'9"	546'10"	668'8"	860'6"
		61'10"	72'6"	83'4"	94'2"	105'3"	133'3"	162'1"	222'0"	285'4"	352'5"	498'10"	664'8"	1193'6"	1982'1"	5841'8"

Note: Circle of confusion = 0.001.

Table 2.18 35mm Depth of Field: 1200mm Lens

F-stop	Hyperfocal Distance (ft.)	Focus Distance 70'	75'	80'	90'	100'	125'	150'	200'	250'	300'	400'	500'	750'	1000'	1500'
2.8	66428.8'	59'11"	69'11"	79'11"	89'11"	99'10"	124'9"	149'8"	199'5"	249'1"	298'8"	397'7"	496'3"	741'8"	985'2"	1466'11"
		60'1"	70'1"	80'1"	90'1"	100'2"	125'3"	150'4"	200'7"	250'11"	301'4"	402'5"	503'10"	758'7"	1015'3"	1534'8"
4	46500.2'	59'11"	69'11"	79'10"	89'10"	99'9"	124'8"	149'6"	199'2"	248'8"	298'1"	396'7"	494'8"	738'1"	978'11"	1453'2"
		60'1"	70'1"	80'2"	90'2"	100'3"	125'4"	150'6"	200'10"	251'4"	301'11"	403'6"	505'5"	762'4"	1022'0"	1550'0"
5.6	33214.4'	59'11"	69'10"	79'10"	89'9"	99'8"	124'6"	149'4"	198'10"	248'2"	297'4"	395'3"	492'7"	733'5"	970'9"	1435'2"
		60'1"	70'2"	80'2"	90'3"	100'4"	125'6"	150'8"	201'3"	251'11"	302'9"	404'11"	507'8"	767'4"	1031'1"	1570'11"
8	23250.1'	59'10"	69'9"	79'9"	89'8"	99'7"	124'4"	149'0"	198'4"	247'4"	296'2"	393'3"	489'6"	726'7"	958'9"	1409'1"
		60'2"	70'3"	80'3"	90'4"	100'5"	125'8"	151'0"	201'9"	252'9"	303'11"	407'0"	511'0"	775'0"	1044'11"	1603'5"
11	16909.2'	59'9"	69'9"	79'7"	89'6"	99'5"	124'1"	148'8"	197'8"	246'4"	294'9"	390'9"	485'8"	718'2"	944'2"	1377'9"
		60'3"	70'3"	80'5"	90'6"	100'7"	125'11"	151'4"	202'5"	253'9"	305'5"	409'8"	515'3"	784'10"	1062'10"	1646'0"
16	11625.0'	59'8"	69'7"	79'5"	89'4"	99'2"	123'8"	148'1"	196'7"	244'9"	292'5"	386'8"	479'5"	704'7"	920'10"	1328'7"
		60'4"	70'5"	80'7"	90'8"	100'10"	126'4"	152'0"	203'6"	255'6"	307'11"	414'3"	522'6"	801'9"	1094'1"	1722'3"
22	8454.6'	59'7"	69'5"	79'3"	89'1"	98'10"	123'2"	146'3"	195'5"	242'10"	289'9"	381'11"	472'1"	688'11"	894'3"	1274'0"
		60'5"	70'7"	80'9"	91'0"	101'2"	126'11"	152'9"	204'10"	257'7"	311'0"	419'10"	531'5"	823'0"	1134'2"	1823'6"
32	5812.5'	59'5"	69'2"	78'11"	88'8"	98'4"	122'4"	146'3"	193'4"	239'8"	285'3"	374'3"	460'5"	664'3"	853'3"	1192'4"
		60'8"	70'10"	81'1"	91'5"	101'9"	127'9"	154'0"	207'2"	261'3"	316'4"	429'7"	547'1"	861'1"	1207'9"	2021'9"
45	4133.3'	59'2"	68'10"	78'6"	88'1"	97'8"	121'4"	144'9"	190'9"	235'9"	279'8"	364'8"	446'1"	634'10"	805'2"	1100'7"
		60'11"	71'2"	81'7"	92'0"	102'6"	128'11"	155'8"	210'2"	266'1"	323'6"	442'10"	568'10"	916'3"	1319'2"	2354'5"
64	2906.3'	58'9"	68'4"	77'10"	87'4"	96'8"	119'10"	142'8"	187'1"	230'2"	271'11"	351'7"	426'7"	596'2"	744'0"	989'4"
		61'3"	71'9"	82'3"	92'11"	103'7"	130'7"	158'2"	214'9"	273'6"	334'6"	463'10"	603'11"	1010'10"	1524'7"	3100'0"

Note: Circle of confusion = 0.001.

Table 2.19 16mm Depth of Field: 10mm Lens

F-stop	Hyperfocal Distance (ft.)	Focus Distance														
		6"	8"	10"	1'	1'6"	2'	2'6"	3'	3'6"	4'	5'	6'	8'	10'	20'
1.4	15.4	0'5.81"	0'7.7"	0'9.4"	0'11.3"	1'4.4"	1'9.2"	2'1.8"	2'6.1"	2'10"	3'2"	3'9"	4'4"	5'3"	6'1"	8'8"
		0'6.2"	0'8.41"	0'10.5"	1'0.8"	1'7.9"	2'3.6"	2'11.8"	3'8.7"	4'6"	5'5"	7'5"	9'10"	16'8"	28'7"	∞
2	10.8	0'5.73"	0'7.57"	0'9.2"	0'11"	1'3.8"	1'8.2"	2'0.3"	2'4.2"	2'8"	2'11"	3'5"	3'10"	4'7"	5'2"	7'0"
		0'6.29"	0'8.57"	0'10.8"	1'1.2"	1'8.9"	2'5.5"	3'3.1"	4'1.9"	5'2"	6'4"	9'4"	13'7"	31'2"	140'11"	∞
2.8	7.7	0'5.6"	0'7.4"	0'9"	0'10.6"	1'3.1"	1'7"	1'10.6"	2'1.9"	2'5"	2'8"	3'0"	3'4"	3'11"	4'4"	5'7"
		0'6.4"	0'8.8"	0'11.2"	1'1.8"	1'10.4"	2'8.4"	3'8.5"	4'11"	6'5"	8'4"	14'4"	27'4"	∞	∞	∞
4	5.4	0'5.5"	0'7.1"	0'8.6"	0'10.1"	1'2.1"	1'5.5"	1'8.5"	1'11.1"	2'1"	2'4"	2'7"	2'10"	3'3"	3'6"	4'3"
		0'6.6"	0'9.2"	0'11.8"	1'2.7"	2'1"	3'2.2"	4'8"	6'9.3"	10'0"	15'7"	70'5"	∞	∞	∞	∞
5.6	3.8	0'5.3"	0'6.8"	0'8.2"	0'9.5"	1'0.9"	1'3.8"	1'6.2"	1'8.2"	1'10"	2'0"	2'2"	2'4"	2'7"	2'9"	3'3"
		0'6.9"	0'9.7"	1'0.7"	1'4.2"	2'5.5"	4'2"	7'1.8"	13'7.9"	39'1"	∞	∞	∞	∞	∞	∞
8	2.7	0'5.1"	0'6.4"	0'7.6"	0'8.7"	0'11.6"	1'1.8"	1'3.6"	1'5"	1'6"	1'7"	1'9"	1'10"	2'0"	2'1"	2'4"
		0'7.4"	0'10.7"	1'2.4"	1'7.1"	3'4.7"	7'9.5"	35'2.7"	∞	∞	∞	∞	∞	∞	∞	∞
11	2.0	0'4.8"	0'6"	0'7"	0'7.9"	0'10.2"	0'11.9"	0'10.5"	1'2.2"	1'3"	1'4"	1'5"	1'6"	1'7"	1'8"	1'9"
		0'8.1"	1'0.2"	1'5.3"	2'0.5"	6'5.1"	∞	∞	∞	∞	∞	∞	∞	∞	∞	∞
16	1.3	0'4.4"	0'5.4"	0'6.2"	0'6.9"	0'8.5"	0'9.7"	0'10.5"	0'11.1"	1'0"	1'0"	1'1"	1'1"	1'2"	1'2"	1'3"
		0'9.5"	1'4"	2'2"	3'10.7"	∞	∞	∞	∞	∞	∞	∞	∞	∞	∞	∞
22	1.0	0'4"	0'4.8"	0'5.4"	0'5.9"	0'7.1"	0'7.9"	0'8.4"	0'8.9"	0'9"	0'9"	0'10"	0'10"	0'10"	0'11"	0'11"
		1'0.3"	2'1.5"	∞	∞	∞	∞	∞	∞	∞	∞	∞	∞	∞	∞	∞
32	0.7	0'3.4"	0'4"	0'4.5"	0'4.8"	0'5.6"	0'6"	0'6.4"	0'6.6"	0'7"	0'7"	0'7"	0'7"	0'7"	0'8"	0'8"
		1'11.4"	164'2.1"	∞	∞	∞	∞	∞	∞	∞	∞	∞	∞	∞	∞	∞

Note: Circle of confusion = 0.0006.

Table 2.20 16mm Depth of Field: 12mm Lens

F-stop	Hyperfocal Distance (ft.)	Focus Distance 6"	8"	10"	1'	1'6"	2'	2'6"	3'	3'6"	4'	5'	6'	8'	10'	20'
1.4	22.1	0'5.87"	0'7.8"	0'9.6"	0'11.5"	1'4.9"	1'10"	2'3"	2'7.7"	3'0"	3'5"	4'1"	4'9"	5'11"	6'11"	10'6"
		0'6.14"	0'8.29"	0'10.3"	1'0.6"	1'7.3"	2'2.4"	2'9.8"	3'5.6"	4'2"	4'11"	6'5"	8'3"	12'6"	18'3"	206'8"
2	15.5	0'5.81"	0'7.71"	0'9.5"	0'11.3"	1'4.4"	1'9.3"	2'1.8"	2'6.2"	2'10"	3'2"	3'9"	4'4"	5'3"	6'1"	8'9"
		0'6.2"	0'8.4"	0'10.5"	1'0.8"	1'7.9"	2'3.6"	2'11.8"	3'8.6"	4'6"	5'5"	7'5"	9'9"	16'6"	28'2"	∞
2.8	11.1	0'5.7"	0'7.6"	0'9.3"	0'11"	1'3.9"	1'8.3"	2'0.5"	2'4.3"	2'8"	2'11"	3'5"	3'11"	4'8"	5'3"	7'2"
		0'6.3"	0'8.6"	0'10.8"	1'1.2"	1'8.8"	2'5.3"	3'2.7"	4'1.4"	5'1"	6'3"	9'1"	13'1"	28'10"	103'4"	∞
4	7.8	0'5.6"	0'7.4"	0'9"	0'10.6"	1'3.1"	1'7.1"	1'10.7"	2'2"	2'5"	2'8"	3'0"	3'5"	3'11"	4'4"	5'7"
		0'6.4"	0'8.8"	0'11.2"	1'1.8"	1'10.3"	2'8.3"	3'8.3"	4'10.7"	6'5"	8'3"	14'1"	26'7"	∞	∞	∞
5.6	5.5	0'5.5"	0'7.2"	0'8.7"	0'10.2"	1'2.2"	1'5.6"	1'8.7"	1'11.3"	2'2"	2'4"	2'8"	2'11"	3'3"	3'7"	4'4"
		0'6.6"	0'9.1"	0'11.7"	1'2.6"	2'0.7"	3'1.6"	4'6.7"	6'6.6"	9'6"	14'5"	51'8"	∞	∞	∞	∞
8	3.9	0'5.3"	0'6.9"	0'8.2"	0'9.5"	1'1"	1'3.8"	1'6.2"	1'8.3"	1'10"	2'0"	2'2"	2'4"	2'7"	2'10"	3'3"
		0'6.9"	0'9.7"	1'0.7"	1'4.2"	2'5.4"	4'1.6"	7'0.5"	13'3.4"	36'2"	∞	∞	∞	∞	∞	∞
11	2.8	0'5.1"	0'6.5"	0'7.7"	0'8.9"	0'11.7"	1'2"	1'1.1"	1'5.4"	1'7"	1'8"	1'10"	1'11"	2'1"	2'2"	2'6"
		0'7.3"	0'10.5"	1'2.1"	1'6.6"	3'2.5"	6'10.7"	22'1.7"	∞	∞	∞	∞	∞	∞	∞	∞
16	1.9	0'4.8"	0'6"	0'7"	0'7.9"	0'10.1"	0'11.8"	1'1.1"	1'2.1"	1'3"	1'4"	1'5"	1'6"	1'7"	1'7"	1'9"
		0'8.1"	1'0.3"	1'5.4"	2'0.8"	6'7.7"	∞	∞	∞	∞	∞	∞	∞	∞	∞	∞
22	1.4	0'4.4"	0'5.4"	0'6.3"	0'7"	0'8.7"	0'9.9"	0'10.8"	0'11.5"	1'0"	1'1"	1'1"	1'2"	1'2"	1'3"	1'4"
		0'9.3"	1'3.3"	2'0.2"	3'5.3"	∞	∞	∞	∞	∞	∞	∞	∞	∞	∞	∞
32	1.0	0'4"	0'4.8"	0'5.4"	0'5.9"	0'7.1"	0'7.8"	0'8.4"	0'8.8"	0'9"	0'9"	0'10"	0'10"	0'10"	0'11"	0'11"
		1'0.4"	2'2.1"	5'9.5"	∞	∞	∞	∞	∞	∞	∞	∞	∞	∞	∞	∞

Note: Circle of confusion = 0.0006.

Table 2.21 16mm Depth of Field: 14mm Lens

F-stop	Hyperfocal Distance (ft.)	Focus Distance														
		6"	8"	10"	1'	1'6"	2'	2'6"	3'	3'6"	4'	5'	6'	8'	10'	20'
1.4	30.1'	0'5.9"	0'7.87"	0'9.7"	0'11.6"	1'5.1"	1'10.5"	2'3.7"	2'8.7"	3'2"	3'6"	4'3"	5'0"	6'4"	7'6"	12'0"
	0'6.1"	0'8.22"	0'10.2"	1'0.4"	1'6.9"	2'1.7"	2'8.7"	3'4"	4'0"	4'7"	6'0"	7'6"	10'11"	15'0"	59'5"	
2	21.1'	0'5.9"	0'7.79"	0'9.6"	0'11.5"	1'4.8"	1'9.9"	2'2.8"	2'7.5"	3'0"	3'4"	4'1"	4'8"	5'10"	6'9"	10'3"
	0'6.1"	0'8.3"	0'10.4"	1'0.6"	1'7.4"	2'2.5"	2'10"	3'6"	4'2"	4'11"	6'7"	8'5"	12'11"	19'0"	384'6"	
2.8	15.1'	0'5.8"	0'7.7"	0'9.4"	0'11.3"	1'4.4"	1'9.2"	2'1.7"	2'6"	2'10"	3'2"	3'9"	4'3"	5'3"	6'0"	8'7"
	0'6.2"	0'8.4"	0'10.5"	1'0.9"	1'8"	2'3.7"	3'0"	3'8.9"	4'7"	5'5"	7'6"	10'0"	17'1"	29'9"	∞	
4	10.5'	0'5.7"	0'7.6"	0'9.2"	0'11"	1'3.8"	1'8.2"	2'0.3"	2'4"	2'8"	2'11"	3'5"	3'10"	4'7"	5'2"	6'11"
	0'6.3"	0'8.6"	0'10.8"	1'1.3"	1'9"	2'5.6"	3'3.3"	4'2.3"	5'3"	6'5"	9'6"	13'11"	33'1"	192'3"	∞	
5.6	7.5'	0'5.6"	0'7.4"	0'9"	0'10.6"	1'3"	1'7"	1'10.5"	2'1.7"	2'5"	2'7"	3'0"	3'4"	3'11"	4'4"	5'6"
	0'6.4"	0'8.8"	0'11.2"	1'1.8"	1'10.5"	2'8.7"	3'8.9"	5'0"	6'6"	8'6"	14'10"	29'5"	∞	∞	∞	
8	5.3'	0'5.5"	0'7.1"	0'8.6"	0'10.1"	1'2"	1'5.4"	1'8.4"	1'11"	2'1"	2'3"	2'7"	2'10"	3'2"	3'5"	4'2"
	0'6.6"	0'9.2"	0'11.8"	1'2.8"	2'1.2"	3'2.7"	4'9"	6'11"	10'5"	16'7"	96'2"	∞	∞	∞	∞	
11	3.8'	0'5.3"	0'6.8"	0'8.2"	0'9.5"	1'0.9"	1'3.8"	1'3.4"	1'8"	1'10"	1'11"	2'2"	2'4"	2'7"	2'9"	3'3"
	0'6.9"	0'9.7"	1'0.7"	1'4.2"	2'5.6"	4'2.1"	7'2.1"	13'9"	40'0"	∞	∞	∞	∞	∞	∞	
16	2.6'	0'5"	0'6.4"	0'7.6"	0'8.7"	0'11.5"	1'1.6"	1'3.4"	1'4.8"	1'6"	1'7"	1'9"	1'10"	2'0"	2'1"	2'4"
	0'7.4"	0'10.8"	1'2.5"	1'7.3"	3'5.7"	8'3.3"	48'0.8"	∞	∞	∞	∞	∞	∞	∞	∞	
22	1.9'	0'4.8"	0'6"	0'7"	0'7.9"	0'10.1"	0'11.7"	1'1"	1'2"	1'3"	1'4"	1'5"	1'5"	1'7"	1'7"	1'9"
	0'8.1"	1'0.4"	1'5.6"	2'1.1"	6'10.6"	∞	∞	∞	∞	∞	∞	∞	∞	∞	∞	
32	1.3'	0'4.4"	0'5.3"	0'6.1"	0'6.8"	0'8.4"	0'9.5"	0'10.4"	0'11"	0'11"	1'0"	1'1"	1'1"	1'2"	1'2"	1'3"
	0'9.7"	1'4.3"	2'2.9"	4'1.7"	∞	∞	∞	∞	∞	∞	∞	∞	∞	∞	∞	

Note: Circle of confusion = 0.0006.

Table 2.22 16mm Depth of Field: 16mm Lens

F-stop	Hyperfocal Distance (ft.)	Focus Distance														
		6"	8"	10"	1'	1'6"	2'	2'6"	3'	3'6"	4'	5'	6'	8'	10'	20'
1.4	39.4	0'5.92"	0'7.91"	0'9.8"	0'11.7"	1'5.3"	1'10.8"	2'4.2"	2'9.5"	3'3"	3'8"	4'5"	5'2"	6'8"	8'0"	13'3"
		0'6.08"	0'8.18"	0'10.2"	1'0.3"	1'6.7"	2'1.3"	2'8"	3'3"	3'10"	4'5"	5'9"	7'1"	10'0"	13'5"	40'8"
2	27.6	0'5.89"	0'7.85"	0'9.7"	0'11.6"	1'5.1"	1'10.4"	2'3.5"	2'8.5"	3'1"	3'6"	4'3"	4'11"	6'2"	7'4"	11'7"
		0'6.11"	0'8.24"	0'10.3"	1'0.5"	1'7"	2'1.9"	2'9"	3'4.4"	4'0"	4'8"	6'1"	7'8"	11'3"	15'8"	72'11"
2.8	19.7	0'5.9"	0'7.8"	0'9.6"	0'11.4"	1'4.7"	1'9.8"	2'2.6"	2'7.2"	2'12"	3'4"	3'12"	4'7"	5'8"	6'8"	9'11"
		0'6.2"	0'8.3"	0'10.4"	1'0.6"	1'7.5"	2'2.7"	2'10.4"	3'6.5"	4'3"	5'0"	6'8"	8'8"	13'6"	20'4"	∞
4	13.8	0'5.8"	0'7.7"	0'9.4"	0'11.2"	1'4.2"	1'9"	2'1.4"	2'5.6"	2'9"	3'1"	3'8"	4'2"	5'1"	5'10"	8'2"
		0'6.2"	0'8.5"	0'10.6"	1'0.9"	1'8.2"	2'4.1"	3'0.7"	3'10"	4'8"	5'8"	7'10"	10'8"	19'1"	36'6"	∞
5.6	9.8	0'5.7"	0'7.5"	0'9.2"	0'10.9"	1'3.6"	1'7.9"	1'11.9"	2'3.6"	2'7"	2'10"	3'4"	3'9"	4'5"	5'0"	6'7"
		0'6.3"	0'8.6"	0'10.9"	1'1.4"	1'9.2"	2'6.1"	3'4.2"	4'3.8"	5'5"	6'9"	10'2"	15'4"	42'9"	∞	∞
8	6.9	0'5.6"	0'7.3"	0'8.9"	0'10.5"	1'2.8"	1'6.6"	1'10"	2'1.1"	2'4"	2'6"	2'11"	3'2"	3'8"	4'1"	5'1"
		0'6.5"	0'8.9"	0'11.3"	1'2"	1'11"	2'9.8"	3'11.1"	5'3.8"	7'1"	9'6"	18'3"	46'6"	∞	∞	∞
11	5.0	0'5.5"	0'7.1"	0'8.5"	0'10"	1'1.9"	1'5.2"	1'5.4"	1'10.5"	2'1"	2'3"	2'6"	2'9"	3'1"	3'4"	4'0"
		0'6.7"	0'9.3"	0'11.9"	1'3"	2'1.7"	3'3.9"	4'11.9"	7'5.7"	11'7"	19'10"	∞	∞	∞	∞	∞
16	3.4	0'5.2"	0'6.7"	0'8"	0'9.3"	1'0.5"	1'3.2"	1'5.4"	1'7.2"	1'9"	1'10"	2'0"	2'2"	2'5"	2'7"	2'11"
		0'7"	0'10"	1'1.1"	1'4.9"	2'7.9"	4'9.2"	9'1.4"	23'3"	∞	∞	∞	∞	∞	∞	∞
22	2.5	0'5"	0'6.3"	0'7.5"	0'8.6"	0'11.3"	1'1.3"	1'3"	1'4.4"	1'6"	1'6"	1'8"	1'9"	1'11"	2'0"	2'3"
		0'7.5"	0'11"	1'2.9"	1'8"	3'8.9"	9'11"	∞	∞	∞	∞	∞	∞	∞	∞	∞
32	1.7	0'4.7"	0'5.8"	0'6.7"	0'7.6"	0'9.6"	0'11.1"	1'0.2"	1'1.1"	1'2"	1'2"	1'3"	1'4"	1'5"	1'6"	1'7"
		0'8.5"	1'1.2"	1'7.2"	2'4.6"	11'7.5"	∞	∞	∞	∞	∞	∞	∞	∞	∞	∞

Note: Circle of confusion = 0.0006.

Table 2.23 16mm Depth of Field: 20mm Lens

F-stop	Hyperfocal Distance (ft.)	Focus Distance														
		6"	8"	10"	1'	1'6"	2'	2'6"	3'	3'6"	4'	5'	6'	8'	10'	15'
1.4	61.5	0'5.95"	0'7.95"	0'9.8"	0'11.8"	1'5.6"	1'11.2"	2'4.8"	2'10.3"	3'4"	3'9"	4'7"	5'6"	7'1"	8'7"	12'1"
		0'6.05"	0'8.13"	0'10.1"	1'0.2"	1'6.4"	2'0.8"	2'7.3"	3'1.8"	3'9"	4'3"	5'5"	6'8"	9'2"	11'11"	19'10"
2	43.1	0'5.93"	0'7.92"	0'9.8"	0'11.7"	1'5.4"	1'10.9"	2'4.4"	2'9.7"	3'3"	3'8"	4'6"	5'3"	6'9"	8'1"	11'1"
		0'6.07"	0'8.17"	0'10.2"	1'0.3"	1'6.6"	2'1.2"	2'7.8"	3'2.7"	3'10"	4'5"	5'8"	7'0"	9'10"	13'0"	23'0"
2.8	30.8	0'5.9"	0'7.9"	0'9.7"	0'11.6"	1'5.2"	1'10.5"	2'3.7"	2'8.8"	3'2"	3'6"	4'4"	5'0"	6'4"	7'7"	10'1"
		0'6.1"	0'8.2"	0'10.2"	1'0.4"	1'6.9"	2'1.7"	2'8.7"	3'3.9"	3'11"	4'7"	6'0"	7'5"	10'10"	14'10"	29'3"
4	21.5	0'5.9"	0'7.8"	0'9.6"	0'11.5"	1'4.8"	1'10"	2'2.9"	2'7.6"	3'0"	3'4"	4'1"	4'8"	5'10"	6'10"	8'10"
		0'6.1"	0'8.3"	0'10.4"	1'0.6"	1'7.3"	2'2.5"	2'9.9"	3'5.8"	4'2"	4'11"	6'6"	8'4"	12'9"	18'8"	49'6"
5.6	15.4	0'5.8"	0'7.7"	0'9.4"	0'11.3"	1'4.4"	1'9.2"	2'1.8"	2'6.1"	2'10"	3'2"	3'9"	4'4"	5'3"	6'1"	7'7"
		0'6.2"	0'8.4"	0'10.5"	1'0.8"	1'7.9"	2'3.6"	2'11.8"	3'8.7"	4'6"	5'5"	7'5"	9'10"	16'8"	28'7"	611'9"
8	10.8	0'5.7"	0'7.6"	0'9.2"	0'11"	1'3.8"	1'8.2"	2'0.3"	2'4.2"	2'8"	2'11"	3'5"	3'10"	4'7"	5'2"	6'3"
		0'6.3"	0'8.6"	0'10.8"	1'1.2"	1'8.9"	2'5.5"	3'3.1"	4'1.9"	5'2"	6'4"	9'4"	13'7"	32'0"	140'11"	∞
11	7.8	0'5.6"	0'7.4"	0'9"	0'10.6"	1'3.1"	1'7.1"	1'8.5"	2'2"	2'5"	2'8"	3'1"	3'5"	3'11"	4'5"	5'2"
		0'6.4"	0'8.8"	0'11.1"	1'1.8"	1'10.3"	2'8.2"	3'8.1"	4'10.4"	6'4"	8'2"	13'10"	25'8"	∞	∞	∞
16	5.4	0'5.5"	0'7.1"	0'8.6"	0'10.1"	1'2.1"	1'5.5"	1'8.5"	1'11.1"	2'1"	2'4"	2'7"	2'10"	3'3"	3'6"	4'0"
		0'6.6"	0'9.2"	0'11.8"	1'2.7"	2'1"	3'2.2"	4'8"	6'9.3"	10'0"	15'7"	70'5"	∞	∞	∞	∞
22	3.9	0'5.3"	0'6.9"	0'8.2"	0'9.6"	1'1"	1'3.9"	1'6.3"	1'8.4"	1'10"	2'0"	2'2"	2'4"	2'8"	2'10"	3'1"
		0'6.9"	0'9.7"	1'0.6"	1'4.1"	2'5.2"	4'1.1"	6'11"	12'10.1"	33'1"	∞	∞	∞	∞	∞	∞
32	2.7	0'5.1"	0'6.4"	0'7.6"	0'8.7"	0'11.6"	1'1.8"	1'3.6"	1'5"	1'6"	1'7"	1'9"	1'10"	2'0"	2'1"	2'3"
		0'7.4"	0'10.7"	1'2.4"	1'7.1"	3'4.7"	7'9.5"	35'2.7"	∞	∞	∞	∞	∞	∞	∞	∞

Note: Circle of confusion = 0.0006.

Table 2.24 16mm Depth of Field: 25mm Lens

F-stop	Hyperfocal Distance (ft.)	Focus Distance														
		6"	8"	10"	1'	1'6"	2'	2'6"	3'	3'6"	4'	5'	6'	8'	10'	15'
1.4	96.1	0'5.97"	0'7.98"	0'9.9"	0'11.9"	1'5.7"	1'11.5"	2'5.2"	2'10.9"	3'5"	3'10"	4'9"	5'8"	7'5"	9'1"	13'0"
		0'6.03"	0'8.1"	0'10"	1'0.1"	1'6.3"	2'0.5"	2'6.8"	3'1.2"	3'8"	4'2"	5'3"	6'5"	8'9"	11'2"	17'9"
2	67.3	0'5.96"	0'7.96"	0'9.8"	0'11.8"	1'5.6"	1'11.3"	2'4.9"	2'10.5"	3'4"	3'9"	4'8"	5'6"	7'2"	8'8"	12'3"
		0'6.04"	0'8.12"	0'10.1"	1'0.2"	1'6.4"	2'0.7"	2'7.2"	3'1.7"	3'8"	4'3"	5'5"	6'7"	9'1"	11'9"	19'4"
2.8	48.1	0'5.9"	0'7.9"	0'9.8"	0'11.8"	1'5.5"	1'11"	2'4.5"	2'9.9"	3'3"	3'8"	4'6"	5'4"	6'10"	8'3"	11'5"
		0'6.1"	0'8.2"	0'10.1"	1'0.3"	1'6.6"	2'1"	2'7.6"	3'2.4"	3'9"	4'4"	5'7"	6'10"	9'7"	12'8"	21'10"
4	33.6	0'5.9"	0'7.9"	0'9.7"	0'11.7"	1'5.2"	1'10.7"	2'3.9"	2'9.1"	3'2"	3'7"	4'4"	5'1"	6'6"	7'9"	10'4"
		0'6.1"	0'8.2"	0'10.2"	1'0.4"	1'6.8"	2'1.5"	2'8.4"	3'3.5"	3'11"	4'6"	5'10"	7'4"	10'6"	14'3"	27'1"
5.6	24.0	0'5.9"	0'7.8"	0'9.6"	0'11.5"	1'4.9"	1'10.2"	2'3.2"	2'8"	3'1"	3'5"	4'2"	4'10"	6'0"	7'1"	9'3"
		0'6.1"	0'8.3"	0'10.3"	1'0.5"	1'7.2"	2'2.2"	2'9.5"	3'5.1"	4'1"	4'10"	6'4"	8'0"	12'0"	17'2"	39'11"
8	16.8	0'5.8"	0'7.7"	0'9.5"	0'11.3"	1'4.5"	1'9.4"	2'2.1"	2'6.6"	2'11"	3'3"	3'10"	4'5"	5'5"	6'3"	7'11"
		0'6.2"	0'8.4"	0'10.5"	1'0.8"	1'7.8"	2'3.2"	2'11.2"	3'7.8"	4'5"	5'3"	7'1"	9'4"	15'3"	24'8"	138'9"
11	12.2	0'5.8"	0'7.6"	0'9.3"	0'11.1"	1'4"	1'8.6"	1'11.1"	2'4.9"	2'9"	3'0"	3'7"	4'0"	4'10"	5'6"	6'9"
		0'6.3"	0'8.5"	0'10.7"	1'1.1"	1'8.5"	2'4.7"	3'1.7"	3'11.7"	4'11"	5'11"	8'5"	11'9"	23'1"	54'10"	∞
16	8.4	0'5.7"	0'7.4"	0'9.1"	0'10.7"	1'3.3"	1'7.4"	1'11.1"	2'2.5"	2'6"	2'9"	3'2"	3'6"	4'1"	4'7"	5'5"
		0'6.4"	0'8.7"	0'11.1"	1'1.6"	1'9.9"	2'7.5"	3'6.7"	4'8"	6'0"	7'8"	12'4"	20'11"	164'4"	∞	∞
22	6.1	0'5.5"	0'7.2"	0'8.8"	0'10.3"	1'2.5"	1'6.1"	1'9.3"	2'0.2"	2'3"	2'5"	2'9"	3'0"	3'6"	3'10"	4'4"
		0'6.5"	0'9"	0'11.5"	1'2.3"	1'11.8"	2'11.7"	4'2.7"	5'10.7"	8'2"	11'7"	27'5"	316'8"	∞	∞	∞
32	4.2	0'5.4"	0'6.9"	0'8.3"	0'9.7"	1'1.3"	1'4.3"	1'6.8"	1'9"	1'11"	2'1"	2'3"	2'6"	2'9"	3'0"	3'3"
		0'6.8"	0'9.6"	1'0.4"	1'3.7"	2'4"	3'9.8"	6'2"	10'5.7"	20'11"	82'2"	∞	∞	∞	∞	∞

Note: Circle of confusion = 0.0006.

Table 2.25 16mm Depth of Field: 35mm Lens

F-stop	Hyperfocal Distance (ft.)	Focus Distance 1'	1'6"	2'	2'6"	3'	3'6"	4'	6'	8'	10'	15'	20'	25'	50'	100'
1.4	188.4	0'11.94"	1'5.9"	1'11.7"	2'5.6"	2'11.4"	3'5.2"	3'11"	5'10"	7'8"	9'6"	13'11"	18'1"	22'1"	33'0"	65'4"
		1'0.06"	1'6.1"	2'0.3"	2'6.4"	3'0.6"	3'6.8"	4'1"	6'2"	8'4"	10'7"	16'4"	22'5"	28'10"	50'9"	213'2"
2	131.9	0'11.91"	1'5.8"	1'11.6"	2'5.4"	2'11.2"	3'4.9"	3'10.6"	5'9"	7'7"	9'4"	13'6"	17'4"	21'0"	30'8"	56'10"
		1'0.09"	1'6.2"	2'0.4"	2'6.6"	3'0.8"	3'7.1"	4'1.5"	6'3"	8'6"	10'10"	16'11"	23'7"	30'10"	57'5"	413'11"
2.8	94.2	0'11.9"	1'5.7"	1'11.5"	2'5.2"	2'10.9"	3'4.5"	3'10"	5'8"	7'4"	9'0"	12'11"	16'6"	19'9"	28'1"	48'6"
		1'0.1"	1'6.3"	2'0.5"	2'6.8"	3'1.2"	3'7.6"	4'2.1"	6'5"	8'9"	11'2"	17'10"	25'5"	34'0"	69'6"	∞
4	65.9	0'11.8"	1'5.6"	1'11.3"	2'4.9"	2'10.4"	3'3.9"	3'9.3"	5'6"	7'2"	8'8"	12'3"	15'4"	18'2"	24'11"	39'9"
		1'0.2"	1'6.4"	2'0.8"	2'7.2"	3'1.7"	3'8.4"	4'3.1"	6'7"	9'1"	11'9"	19'5"	28'9"	40'3"	101'8"	∞
5.6	47.1	0'11.8"	1'5.4"	1'11"	2'4.5"	2'9.8"	3'3.1"	3'8.2"	5'4"	6'10"	8'3"	11'5"	14'0"	16'4"	21'8"	32'0"
		1'0.3"	1'6.6"	2'1.1"	2'7.7"	3'2.4"	3'9.4"	4'4.5"	6'11"	9'8"	12'8"	22'0"	34'9"	53'3"	265'7"	∞
8	33.0	0'11.6"	1'5.2"	1'10.6"	2'3.9"	2'9"	3'2"	3'6.8"	5'1"	6'5"	7'8"	10'4"	12'5"	14'3"	18'1"	24'10"
		1'0.4"	1'6.9"	2'1.6"	2'8.5"	3'3.6"	3'11"	4'6.6"	7'4"	10'7"	14'4"	27'6"	50'10"	103'6"	∞	∞
11	24.0	0'11.5"	1'4.9"	1'10.2"	2'3.2"	2'8"	2'10.6"	3'5.1"	4'10"	6'0"	7'1"	9'3"	10'11"	12'3"	15'0"	19'4"
		1'0.5"	1'7.2"	2'2.2"	2'9.5"	3'5.1"	4'1.2"	4'9.6"	8'0"	12'0"	17'2"	40'1"	120'8"	∞	∞	∞
16	16.5	0'11.3"	1'4.5"	1'9.4"	2'2"	2'6.5"	2'10.6"	3'2.6"	4'5"	5'5"	6'3"	7'10"	9'0"	9'11"	11'8"	14'2"
		1'0.8"	1'7.8"	2'3.3"	2'11.4"	3'8"	4'5.3"	5'3.4"	9'5"	15'7"	25'5"	166'10"	∞	∞	∞	∞
22	12.0	0'11.1"	1'4"	1'8.6"	2'0.8"	2'4.8"	2'8.5"	2'12"	3'12"	4'10"	5'5"	6'8"	7'6"	8'1"	9'3"	10'8"
		1'1.1"	1'8.6"	2'4.8"	3'1.9"	4'0"	4'11.3"	6'0"	12'0"	24'1"	60'4"	∞	∞	∞	∞	∞
32	8.2	0'10.7"	1'3.2"	1'7.3"	1'11"	2'2.4"	2'5.5"	2'8.3"	3'6"	4'1"	4'6"	5'4"	5'10"	6'2"	6'10"	7'7"
		1'1.7"	1'10"	2'7.7"	3'7.1"	4'8.6"	6'1"	7'9.3"	22'1"	273'5"	∞	∞	∞	∞	∞	∞

Note: Circle of confusion = 0.0006.

Table 2.26 16mm Depth of Field: 50mm Lens

F-stop	Hyperfocal Distance (ft.)	Focus Distance														
		1'	1'6"	2'	2'6"	3'	3'6"	4'	6'	8'	10'	15'	20'	25'	50'	100'
1.4	384.4	0'11.97"	1'5.9"	1'11.9"	2'5.8"	2'11.7"	3'5.6"	3'11.5"	5'11"	7'10"	9'9"	14'5"	19'0"	23'6"	44'3"	79'4"
		1'0.03"	1'6.1"	2'0.1"	2'6.2"	3'0.3"	3'6.4"	4'0.5"	6'1"	8'2"	10'3"	15'7"	21'1"	26'9"	57'6"	135'2"
2	269.1	0'11.96"	1'5.9"	1'11.8"	2'5.7"	2'11.6"	3'5.5"	3'11.3"	5'10"	7'9"	9'8"	14'2"	18'7"	22'10"	42'2"	72'11"
		1'0.04"	1'6.1"	2'0.2"	2'6.3"	3'0.4"	3'6.6"	4'0.7"	6'2"	8'3"	10'5"	15'11"	21'7"	27'7"	61'5"	159'2"
2.8	192.2	0'11.9"	1'5.9"	1'11.8"	2'5.6"	2'11.4"	3'5.2"	3'11"	5'10"	7'8"	9'6"	13'11"	18'1"	22'1"	39'8"	65'9"
		1'0.1"	1'6.1"	2'0.3"	2'6.4"	3'0.6"	3'6.8"	4'1"	6'2"	8'4"	10'7"	16'3"	22'4"	28'9"	67'7"	208'5"
4	134.5	0'11.9"	1'5.8"	1'11.6"	2'5.5"	2'11.2"	3'4.9"	3'10.6"	5'9"	7'7"	9'4"	13'6"	17'5"	21'1"	36'5"	57'4"
		1'0.1"	1'6.2"	2'0.4"	2'6.6"	3'0.8"	3'7.1"	4'1.5"	6'3"	8'6"	10'10"	16'11"	23'6"	30'8"	79'7"	389'5"
5.6	96.1	0'11.9"	1'5.7"	1'11.5"	2'5.2"	2'10.9"	3'4.5"	3'10.1"	5'8"	7'5"	9'1"	13'0"	16'7"	19'10"	32'11"	49'0"
		1'0.1"	1'6.3"	2'0.5"	2'6.8"	3'1.2"	3'7.6"	4'2.1"	6'5"	8'9"	11'2"	17'9"	25'3"	33'9"	104'3"	∞
8	67.3	0'11.8"	1'5.6"	1'11.3"	2'4.9"	2'10.5"	3'3.9"	3'9.3"	5'6"	7'2"	8'8"	12'3"	15'5"	18'3"	28'8"	40'3"
		1'0.2"	1'6.4"	2'0.7"	2'7.2"	3'1.7"	3'8.3"	4'3"	6'7"	9'1"	11'9"	19'4"	28'6"	39'9"	194'9"	∞
11	48.9	0'11.8"	1'5.5"	1'11.1"	2'4.5"	2'9.9"	3'2"	3'8.4"	5'4"	6'11"	8'4"	11'6"	14'2"	16'7"	24'9"	32'10"
		1'0.3"	1'6.6"	2'1"	2'7.6"	3'2.4"	3'9.2"	4'4.3"	6'10"	9'7"	12'7"	21'8"	33'10"	51'1"	∞	∞
16	33.6	0'11.7"	1'5.2"	1'10.7"	2'3.9"	2'9.1"	3'2"	3'6.9"	5'1"	6'6"	7'9"	10'4"	12'7"	14'4"	20'1"	25'2"
		1'0.4"	1'6.8"	2'1.5"	2'8.4"	3'3.5"	3'10.9"	4'6.5"	7'4"	10'6"	14'3"	27'1"	49'4"	97'4"	∞	∞
22	24.5	0'11.5"	1'5"	1'10.2"	2'3.2"	2'8.1"	3'0.7"	3'5.3"	4'10"	6'0"	7'1"	9'4"	11'0"	12'4"	16'5"	19'8"
		1'0.5"	1'7.2"	2'2.1"	2'9.4"	3'5"	4'1"	4'9.4"	7'11"	11'11"	16'11"	38'9"	109'7"	∞	∞	∞
32	16.8	0'11.3"	1'4.5"	1'9.4"	2'2.1"	2'6.6"	2'10.8"	3'2.8"	4'5"	5'5"	6'3"	7'11"	9'2"	10'1"	12'7"	14'5"
		1'0.8"	1'7.8"	2'3.2"	2'11.2"	3'7.8"	4'5"	5'3"	9'4"	15'3"	24'8"	138'9"	∞	∞	∞	∞

Note: Circle of confusion = 0.0006.

Table 2.27 16mm Depth of Field: 85mm Lens

F-stop	Hyperfocal Distance (ft.)	Focus Distance 2'	3'	4'	5'	6'	7'	8'	10'	12'	15'	25'	50'	100'	200'	400'
1.4	1111.0'	1'11.96"	2'11.9"	3'11.8"	4'11.7"	5'11.6"	6'11.5"	7'11.3"	9'11"	11'10"	14'10"	24'5"	47'10"	91'9"	169'6"	294'1"
		2'0.04"	3'0.1"	4'0.2"	5'0.3"	6'0.4"	7'0.5"	8'0.7"	10'1"	12'2"	15'2"	25'7"	52'4"	109'11"	243'11"	625'0"
2	777.7'	1'11.94"	2'11.86"	3'11.8"	4'11.6"	5'11.4"	6'11.3"	7'11"	9'10"	11'10"	14'9"	24'3"	47'0"	88'7"	159'1"	264'2"
		2'0.06"	3'0.14"	4'0.2"	5'0.4"	6'0.6"	7'0.8"	8'1"	10'2"	12'2"	15'4"	25'10"	53'5"	114'9"	269'3"	823'7"
2.8	555.5'	1'11.9"	2'11.8"	3'11.7"	4'11.5"	5'11.2"	6'11"	7'10.6"	9'10"	11'9"	14'7"	23'11"	45'10"	84'9"	147'1"	232'7"
		2'0.1"	3'0.2"	4'0.3"	5'0.5"	6'0.8"	7'1.1"	8'1.4"	10'2"	12'3"	15'5"	26'2"	54'11"	121'11"	312'6"	1249'0"
4	388.8'	1'11.9"	2'11.7"	3'11.5"	4'11.2"	5'10.9"	6'10.5"	7'10.1"	9'9"	11'8"	14'5"	23'6"	44'4"	79'7"	132'1"	197'2"
		2'0.1"	3'0.3"	4'0.5"	5'0.8"	6'1.1"	7'1.5"	8'2"	10'3"	12'5"	15'7"	26'9"	57'5"	134'7"	411'10"	∞
5.6	277.7'	1'11.8"	2'11.6"	3'11.3"	4'10.9"	5'10.5"	6'9.9"	7'9.3"	9'8"	11'6"	14'3"	22'11"	42'4"	73'6"	116'3"	163'11"
		2'0.2"	3'0.4"	4'0.7"	5'1.1"	6'1.6"	7'2.2"	8'2.8"	10'4"	12'7"	15'10"	27'6"	61'0"	156'3"	714'6"	∞
8	194.4'	1'11.8"	2'11.5"	3'11"	4'10.5"	5'9.8"	6'9.1"	7'8.2"	9'6"	11'4"	13'11"	22'2"	39'9"	66'0"	98'7"	130'10"
		2'0.2"	3'0.6"	4'1"	5'1.6"	6'2.3"	7'3.1"	8'4.1"	10'7"	12'9"	16'3"	28'8"	67'4"	205'11"	∞	∞
11	141.4'	1'11.7"	2'11.3"	3'10.7"	4'10"	5'9.1"	6'8"	7'4.7"	9'4"	11'1"	13'7"	21'3"	36'11"	58'7"	82'10"	104'6"
		2'0.3"	3'0.8"	4'1.4"	5'2.2"	6'3.2"	7'4.4"	8'5.8"	10'9"	13'1"	16'9"	30'4"	77'4"	341'7"	∞	∞
16	97.2'	1'11.5"	2'10.9"	3'10.1"	4'9.1"	5'7.8"	6'6.4"	7'4.7"	9'1"	10'8"	13'0"	19'11"	33'0"	49'4"	65'5"	78'2"
		2'0.5"	3'1.1"	4'2.1"	5'3.3"	6'4.7"	7'6.5"	8'8.6"	11'2"	13'8"	17'9"	33'8"	102'11"	∞	∞	∞
22	70.7'	1'11.3"	2'10.5"	3'9.4"	4'8"	5'6.4"	6'4.4"	7'2.2"	8'9"	10'3"	12'4"	18'6"	29'3"	41'5"	52'3"	60'1"
		2'0.7"	3'1.6"	4'2.9"	5'4.6"	6'6.7"	7'9.2"	9'0.2"	11'8"	14'5"	19'0"	38'8"	170'9"	∞	∞	∞
32	48.6'	1'11.1"	2'9.9"	3'8.4"	4'6.4"	5'4.1"	6'1.4"	6'10.4"	8'4"	9'7"	11'6"	16'6"	24'8"	32'8"	39'1"	43'4"
		2'1"	3'2.4"	4'4.3"	5'6.9"	6'10.1"	8'2.1"	9'6.9"	12'7"	15'11"	21'8"	51'6"	∞	∞	∞	∞

Note: Circle of confusion = 0.0006.

Table 2.28 16mm Depth of Field: 100mm Lens

F-stop	Hyperfocal Distance	Focus Distance 4'	5'	6'	8'	9'	10'	12'	15'	20'	25'	30'	50'	100'	200'	400'
1.4	1537.7	3'11.88"	4'11.8"	5'11.7"	7'11.5"	8'11.4"	9'11.2"	11'10.9"	14'10"	19'9"	24'7"	29'5"	48'5"	93'11"	177'0"	317'5"
		4'0.13"	5'0.2"	6'0.3"	8'0.5"	9'0.6"	10'0.8"	12'1.1"	15'2"	20'3"	25'5"	30'7"	51'8"	103'0"	229'11"	540'8"
2	1076.4'	3'11.82"	4'11.7"	5'11.6"	7'11.3"	8'11.1"	9'10.9"	11'10.4"	14'10"	19'8"	24'5"	29'2"	49'0"	91'6"	168'8"	291'8"
		4'0.18"	5'0.3"	6'0.4"	8'0.7"	9'0.9"	10'1.1"	12'1.6"	15'3"	20'5"	25'7"	30'10"	52'5"	110'3"	245'8"	636'7"
2.8	768.9'	3'11.8"	4'11.6"	5'11.4"	7'11"	8'10.8"	9'10.5"	11'9.8"	14'9"	19'6"	24'3"	28'10"	46'11"	88'6"	158'9"	263'1"
		4'0.3"	5'0.4"	6'0.6"	8'1"	9'1.3"	10'1.6"	12'2.3"	15'4"	20'6"	25'10"	31'3"	53'6"	114'11"	270'4"	833'9"
4	538.2'	3'11.6"	4'11.4"	5'11.2"	7'10.6"	8'10.2"	9'9.8"	11'8.9"	14'7"	19'3"	23'11"	28'5"	45'9"	84'4"	145'10"	229'6"
		4'0.4"	5'0.6"	6'0.8"	8'1.4"	9'1.8"	10'2.3"	12'3.3"	15'5"	20'9"	26'3"	31'9"	55'1"	122'10"	318'3"	1557'9"
5.6	384.4'	3'11.5"	4'11.2"	5'10.9"	7'10"	8'9.5"	9'9"	11'7.6"	14'5"	19'0"	23'6"	29'0"	44'3"	79'4"	131'7"	196'0"
		4'0.5"	5'0.8"	6'1.1"	8'2"	9'2.6"	10'3.2"	12'4.6"	15'7"	21'1"	26'9"	32'6"	57'6"	135'2"	416'11"	∞
8	269.1'	3'11.3"	4'10.9"	5'10.4"	7'9.2"	8'8.5"	9'7.7"	11'5.9"	14'2"	18'7"	22'10"	27'0"	42'2"	72'11"	114'9"	160'10"
		4'0.7"	5'1.1"	6'1.6"	8'2.9"	9'3.7"	10'4.6"	12'6.7"	15'11"	21'7"	27'7"	33'9"	61'5"	159'2"	778'11"	∞
11	195.7'	3'11"	4'10.5"	5'9.9"	7'8.2"	8'7.3"	9'3.7"	11'3.7"	13'11"	18'2"	22'2"	26'0"	39'10"	66'2"	98'11"	131'5"
		4'1"	5'1.6"	6'2.3"	8'4.1"	9'5.2"	10'6.5"	12'9.4"	16'3"	22'3"	28'8"	35'5"	67'2"	204'6"	∞	∞
16	134.5'	3'10.6"	4'9.9"	5'8.9"	7'6.6"	8'5.2"	9'3.7"	11'0.2"	13'6"	17'5"	21'1"	24'6"	36'5"	57'4"	80'5"	100'8"
		4'1.5"	5'2.3"	6'3.4"	8'6.1"	9'7.7"	10'9.6"	13'2.1"	16'11"	23'6"	30'8"	38'7"	79'7"	389'5"	∞	∞
22	97.9'	3'10.1"	4'9.1"	5'7.8"	7'4.7"	8'2.9"	9'0.9"	10'8.3"	13'0"	16'7"	19'11"	23'0"	33'1"	49'5"	65'8"	78'7"
		4'2"	5'3.2"	6'4.7"	8'8.5"	9'10.9"	11'1.7"	13'8.1"	17'9"	22'0"	33'7"	43'3"	102'3"	∞	∞	∞
32	67.3'	3'9.3"	4'7.8"	5'6.1"	7'1.8"	7'11.3"	8'8.5"	10'2.2"	12'3"	15'5"	18'3"	20'9"	28'8"	40'3"	50'4"	57'7"
		4'3"	5'4.8"	6'7.1"	9'1"	10'4.7"	11'9"	14'7.3"	19'4"	28'6"	39'9"	54'2"	194'9"	∞	∞	∞

Note: Circle of confusion = 0.0006.

Table 2.29 16mm Depth of Field: 150mm Lens

F-stop	Hyperfocal Distance (ft.)	Focus Distance 4'	5'	6'	8'	9'	10'	12'	15'	20'	25'	30'	50'	100'	200'	400'
1.4	3459.8'	3'11.94"	4'11.9"	5'11.9"	7'11.8"	8'11.7"	9'11.7"	11'11.5"	14'11"	19'11"	24'10"	29'9"	49'3"	97'2"	189'1"	358'7"
		4'0.06"	5'0.1"	6'0.1"	8'0.2"	9'0.3"	10'0.3"	12'0.5"	15'1"	20'1"	25'2"	30'3"	50'9"	103'0"	212'3"	452'3"
2	2421.9'	3'11.92"	4'11.9"	5'11.8"	7'11.7"	8'11.6"	9'11.5"	11'11.3"	14'11"	19'10"	24'9"	29'8"	49'0"	96'0"	184'9"	343'4"
		4'0.08"	5'0.1"	6'0.2"	8'0.3"	9'0.4"	10'0.5"	12'0.7"	15'1"	20'2"	25'3"	30'5"	51'1"	104'4"	218'0"	479'2"
2.8	1729.9'	3'11.9"	4'11.8"	5'11.8"	7'11.6"	8'11.4"	9'11.3"	11'11"	14'10"	19'9"	24'8"	29'6"	48'7"	94'6"	179'3"	324'11"
		4'0.1"	5'0.2"	6'0.3"	8'0.4"	9'0.6"	10'0.7"	12'1"	15'2"	20'3"	25'4"	30'6"	51'6"	106'2"	226'2"	520'4"
4	1210.9'	3'11.8"	4'11.8"	5'11.6"	7'11.4"	8'11.2"	9'11"	11'10.6"	14'10"	19'8"	24'6"	29'3"	48'0"	92'4"	171'8"	300'8"
		4'0.2"	5'0.2"	6'0.4"	8'0.6"	9'0.8"	10'1"	12'1.4"	15'2"	20'4"	25'6"	30'9"	52'2"	109'0"	239'7"	597'4"
5.6	865.0'	3'11.8"	4'11.7"	5'11.5"	7'11.1"	8'10.9"	9'10.6"	11'10"	14'9"	19'7"	24'4"	29'0"	47'3"	89'8"	162'5"	273'6"
		4'0.2"	5'0.3"	6'0.5"	8'0.9"	9'1.1"	10'1.4"	12'2"	15'3"	20'6"	25'9"	31'1"	53'1"	113'1"	260'2"	744'1"
8	605.5'	3'11.7"	4'11.5"	5'11.3"	7'10.7"	8'10.4"	9'10.1"	11'9.2"	14'8"	19'4"	24'0"	28'7"	46'2"	85'10"	150'4"	240'10"
		4'0.3"	5'0.5"	6'0.7"	8'1.3"	9'1.6"	10'2"	12'2.9"	15'5"	20'8"	26'1"	31'7"	54'6"	119'9"	298'8"	1178'8"
11	440.3'	3'11.6"	4'11.3"	5'11"	7'10.3"	8'9.8"	9'8.2"	11'8.2"	14'6"	19'2"	23'8"	28'1"	44'11"	81'6"	137'6"	209'7"
		4'0.4"	5'0.7"	6'1"	8'1.8"	9'2.3"	10'2.8"	12'4"	15'6"	20'11"	26'6"	32'2"	56'5"	129'5"	366'5"	4366'1"
16	302.7'	3'11.4"	4'11"	5'10.6"	7'9.5"	8'8.9"	9'8.2"	11'6.5"	14'4"	18'9"	23'1"	27'4"	42'11"	75'2"	120'5"	172'4"
		4'0.6"	5'1"	6'1.5"	8'2.6"	9'3.3"	10'4.1"	12'5.9"	15'9"	21'5"	27'3"	33'4"	59'11"	149'4"	589'4"	∞
22	220.2'	3'11.1"	4'10.7"	5'10.1"	7'8.6"	8'7.8"	9'6.8"	11'4.6"	14'1"	18'4"	22'5"	26'5"	40'9"	68'9"	104'10"	142'0"
		4'0.9"	5'1.4"	6'2"	8'3.6"	9'4.6"	10'5.7"	12'8.3"	16'1"	22'0"	28'2"	34'9"	64'8"	183'3"	2183'0"	∞
32	151.4'	3'10.8"	4'10.1"	5'9.3"	7'7.2"	8'5.9"	9'4.6"	11'1.4"	13'8"	17'8"	21'5"	25'0"	37'7"	60'3"	86'2"	109'10"
		4'1.3"	5'2"	6'3"	8'5.4"	9'6.8"	10'8.5"	13'0.4"	16'8"	23'1"	29'11"	37'5"	74'8"	294'8"	∞	∞

Note: Circle of confusion = 0.0006.

Table 2.30 16mm Depth of Field: 200mm Lens

F-stop	Hyperfocal Distance (ft.)	Focus Distance 6'	7'	8'	9'	10'	15'	20'	25'	30'	50'	100'	150'	200'	300'	500'
1.4	6150.8'	5'11.9"	6'11.9"	7'11.9"	8'11.8"	9'11.8"	14'11.6"	19'11"	24'11"	29'10"	49'7"	98'5"	146'5"	193'8"	286'1"	462'5"
		6'0.1"	7'0.1"	8'0.1"	9'0.2"	10'0.2"	15'0.4"	20'1"	25'1"	30'2"	50'5"	101'8"	153'9"	206'9"	315'5"	544'3"
2	4305.6'	5'11.9"	6'11.9"	7'11.8"	8'11.8"	9'11.7"	14'11.4"	19'11"	24'10"	29'10"	49'5"	97'9"	144'11"	191'1"	280'6"	448'0"
		6'0.1"	7'0.1"	8'0.2"	9'0.2"	10'0.3"	15'0.6"	20'1"	25'2"	30'3"	50'7"	102'5"	155'5"	209'9"	322'6"	565'8"
2.8	3075.4'	5'11.9"	6'11.8"	7'11.8"	8'11.7"	9'11.6"	14'11.1"	19'10"	24'10"	29'9"	49'2"	96'10"	143'0"	187'9"	273'4"	430'1"
		6'0.1"	7'0.2"	8'0.3"	9'0.3"	10'0.4"	15'0.9"	20'2"	25'2"	30'4"	50'10"	103'4"	157'8"	213'11"	332'5"	597'1"
4	2152.8'	5'11.8"	6'11.7"	7'11.6"	8'11.6"	9'11.4"	14'10.8"	19'10"	24'9"	29'7"	48'10"	95'7"	140'3"	183'0"	263'4"	405'9"
		6'0.2"	7'0.3"	8'0.4"	9'0.5"	10'0.6"	15'1.3"	20'2"	25'4"	30'5"	51'2"	104'10"	161'3"	220'6"	348'7"	651'3"
5.6	1537.7'	5'11.7"	6'11.6"	7'11.5"	8'11.4"	9'11.2"	14'10.3"	19'9"	24'7"	29'5"	48'5"	93'11"	136'8"	177'0"	251'0"	377'4"
		6'0.3"	7'0.4"	8'0.5"	9'0.6"	10'0.8"	15'1.8"	20'3"	25'5"	30'7"	51'8"	106'11"	166'3"	229'11"	372'9"	740'11"
8	1076.4'	5'11.6"	6'11.5"	7'11.3"	8'11.1"	9'10.9"	14'9.5"	19'8"	24'5"	29'2"	47'9"	91'6"	131'8"	168'8"	234'7"	341'5"
		6'0.4"	7'0.5"	8'0.7"	9'0.9"	10'1.1"	15'2.5"	20'5"	25'7"	30'10"	52'5"	110'3"	174'3"	245'8"	415'11"	933'9"
11	782.8'	5'11.5"	6'11.3"	7'11"	8'10.8"	9'10.5"	14'7.1"	19'6"	24'3"	28'11"	47'0"	88'8"	125'11"	159'4"	216'11"	305'1"
		6'0.6"	7'0.8"	8'1"	9'1.3"	10'1.6"	15'3.5"	20'6"	25'10"	31'2"	53'5"	114'8"	185'7"	268'8"	486'5"	1383'11"
16	538.2'	5'11.2"	6'10.9"	7'10.6"	8'10.2"	9'9.8"	14'7.1"	19'3"	23'11"	28'5"	45'9"	84'4"	117'4"	145'10"	192'8"	259'2"
		6'0.8"	7'1.1"	8'1.4"	9'1.8"	10'2.3"	15'5.2"	20'9"	26'3"	31'9"	55'1"	122'10"	208'0"	318'3"	677'10"	7045'1"
22	391.4'	5'10.9"	6'10.5"	7'10.1"	8'9.6"	9'9"	14'5.4"	19'0"	23'6"	27'10"	44'4"	79'8"	108'5"	132'4"	169'10"	219'7"
		6'1.1"	7'1.5"	8'2"	9'2.5"	10'3.1"	15'7.2"	21'1"	26'8"	32'6"	57'4"	134'4"	243'2"	409'0"	1284'6"	∞
32	269.1'	5'10.4"	6'9.9"	7'9.2"	8'8.5"	9'7.7"	14'2.5"	18'7"	22'10"	27'0"	42'2"	72'11"	96'4"	114'9"	141'10"	174'11"
		6'1.6"	7'2.2"	8'2.9"	9'3.7"	10'4.6"	15'10.6"	21'7"	27'7"	33'9"	61'5"	159'2"	338'11"	778'11"	∞	∞

Note: Circle of confusion = 0.0006.

Table 2.31 16mm Depth of Field: 300mm Lens

F-stop	Hyperfocal Distance (ft.)	Focus Distance														
		8'	9'	10'	11'	12'	15'	20'	25'	30'	50'	100'	150'	200'	300'	500'
2	13839.3'	7'11.9"	8'11.9"	9'11.9"	10'11.9"	11'11.9"	14'11.8"	19'11.7"	24'11"	29'11"	49'10"	99'3"	148'5"	197'2"	293'8"	482'7"
		8'0.1"	9'0.1"	10'0.1"	11'0.1"	12'0.1"	15'0.2"	20'0.3"	25'1"	30'1"	50'2"	100'9"	151'8"	202'11"	306'8"	518'9"
2	9687.5'	7'11.9"	8'11.9"	9'11.9"	10'11.9"	11'11.8"	14'11.7"	19'11.5"	24'11"	29'11"	49'9"	99'0"	147'9"	195'11"	291'0"	475'6"
		8'0.1"	9'0.1"	10'0.1"	11'0.2"	12'0.2"	15'0.3"	20'0"	25'1"	30'1"	50'3"	101'1"	152'4"	204'3"	309'7"	527'3"
2.8	6919.7'	7'11.9"	8'11.9"	9'11.8"	10'11.8"	11'11.8"	14'11.6"	19'11"	24'11"	29'10"	49'8"	98'7"	146'10"	194'5"	287'6"	466'4"
		8'0.1"	9'0.1"	10'0.2"	11'0.2"	12'0.3"	15'0.4"	20'1"	25'1"	30'2"	50'4"	101'6"	153'4"	205'11"	313'7"	538'11"
4	4843.8'	7'11.8"	8'11.8"	9'11.8"	10'11.7"	11'11.6"	14'11.4"	19'11"	24'10"	29'10"	49'6"	98'0"	145'6"	192'1"	282'6"	453'3"
		8'0.2"	9'0.2"	10'0.2"	11'0.3"	12'0.4"	15'0.6"	20'1"	25'2"	30'2"	50'6"	102'1"	154'10"	208'7"	319'10"	557'7"
5.6	3459.8'	7'11.8"	8'11.7"	9'11.7"	10'11.6"	11'11.5"	14'11.2"	19'11"	24'10"	29'9"	49'3"	97'2"	143'9"	189'1"	276'1"	436'10"
		8'0.2"	9'0.3"	10'0.3"	11'0.4"	12'0.5"	15'0.8"	20'1"	25'2"	30'3"	50'9"	103'0"	156'10"	212'3"	328'6"	584'6"
8	2421.9'	7'11.7"	8'11.6"	9'11.5"	10'11.4"	11'11.3"	14'10.9"	19'10"	24'9"	29'8"	49'0"	96'0"	141'3"	184'9"	266'11"	414'5"
		8'0.3"	9'0.4"	10'0.5"	11'0.6"	12'0.7"	15'1.1"	20'2"	25'3"	30'5"	51'1"	104'4"	159'11"	218'0"	342'5"	630'1"
11	1761.4'	7'11.6"	8'11.5"	9'11.3"	10'11.2"	11'11"	14'9.8"	19'9"	24'8"	29'6"	48'7"	94'8"	138'3"	179'7"	256'4"	389'5"
		8'0.4"	9'0.6"	10'0.7"	11'0.8"	12'1"	15'1.5"	20'3"	25'4"	30'6"	51'6"	106'0"	164'0"	225'7"	361'7"	698'2"
16	1210.9'	7'11.4"	8'11.2"	9'11"	10'10.8"	11'10.6"	14'9.8"	19'8"	24'6"	29'3"	48'0"	92'4"	133'6"	171'8"	240'5"	353'11"
		8'0.6"	9'0.8"	10'1"	11'1.2"	12'1.4"	15'2.3"	20'4"	25'6"	30'9"	52'2"	109'0"	171'2"	239'7"	398'10"	851'8"
22	880.7'	7'11.1"	8'10.9"	9'10.7"	10'10.4"	11'10.1"	14'9"	19'7"	24'4"	29'0"	47'4"	89'10"	128'2"	163'0"	223'9"	318'11"
		8'0.9"	9'1.1"	10'1.4"	11'1.7"	12'2"	15'3.1"	20'6"	25'9"	31'1"	53'0"	112'10"	180'10"	258'9"	455'0"	1156'9"
32	605.5'	7'10.7"	8'10.4"	9'10.1"	10'9.6"	11'9.2"	14'7.6"	19'4"	24'0"	28'7"	46'2"	85'10"	120'3"	150'4"	200'7"	273'10"
		8'1.3"	9'1.6"	10'2"	11'2.4"	12'2.9"	15'4.6"	20'8"	26'1"	31'7"	54'6"	119'9"	199'5"	298'8"	594'8"	2870'4"

Note: Circle of confusion = 0.0006.

LENS EXTENDERS

Optical devices that increase the focal length of the lens have a corresponding effect on the T-stop. To find the filter factor, square the extension factor. For example, a 2x optic has a filter factor of 4, and a 3x extender has a filter factor of 9. A factor of 4 translates to two stops, and 9 translates to approximately three stops; thus, a 2x extender turns a 200mm f/4 lens into a 400mm f/8 lens. When combining extenders, the factors must be multiplied. For example, a 2x extender and a 3x extender used together have a factor of 36 and a five-stop increase in exposure. See Table 3.1 for exposure increase due to factors. For best results, extenders must generally be stopped down.

MACROPHOTOGRAPHY

Regular prime lenses can seldom focus closer than 9 or 10 inches. Zooms generally have a minimum focus of around 2 to 3 feet.

Extreme close-up photography has a set of problems all its own. The most critical aspect of macro work is the degree of magnification. A magnification of 1:1 means that the object will be reproduced on film at its actual size; that is, an object that is 1/2 inch in reality will produce an image on the negative or video tube of 1/2 inch. A reproduction ratio of 1:2 results in an image that is one-half its normal size, 1:3 produces an image of one-third its normal size, and so on.

In film, the 35mm academy frame is 16mm high and 22mm wide. In 1:1 reproduction, a 22mm object will fill the entire frame. Most lenses of ordinary design can focus no closer than a ratio of 1:8 or 1:10.

Exposure Compensation in Macrophotography

When a small image is spread over a large piece of film, it naturally produces less exposure. With reproduction ratios of greater than 1:10, exposure compensation is necessary. The formula for exposure compensation is as follows:

$$\text{shooting f-stop} = \frac{\text{f-stop determined by meter}}{1 + \text{magnification ratio}}$$

For example, if the meter reading is f/8 and the reproduction ratio is 1:2, or one-half size, the calculation is as follows:

$$\frac{8}{(1 + 0.5)} = 5.3$$

Depth of Field in Close-up Work

Many misconceptions are associated with macrophotography. Perhaps the most basic is that wide angle lenses have greater depth of field. Depth of field is a function of image size, not focal length. It is true that wide-angle lenses have greater depth of field, but once you have attached a wider lens, you still want the same image you had before. To accomplish that, you must move the camera closer to the subject. Once you have done this, the depth of field is exactly the same as it was before because focus distance is also an important determinant of depth of field.

The important aspects of close-up photography are these:

- Depth of field decreases as magnification increases.
- Depth of field decreases as focus distance decreases.
- Depth of field is doubled by closing down the lens two stops.

Depth of Field in Extreme Close-up Work

The calculation of depth of field in extreme close-up work differs from normal calculations. At magnifications greater than 1:10, the depth of field is extremely small, and it is easier to calculate the total depth of field rather than a near and far limit of the zone of focus.

The total depth of field is calculated by the following formula:

$$D^t = \frac{2Cc \times f\ (1 + m)}{m^2}$$

total depth of field =

$$\frac{2 \times \text{circle of confusion} \times \text{f-stop}\ (1 + \text{magnification})}{\text{magnification}^2}$$

Magnification is calculated by the following formula:

$$\text{magnification} = \frac{\text{image size}}{\text{object size}}$$

Tables 2.32 and 2.33 list the total depth of field, in decimal inches, for 35mm and 16mm formats. They also give the exposure factor and the increase in T-stop when shooting at a particular magnification.

Table 2.32 Extreme Close-up Depth of Field (in Inches) and Exposure: 35mm Format

	F/number													Exposure	T-stop
Magnification	f/1	f/1.4	f/2	f/2.8	f/4	f/5.6	f/8	f/11	f/16	f/22	f/32	f/45	f/64	Factor	Increase
1:10	0.22	0.31	0.44	0.62	0.88	1.23	1.76	2.42	3.52	4.84	7.04	9.90	14.08	1.21	1/4
1:9	0.18	0.25	0.36	0.50	0.72	1.01	1.44	1.98	2.88	3.96	5.76	8.10	11.52	1.23	1/4
1:8	0.00	0.01	0.01	0.01	0.58	0.81	1.15	1.58	2.30	3.17	4.61	6.48	9.22	1.27	1/3
1:7	0.00	0.01	0.22	0.31	0.45	0.63	0.90	1.23	1.79	2.46	3.58	5.04	7.17	1.31	1/3
1:6	0.08	0.12	0.17	0.24	0.34	0.47	0.67	0.92	1.34	1.85	2.69	3.78	5.38	1.36	1/2
1:5	0.06	0.08	0.12	0.17	0.24	0.34	0.48	0.66	0.96	1.32	1.92	2.70	3.84	1.44	1/2
1:4	0.04	0.06	0.08	0.11	0.16	0.22	0.32	0.44	0.64	0.88	1.28	1.80	2.56	1.56	2/3
1:3	0.02	0.03	0.05	0.07	0.10	0.13	0.19	0.26	0.38	0.53	0.77	1.08	1.54	1.78	1 3/4
1:2	0.01	0.02	0.02	0.03	0.05	0.07	0.10	0.13	0.19	0.26	0.38	0.54	0.77	2.25	1 1/3
2:3	0.01	0.01	0.02	0.02	0.03	0.04	0.06	0.08	0.12	0.17	0.24	0.34	0.48	2.78	1 1/2
3:4	0.01	0.01	0.01	0.02	0.02	0.03	0.05	0.07	0.10	0.14	0.20	0.28	0.40	3.06	1 2/3
7:8	0.00	0.01	0.01	0.01	0.02	0.03	0.04	0.05	0.08	0.11	0.16	0.22	0.31	3.52	1 3/4
1:1	0.00	0.01	0.01	0.01	0.02	0.02	0.03	0.04	0.06	0.09	0.13	0.18	0.26	4	2

Note: Circle of confusion = 0.002.

Table 2.33 Extreme Close-up Depth of Field (in Inches) and Exposure: 16mm Format

	F/number														
Magnification	f/1	f/1.4	f/2	f/2.8	f/4	f/5.6	f/8	f/11	f/16	f/22	f/32	f/45	f/64	Exposure Factor	T-stop Increase
1:10	0.13	0.18	0.26	0.37	0.53	0.74	1.06	1.45	2.11	2.90	4.22	5.94	8.45	1.21	1/4
1:9	0.11	0.15	0.22	0.30	0.43	0.60	0.86	1.19	1.73	2.38	3.46	4.86	6.91	1.23	1/4
1:8	0.00	0.00	0.00	0.01	0.35	0.48	0.69	0.95	1.38	1.90	2.76	3.89	5.53	1.27	1/3
1:7	0.00	0.00	0.13	0.19	0.27	0.38	0.54	0.74	1.08	1.48	2.15	3.02	4.30	1.31	1/3
1:6	0.05	0.07	0.10	0.14	0.20	0.28	0.40	0.55	0.81	1.11	1.61	2.27	3.23	1.36	1/2
1:5	0.04	0.05	0.07	0.10	0.14	0.20	0.29	0.40	0.58	0.79	1.15	1.62	2.30	1.44	1/2
1:4	0.02	0.03	0.05	0.07	0.10	0.13	0.19	0.26	0.38	0.53	0.77	1.08	1.54	1.56	2/3
1:3	0.01	0.02	0.03	0.04	0.06	0.08	0.12	0.16	0.23	0.32	0.46	0.65	0.92	1.78	1 3/4
1:2	0.01	0.01	0.01	0.02	0.03	0.04	0.06	0.08	0.12	0.16	0.23	0.32	0.46	2.25	1 1/3
2:3	0.00	0.01	0.01	0.01	0.02	0.03	0.04	0.05	0.07	0.10	0.14	0.20	0.29	2.78	1 1/2
3:4	0.00	0.01	0.01	0.01	0.01	0.02	0.03	0.04	0.06	0.08	0.12	0.17	0.24	3.06	1 2/3
7:8	0.00	0.00	0.01	0.01	0.01	0.02	0.02	0.03	0.05	0.06	0.09	0.13	0.19	3.52	1 3/4
1:1	0.00	0.00	0.00	0.01	0.01	0.01	0.02	0.03	0.04	0.05	0.08	0.11	0.15	4	2

Note: Circle of confusion = 0.0006.

A simplified way of determining the degree of magnification is to use Figure 2.2 for 35mm or 2.3 for 16mm. Place the chart at the same distance from the focal plane as the subject, and focus on it. The rectangles on the chart are based on full aperture sizes in 35mm or 16mm. The rectangle that fills the aperture in the viewfinder indicates the degree of magnification.

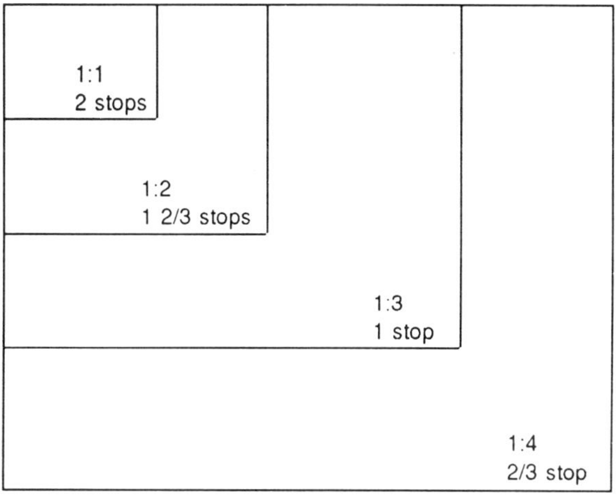

Figure 2.2 35mm close focus chart

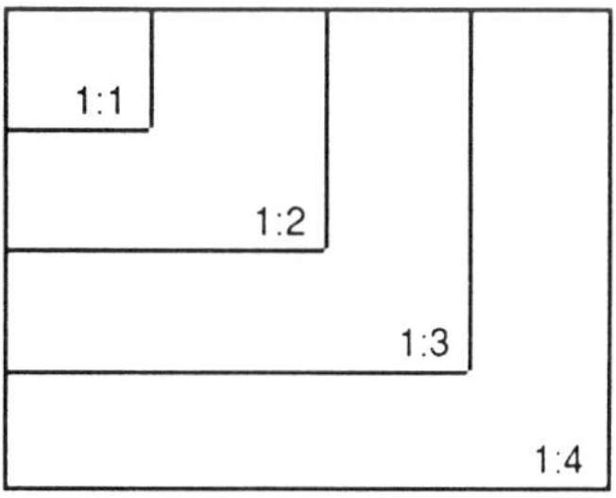

Figure 2.3 16mm close focus chart

Lens Displacement

When focused closer than infinity, the front elements of the lens (or all of the elements) are moved away from the focal plane. This is important in calculating exposure loss in extreme close-up work. The following calculation is used:

$$d = \frac{f^2}{a - f}$$

lens displacement from infinity position =

$$\frac{\text{focal length (inches)}^2}{\text{focus distance (inches)} - \text{focal length (inches)}}$$

Close-up Tools

Extreme close-up photography can be be accomplished with a variety of tools.

Diopters

Commonly referred to as *proxars*, diopters are simple meniscus lenses that are placed in front of the camera lens and reduce the minimum focusing distance of the lens. These lenses are measured in diopters. A diopter is the reciprocal of the focal length as measured in meters. A +1 diopter has a focal length of 1 meter, a +2 diopter has a focal length of 1/2 meter, and so on. Minimum focusing distance with the lens set at infinity is determined by dividing the diopter number into 100 cm. For example, a +2 diopter has a minimum focusing distance of 50 centimeters (100÷2 = 50) or 19.68 inches. You will actually be able to focus a bit closer by changing the focus of the lens itself. Closer focusing is possible by setting the lens to its minimum focus. Table 2.34 gives the minimum focusing distance of various diopters with the lens set at infinity.

Table 2.34 Diopter Focus with Lens at Infinity

	Minimum Focus	
Diopter	**Millimeters**	**Inches**
1/4D	4000	157.48
1/2D	2000	78.74
1D	1000	39.37
1 1/2D	666	26.22
2D	500	19.69
3D	333.33	13.12

The following guidelines are recommended for diopter use:

- Use a diopter with the lowest power possible. Combine it with a longer focal length lens, if necessary.
- Stop down as much as possible.
- There is no need for exposure compensation with diopters.
- When using two diopters together, add the diopter factors, and always place the diopter with the highest power closest to the lens.

Extension Tubes or Bellows

The advantage of extension tubes or bellows is that they do not alter the optics at all; thus, there is no degradation of the image. Extension tubes are simple rigid tubes that hold the lens farther away from the film plane than it normally sits, thus reducing the minimum focus distance. A bellows unit operates on the same principle but is continuously variable with a rack and pinion. Both devices give good results down to about 1:2.

Extension tubes are generally incompatible with wide-angle or zoom lenses. Lenses with larger minimum apertures generally give better results than high-speed lenses. To achieve 1:1 reproduction, the extension must equal the focal length of the lens. For 1:1 reproduction with a 50mm lens, for example, you need a 50mm extension. Optically, the best results at very high magnifications are obtained by reversing the lens (so that the back of the lens faces the subject) and mounting it on a bellows unit.

Macro Lenses

Macro lenses are specially designed optics that are optimized for close-up work. They are good in the 1:2 to 1:1 reproduction range. Some macros have barrel markings for magnification ratio as well as focus distance; this facilitates calculating the exposure compensation.

Close-Focus Lenses

Unlike macros, close-focus lenses are no different in design from ordinary prime lenses. For the most part, close-focus lenses are primes that have had the stop pins removed so that the focus barrel can rotate more than a full rotation and thus focus closer than normal.

Snorkles and Innovision

Several types of snorkle lenses, which are like periscopes, are available. They generally allow for extremely close focus and for getting the lens into incredibly small spaces. Century Precision Optics, Cine Photo Tech, and other companies make excellent snorkle units. Some require exposure compensation, and others have the compensation built-in. Be sure to determine which type you are using.

Innovision is a snorkle-type lens that can be fitted on both video and motion-picture cameras for extreme close-up work. It has the advantage of an extremely narrow barrel that can reach inside very small areas, even inside flowers. The f-stop is fixed and is very high, around f/32 to f/45, depending on the application. A high f-stop is generally needed for extreme close-up work. Innovision has its own light source: a small ring around the front element of the lens. It is a fiber-optic ring, remotely lit from a separate unit. It is approximately daylight-balanced and can be gelled inside the power unit.

LENS CARE

- Protect all lenses from shock. During shipping, each lens should have a minimum of 3 inches of foam surrounding it.
- Never clean a lens with dry lens tissue.
- Never put lens cleaning fluid on a lens; put it on the lens tissue instead.
- Brush or blow off loose grit before wiping the lens with lens tissue.
- Never use eyeglass cleaning cloths, which may contain silicon.
- In dusty or sandy conditions, try to keep a filter on the lens.
- Never use rubber cement or nail polish to attach a filter to the rear of the lens. Use 1/2-inch transfer tape, or snot tape (Scotch ATG-924).

SECTION 3

Color and Filters

FILTERS IN BLACK-AND-WHITE FILM

Contrast Filters

Filters function by transmitting some colors and absorbing others. This characteristic makes color filters valuable in controlling black-and-white images. The basic principle of contrast-control filtration in black-and-white cinematography is that a filter lightens colors in its own area of the spectrum and darkens complementary colors. Keep in mind that color filters increase or decrease contrast on black-and-white film only when there is a color difference in the scene. In a scene composed only of black, white, and gray objects, a color filter reduces exposure. It does not alter the contrast.

Exposure Compensation

Anytime a filter is used, it reduces the total amount of light reaching the film. You must compensate for it by allowing more overall exposure. The exposure compensation necessary for each filter is called the *filter factor*. Filter factors and the resulting exposure compensation, in stops, are given in Table 3.1.

Table 3.1 Filter Factors and Exposure Compensation

Filter Factor	Exposure Increase (Stops)
1.25	1/3
1.5	2/3
2	1
2.5	1 1/3
3	1 2/3
4	2
5	2 1/3
6	2 2/3
8	3
10	3 1/3
12	3 2/3
40	5 1/3
100	6 2/3
1000	10

Different filter factors are given for daylight and tungsten light. In the warm colors (red, orange, and yellow), the daylight filter factors are greater than the tungsten filter factors. In the violet and blue range, the daylight factors are less than the tungsten factors. In the cyan and green range of the spectrum, the daylight and tungsten filter factors are nearly all equal. The same is true for magenta, which is equally red and blue.

A simple rule of thumb is to expose for the darkest subject in the scene that is substantially the same color as the filter, and let the filter take care of the highlights.

The System Used to Designate Kodak Wratten Filters
With color-compensating filters (CC series), the definition of the color value of the filter is quite simple: a CC10Y filter has a peak density of 10 yellow. For other filters that are not "pure" color (that is, are not restricted to a narrow band of the spectrum), it is not as simple to affix a designation. There are many systems for naming filters, but the most widely accepted is the system used to designate Kodak Wratten filters. Most manufacturers at least provide an equivalence expressed in the Wratten system. The system used to designate Kodak Wratten gelatin filters is shown in Table 3.2.

Table 3.2 Designation System for Kodak Wratten Gelatin Filters

Number	Color	Use
1A	Pale pink	Absorbs UV. Reduces excess blue in open shade scenes.
2A	Pale yellow	Absorbs UV. Reduces atmospheric haze.
2B	Pale yellow	Absorbs UV. Stronger haze reduction than 2C.
8	Yellow	Darkens sky and shadows lit by blue skylight. Lightens foliage. Gives a normal rendition of day scenes with pan film. Formerly known as K2.
11	Yellow-green	Corrects color response of type B panchromatic emulsions to match response of the eye to objects exposed to tungsten illumination. Gives better flesh tones in portraits against sky. Formerly known as X1.
12	Deep yellow	Minus-blue. Haze penetration in aerial work.
15	Deep yellow	Darkens sky more dramatically than #8 or #9. Used with black-and-white infrared film. Absorbs some green. Formerly known as G.
16	Yellow-orange	Greater correction of sky than #15. Absorbs small amount of green. Sometimes used to check blue-screen backgrounds.
21	Orange	Contrast filter for blue and blue-green absorption.
23A	Light red	Contrast filter with greater green absorption than #21 or #22. Used for color separation work. Darkens blue sky and skylit shadows, producing strong contrast effects.

(continued)

Table 3.2 Designation System for Kodak Wratten Gelatin Filters *(continued)*

Number	Color	Use
25	Red tricolor	For color separation work. Haze penetration in aerial work. Darkens sky and skylit shadows. Formerly known as A.
29	Deep red	Deep red tricolor. Maximum contrast with landscapes. Formerly known as F.
34A	Violet	For minus-green and plus-blue separation.
44A	Light blue-green	Minus-red. (#12 is minus-blue and #32 is minus-green). When used with panchromatic emulsion, simulates the effect of an orthochromatic film, emphasizing blue and green.
47	Blue	Lightens the sky and darkens green foliage and reds. Exaggerates atmospheric effects. Formerly known as C5.
47B	Deep blue	Color separation blue. Used with #25 (red) and #58 (green). Used for Polaroid check of blue-screen illumination.
58	Green	Separation tricolor green. Produces very light foliage.

Note: Courtesy Eastman Kodak Co.

Combining Filters

Combining contrast filters for black-and-white does not have the cumulative effect that you might expect. For example, combining a #8 filter and a #15 filter gives the same visual effect as a #15 filter alone, although the filter factor is changed by the combination of the two. Combining two

Table 3.3 Exposure Compensation for Panchromatic Films

Filter Number	Name	F-stop Loss, Daylight	F-stop Loss, Tungsten
1A	UV	—	—
2A	Haze	—	—
6	Yellow 1	2/3	2/3
8	Yellow 2	1	2/3
11	Green 1	2	1 2/3
12	Yellow	1	2/3
13	Green 2	2 1/3	2
15	Deep yellow	1 2/3	1
16	Orange	1 2/3	1 2/3
21	Orange	2 1/3	2
23A	Light red	2 2/3	1 2/3
25A	Red 1	3	2 2/3
29	Dark red	4 1/3	2
47	Dark blue	2 1/3	3
47B	Dark blue	3	4
58	Dark green	3	3

filters of different groups is seldom necessary because there is almost always a single filter that will accomplish the same effect.

Polarizers

Natural light vibrates in all directions around its path of travel. A polarizer transmits the light that is vibrating in one direction only. Brewster's angle—56° from normal, or 34° from the surface—is the zone of maximum polarization. Brewster's angle is illustrated in Figure 3.1.

In copy work or in product photography with reflective surfaces, the lighting units can be polarized with polascreens, and then a polarizer on the lens can be used to select the desired amount of reflection. As with glare on water and on windows, it is seldom desirable to eliminate all reflections, as this creates an unnatural effect.

Polarizers carry a heavy penalty in terms of light loss, generally at least one and two-thirds to two stops as a filter factor. The filter factor does not change as you rotate the polarizer.

Polarizers can be used with color film to darken the sky. Maximum polarization occurs at about 90° from the sun. This works well for static shots, but care must be taken if a pan or tilt is required because the degree of polarization may change as the camera moves. If the sky is overcast, the polarizer will have little effect.

Neutral-Density Filters

Neutral-density (ND) filters are used to reduce overall exposure without affecting color rendition. They are also known as *Wratten #96* filters. The opacity of ND filters is given in density units: 0.3 equals one stop, 0.6 equals two

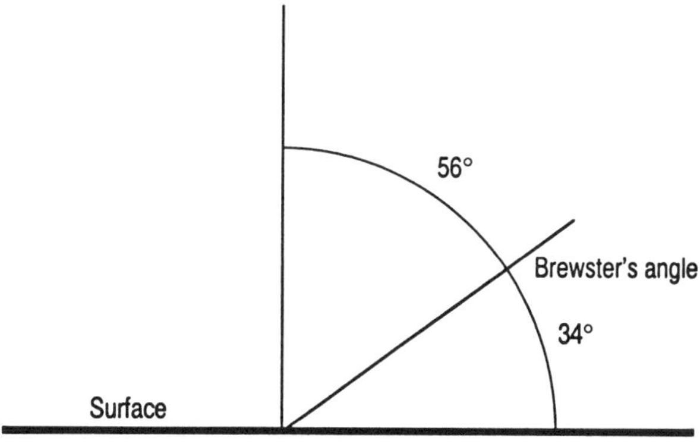

Figure 3.1 Brewster's angle.

Table 3.4 Neutral-Density Filters

ND Filter Number	Transmission (%)	Filter Factor	Exposure Increase (Stops)
0.1	80	$1\frac{1}{4}$	$\frac{1}{3}$
0.2	63	$1\frac{1}{2}$	$\frac{2}{3}$
0.3	50	2	1
0.4	40	$2\frac{1}{2}$	$1\frac{1}{3}$
0.5	32	3	$1\frac{2}{3}$
0.6	25	4	2
0.7	20	5	$2\frac{1}{3}$
0.8	16	6	$2\frac{2}{3}$
0.9	13	8	3
1.0	10	10	$3\frac{1}{3}$
2.0	1	100	$6\frac{2}{3}$
3.0	0.1	1000	10
4.0	0.01	10,000	$13\frac{1}{3}$

stops, and 0.9 equals three stops. ND filters are available combined with #85 correction filters (85N3, 85N6, and 85N9).

In gelatin filters, NDs are available in 0.1 increments (one-third of a stop). If you combine ND filters, the density values are *added.* If you are using the arithmetic exposure factors, do not forget to *multiply* the exposure factor. Common ND filters are given in Table 3.4.

COLOR

Additive Color System

The electromagnetic spectrum is divided into the major hues: violet, indigo, blue, green, yellow, orange, and red. Red, blue, and green have special properties. By mixing various combinations of these three colors, any known color can be produced. For this reason, they are known as *primary colors.*

Table 3.5 Filter Sizes

Series Number	Size (in.)	Size (mm)	Adaptation
4	$\frac{13}{16}$	22	14.2mm to 23mm
5	$1\frac{3}{16}$	30	23.4mm to 34.6mm
6	$1\frac{5}{8}$	41	34.8mm to 44mm
7	2	51	44.4mm to 55mm
8	$2\frac{1}{2}$	63.5	55.2mm to 65.7mm
9	$3\frac{1}{4}$	82.5	66.7mm to 85.2mm
10	$4\frac{1}{2}$	115	
11	$5\frac{7}{16}$	138	

Table 3.6 Square and Rectangular Filter Sizes

Series Number	Size (in.)	Size (mm)
5	2 x 2	50 x 50
6	3 x 3	76 x 76
7	4 x 4	102 x 102
8	4 x 5.65	102 x 143
$8^1/_2$	6.6 x 6.6	167 x 167
9	6 x 4	152 x 102

The colors that are combinations of two primaries are known as *complementary*, or *secondary, colors*:

RED + BLUE = magenta
BLUE + GREEN = cyan
RED + GREEN = yellow

magenta + cyan = BLUE
cyan + yellow = GREEN
yellow + magenta = RED

RED + cyan = neutral gray
BLUE + yellow = neutral gray
GREEN + magenta = neutral gray

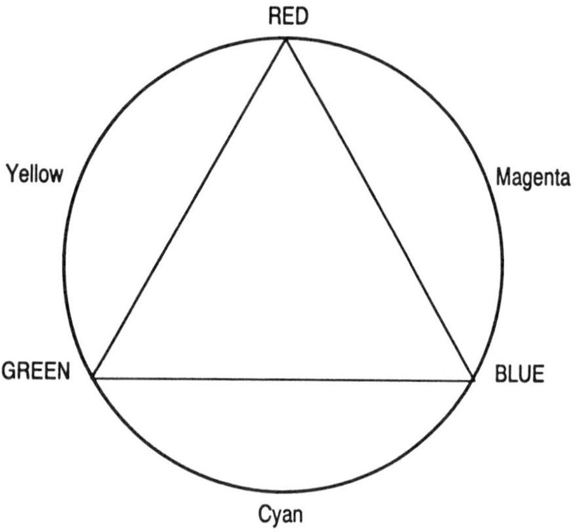

Figure 3.2 Color circle.

Subtractive Color System

We can approach this from another direction by starting with white light. If we *subtract* yellow from white light, we have blue. If we subtract magenta from white light, we are left with green. For this reason, the complementary colors are also known as the *subtractive primaries*. The combination of all three subtractive colors produces black: All light is absorbed.

yellow (RED + GREEN) = white – BLUE
magenta (RED + BLUE) = white – GREEN
cyan (BLUE + GREEN) = white – RED

There are several advantages to using the subtractive system in color photographic film; the most basic advantage is efficiency. In the additive method, to obtain white, three filters are needed (red + blue + green), each of which absorbs a great deal of light. In the subtractive system, nothing is needed to produce white. No filter at all is put in front of the white light. Similarly, to obtain yellow in the additive system, two filters are needed (red + green), which absorb two-thirds of the spectrum. In the subtractive system, only one filter is needed (blue), which absorbs only one-third of the spectrum.

cyan removes RED
yellow removes BLUE
magenta removes GREEN
RED removes cyan
BLUE removes yellow
GREEN removes magenta

Color Temperature

An approximate measure of how close a source is to a pure black-body radiator can be derived through the Color-Rendering index (CRI), a scale of 1 to 100 that gives some indication of the ability of a light source to render color accurately. For photographic purposes, only sources with a CRI of 90 or above are generally considered acceptable.

Typical color temperatures of common light sources are given in Table 3.7.

Mireds

Mired stands for microreciprocal degree. Mireds are derived by dividing 1,000,000 by the Kelvin value. For example, 3200K equals 312 mireds (1,000,000 ÷ 3200 = 312).

To compute how much color correction is required, use the mired values of the source and the final desired color.

Table 3.7 Color Temperatures of Common Light Sources

Light Source	Color Temperature (K)
Candle	2000
Sunlight at dawn	2000
Low-wattage tungsten bulb	2900
Tungsten-halogen bulb	3200
Photo bulb	3400
Morning/afternoon sun	4400
Arc with white-flame carbon	5000
Midday sun	5500
HMIs	5600–5800
Midday sunlight plus skylight	6500
Cloudy sky	6800
Clear blue sky	10,000–20,000

To convert a 5500K source to 3200K, derive the mired values from the color temperatures, and subtract the mired value of the desired color from that of the source.

5000K = 200 mireds

3200K = 312 mireds

312 – 200 = 112 mireds

Filter #85 orange has a mired value of +112.

On the mired scale, a positive shift value means that the filter is yellowish; a negative value means that the filter will give a blue shift. When combining filters, add the mired values.

FILTERS IN COLOR FILM

The basic filter families are shown in Table 3.8.

Table 3.8 Basic Filter Families

Number	Type	Use
85	Conversion	Correct daylight to tungsten balance
80	Conversion	Correct tungsten to daylight
82	Light-balancing	Cool
81	Light-balancing	Warm
CC	Color-compensating	Primary and secondary colors

Table 3.9 80 Series Filters

Number	Conversion (K)	Mired Shift	Compensation (stops)
80A	3200 to 5500	–131	2
80B	3400 to 5500	–112	1 2/3
80C	3800 to 5500	–81	1
80D	4200 to 5500	–56	1/3

Conversion Filters

Conversion filters work in the blue–orange axis and affect fundamental color balance in relation to the color sensitivity of the emulsion. Conversion filters affect all parts of the spectral energy distribution (SED) for smooth color rendition. The 80 series filters, which are blue conversion filters, are given in Table 3.9.

Light-Balancing Filters

Light-balancing filters are warming and cooling filters. They work on the entire SED like conversion filters, but they are used to make smaller shifts in the blue–orange axis.

81 and 82 Series Filters

The 81 series of warming filters (81, 81A, 81B, 81C, 81O, 81EF) increases the warmth of the light by lowering its color temperature in 200K increments. The #81 filter shifts the color temperature by the minimum amount required for the eye to perceive any change: –200K. The 82 series works in the same fashion but reduces the warmth of the light. The #82 filter shifts the overall color temperature by +200K. As with most color-temperature-correction filters, excess magenta or green is not dealt with and must be handled separately. The 81 and 82 series filters are given in Table 3.10.

Color-Compensating Filters

CC filters are manufactured in the primary and secondary colors. They are used to make corrections in a specific area of the spectrum or to create special effects. They affect only their own narrow band of the SED. CC filters cannot be used to correct overall color balance. Primary filters work in a limited band of the spectrum and correct only one wavelength. Information on a variety of CC filters is presented in Tables 3.11 to 3.14.

Fluorescent Lights

Because CC filters are not confined to the blue–orange axis, they can be used to correct imbalances in the magenta–green axis, such as the imbalances that occur with fluores-

Table 3.10 81 and 82 Series Filters

Type of Filter	Number	Exposure Increase (Stops)	Mired Shift	To Obtain 3200K From
	82C + 82C	1 1/3	–89	2490K
	82C + 82B	1 1/3	–77	2570K
	82C + 82A	1	–65	2650K
Cooling	82C + 82	1	–55	2720K
	82C	2/3	–45	2800K
	82B	2/3	–32	2900K
	82A	1/3	–21	3000K
	82	1/3	–10	3100K
	81	1/3	+9	3300K
	81A	1/3	+18	3400K
Warming	81B	1/3	+27	3500K
	81C	1/3	+35	3600K
	81D	2/3	+42	3700K
	81EF	2/3	+52	3850K

Table 3.11 Color-Compensating Filters: Secondary Colors

Color	Designation	Exposure Compensation (Stops)
	CC025Y	None
	CC05Y	None
	CC10Y	1/3
Yellow	CC20Y	1/3
(absorbs blue)	CC30Y	1/3
	CC40Y	1/3
	CC50Y	2/3
	CC025M	None
	CC05M	1/3
	CC10M	1/3
Magenta	CC20M	1/3
(absorbs green)	CC30M	2/3
	CC40M	2/3
	CC50M	2/3
	CC025C	None
	CC05C	1/3
	CC10C	1/3
Cyan	CC20C	1/3
(absorbs red)	CC30C	2/3
	CC40C	2/3
	CC50C	1

Table 3.12 Color-Compensating Filters: Primary Colors

Color	Designation	Exposure Compensation (Stops)
Red (absorbs blue and green)	CC025R	None
	CC05R	1/3
	CC10R	1/3
	CC20R	1/3
	CC30R	2/3
	CC40R	2/3
	CC50R	1
Green (absorbs blue and red)	CC025G	None
	CC05G	1/3
	CC10G	1/3
	CC20G	1/3
	CC30G	2/3
	CC40G	2/3
	CC50G	1
Blue (absorbs green and red)	CC025B	None
	CC05B	1/3
	CC10B	1/3
	CC20B	2/3
	CC30B	2/3
	CC40B	1
	CC50B	1 1/3

Table 3.13 CTO Filters: Daylight to Tungsten

Name	Typical Conversion	Mired Value	Light Loss (Stops)
85	5500K to 3200K	+131	3/4
Full CTO	5500K to 2900K, 6500K to 3125K	+167	2/3
Half CTO	5500K to 3800K, 4400K to 3200K	+81	1/2
Quarter CTO	5500K to 4500K, 3800K to 3200K	+42	1/3
Eighth CTO	5500K to 4900K, 3400K to 3200K	+20	1/3

Table 3.14 CTB Filters: Tungsten to Daylight

Name	Typical Conversion	Mired Value	Light Loss (Stops)
CTB, full blue	3200K to 5500K	–131	1 1/2
Half CTB, half blue	3200K to 4100K	–68	1
Third CTB, third blue	3200K to 3800K	–49	2/3
Quarter CTB, quarter blue	3200K to 3500K	–30	1/2
Eighth CTB, eighth blue	3200K to 3300K	–12	1/3

cent lamps. A CC30M filter is often part of the basic filter package for standard fluorescent tubes. Filters used to correct fluorescent lights are given in Tables 3.15 to 3.19.

Table 3.15 Correcting Off-Balance Sources

Existing Source	Your Lights	Strategy	Comments
Any fluorescents	None or fluorescents	Shoot fluorescent balance	Use fluorescents only, (adding fluorescent fill if necessary),and let the lab time the green out of the print or use 30ccM on lens.
Any fluorescents	Tungsten or HMIs	Replace the lamps	Replace existing fluorescent lamps with full-spectrum fluorescent bulbs, which provide photographic daylight or tungsten balance.
Cool white fluorescents	HMIs	Gel the fluorescents (daylight balance)	Add minusgreen gel to the existing fluorescents to remove the green. With cool white fluorescents,this will result in daylight balance.
Cool white fluorescents	HMIs	Gel the HMIs	Add plusgreen to the HMIs to match them to the heavy green output of the fluorescents. Then use a camera filter to remove the green, or have the lab time it out.
Cool white fluorescents	Tungsten	Gel the tungsten, and convert to daylight	Add plusgreen 50 to the lights to adds green and blue for daylight balance.
Cool white fluorescents	Tungsten	Gel the fluorescents, and convert to 3200K	Add fluorofilter to the fluorescents to reduce green and convert them to tungsten balance.
Warm white fluorescents	Tungsten	Gel the fluorescents (tungsten balance)	Add minusgreen gel. With warm white fluorescents, this will result in a tungsten balance. Tungsten lights or HMIs with #85 filter may be used

Table 3.16 Fluorescent-Balance Filters to Reduce Green

Filter	Nominal CC Equivalent	Use When CC Index Is Approximately
Minusgreen	30M	–12G
Half minusgreen	15M	–5G
Quarter minusgreen	7.5M	–2G

Table 3.17 Fluorescent-Balance Filters to Add Green

Filter	Nominal CC Equivalent	Use When CC Index Is Approximately
Plusgreen (windowgreen)	30G	+13M
Half plusgreen	15G	–5M
Quarter plusgreen	7.5G	–3M

Table 3.18 Fluorescent-Balance Combination Filters

Filter	Use
Fluorofilter	Reduces green and corrects cool white fluorescents to nominal 3200K
Plusgreen 50	Increases green and corrects 3200K sources to balance cool white fluorescents

Table 3.19 Fluorescent-Balance Filters for Use with Lee Camera Filters

Filtration on Tungsten Light	Effect	Lee Camera Filter
Fluorescent 5700	Converts tungsten to match cool white/daylight tubes (5700K)	FL 5700-B
Fluorescent 4300	Converts tungsten to match white tubes (4300K)	FL 4300-B
Fluorescent 3600	Converts tungsten to match warm white tubes (3600K)	FL 3600-B

Carbon Arcs

Carbon arcs give off heavy ultraviolet (UV) radiation. Rosco Y-1 and Lee LCT yellow reduce the UV output. For correction of white-flame carbon arcs to tungsten balance, use Rosco MT2 (together with Y-1) or Lee 232. Rosco MTY is a combination of MT2 and Y-1.

HMIs

HMIs generally run slightly blue and are voltage-dependent. Unlike tungsten lamps, their color temperature goes up as voltage decreases. It is important to check each lamp with a color temperature meter or color Polaroid and write the actual color temp on a piece of tape attached to the fixture. For slight correction, Y-1 or Rosco MT54 can be used. For more correction, use eighth or quarter CTO. Many HMIs also run green. Have eighth and quarter minusgreen available for correction.

Correction filters for carbon arcs and HMIs are given in Table 3.20.

Tungsten Lights

Tungsten bulbs and lamp reflectors yellow with age. For critical color balance, use eighth or quarter CTB. Soft lights

Table 3.20 Lamp Correction Filters

Filter	Description	Use	Mired Shift
Y1, LCT yellow	Pale straw	HMIs and white-flame carbons to absorb UV and reduce Kelvin to daylight balance	+45
WF (white flame)	Similar to Y1, but less color warming	HMIs and white-flame carbons to absorb UV and reduce Kelvin to daylight balance	+20
MT2	Similar to CTO	Used with Y-1 to convert white-flame carbons to 3200K; also used as amber conversion on HMIs and CIDs	+110
MTY	Combination of MT2 and Y1	Converts white-flame carbons to 3200K and reduces UV	+131
Half MT2	Amber	Partially converts white-flame carbons and HMIs	+38
Quarter MT2	Pale Amber	Partially converts white-flame carbons and HMIs	+20
MT54	Pale straw	Corrects white-flame carbons and HMIs	+35
UV filter	Very pale straw	Absorbs 90% of UV below 390 nanometers	+8

always run a little yellow because of the reflector. Putting a light through diffusion usually warms it.

Industrial Lamps

There are three general categories of industrial light sources: sodium vapor, metal halide, and mercury vapor. All of these lights have discontinuous spectrums and are dominant in one color. They all have very low CRIs. It is possible to shoot with these light sources if some corrections are made. Table 3.21 lists the filtration required with various industrial light sources.

High-pressure sodium lamps are very orange and contain a great deal of green. Low-pressure sodium lamps are monochromatic and impossible to correct.

Shown in Tables 3.22 to 3.24 are recommended starting points for using camera filtration to correct off-balance industrial sources. They are approximations only and should

Table 3.21 Industrial Sources

Existing Source	Your Lights	Filtration on Your Lights
High-pressure sodium	Tungsten	Double plusgreen
	HMI or other daylight source	Double plusgreen + full CTO
Metal halide	Tungsten	Plusgreen + full CTB
	HMI or other daylight source	Plusgreen (and possibly some blue)
Mercury vapor	Tungsten	Full CTB + half CTB + double plusgreen
	HMI or other daylight source	Full CTB + double plusgreen

Table 3.22 Camera Filtration for Industrial Sources

Film Type	Existing Source	Camera Filters
Tungsten	High-pressure sodium	80B + CC30M
	Metal halide	85 + CC50M
	Mercury vapor	85 + CC50M
Daylight	High-pressure sodium	80B + CC50B
	Metal halide	81A + CC30M
	Mercury vapor	81A + CC50M

Table 3.23 Effect of Diffusion on Color Temperature of 3200K Source

Diffusion	Color Temperature (K)
Tough Spun	3180
Light Tough Spun	3180
Quarter Tough Spun	3200
Tough Frost	3000
Light Tough Frost	3060
Opal Tough Frost	3100
Tough White (216)	3120
Tough Half White	3150
Tough Quarter White	3150
Grid Cloth	2960
Tough Silk	3160
Soft Frost	2840
Half Soft Frost	3180
Hilite	3050
Hamburg Frost	3200

Data courtesy of Rosco Laboratories.

Table 3.24 Color Meter Readings and Filters

Meter Readout	Gel	Color Compensation
+1	Eighth minusgreen	3.75M
+3	Quarter minusgreen	7.5M
+6	Half minusgreen	15M
+13	Minusgreen	30M
–2	Quarter plusgreen	5G
–5	Half plusgreen	15G
–12	Plusgreen	30G

be confirmed with metering and testing. Always shoot a gray scale and some skin tone to serve as a guide for the timer.

IMAGE MANIPULATION WITH FLASHING

Flashing film, before or after exposure, is a method of reducing contrast or adding a color cast to the film. It consists of giving the film a uniform exposure to light,

Table 3.25 Exposure Before Flashing

Zone	Exposure Units
I	1
II	2
III	4
IV	8
V	16
VI	32
VII	64
VIII	128
IX	256

either in the camera or at the lab. In video, similar effects can be achieved with the camera control unit or during the film-to-video transfer.

The exposure of film is simply a matter of allowing enough light to fall on the emulsion to produce a proportional chemical change. If the scene is underexposed (the shadows are too dark), the silver halide crystals do not get enough light to create the proper chemical change, particularly in the shadows. Flashing is a way of jump-starting the shadow areas to bring them up to a more suitable relationship with the highlights. The most logical question to ask about flashing is this: If we are exposing the film to uniform light, aren't we preexposing the highlight areas in exactly the same way as the shadows?

Exposure is basically geometric. One stop (one zone) more exposure is *twice* as much light. Table 3.25 gives the exposure units for a basic nine-zone exposure. Suppose we expose the film to a uniform Zone II—two units of exposure—as shown in Table 3.26. The effect is evident. We

Table 3.26 Exposure After Flashing

Zone	Exp Units	Added Exp	Total Exp
I	1	2	3
II	2	2	4
III	4	2	6
IV	8	2	10
V	16	2	18
VI	32	2	34
VII	64	2	66
VIII	128	2	130
IX	256	2	258

have made a substantial difference in the lower zones. For example, we have raised Zone II one entire stop of exposure, making it Zone III. At the other end of the scale, however, the effect is negligible. The difference between 256 units of exposure and 258 units cannot be detected even with scientific instruments. We have effectively reduced the contrast range of the negative.

Too much flashing can lead to a veiling effect or a false tonality. The mere suggestion of exposing valuable, undeveloped footage to light is enough to give some producers and directors apoplexy and may be useful in getting them to approve an additional lighting order as an alternative.

The problem with preflashing is that there is no uniform terminology or method among motion-picture labs. If you plan to preflash or post-flash a film, extensive discussion with the lab and testing beforehand are essential. The most common method is to specify a density above base density plus fog (the basic density of unexposed developed film).

SECTION 4

Exposure

F-STOP

The f-stop is a mathematical measure of the ability of a lens to pass light. The variable opening inside the lens is the aperture or iris. The maximum f-stop of a lens is a measure of its ability to pass light with the aperture fully open. A lens with a maximum of f/1 would theoretically allow all light passing through it to reach the film. Beyond this maximum, the scale of f-stops (more commonly called *stops*) is a doubling of the amount of light. In other words, by opening up the lens one stop, you allow twice as much light to pass. Conversely, by closing down one stop, you decrease the amount of light by 50%.

Strictly speaking, the term *f-stop* refers only to a lens aperture, but it has gained a more general usage to describe variations in light value, reflectance, and exposure. More technically, an f-stop on a lens is the number derived by dividing the focal length of the lens by its effective aperture, which is the diameter of the beam of light that can pass through the lens at a given setting.

$$f = \frac{F}{d}$$

$$\text{f-stop} = \frac{\text{focal length}}{\text{diameter of lens opening}}$$

The actual f-number series is shown in Table 4.1. The series is based on the square root of 2 (approximately equal to 1.4), and every other f-number represents a doubling of 1.4: 1.4, 2.8, 5.6, 11, etc. There is some rounding, particularly above f/8. An increase of two stops indicates a *quadrupling* of the amount of light (a factor of four), three stops represents an *eightfold* increase in light (a factor of eight), and so on.

T-STOP

A T-stop is an adjusted f-stop. The f-stop of a lens is a purely mathematical calculation. In reality, some lens designs are more efficient than others. Zoom lenses, in par-

Table 4.1 The F-stop Series

f/1
f/1.4
f/2
f/2.8
f/4
f/5.6
f/8
f/11
f/16
f/22
f/32
f/45
f/64
f/90

Table 4.2 F-stop Series with Third and Half Stops

Full Stops	Third Stops	Half Stops
1		
	1.1	
		1.2
	1.3	
1.4		
	1.6	
		1.7
	1.8	
2		
	2.2	
		2.4
	2.5	
2.8		
	3.2	
		3.4
	3.5	
4		
	4.5	
		4.8
	5	
5.6		

(continued)

Table 4.2 F-stop Series with Third and Half Stops *(continued)*

Full Stops	Third Stops	Half Stops
	6.3	
		6.8
	7	
8		
	9	
		9.6
	10	
11		
	13	
		13.6
	14	
16		
	18	
		19
	20	
22		
	25	
		27
	28	
32		
	35	
		38
	40	
45		
	50	
		54
	57	
64		
	72	
		77
	80	
90		

ticular, are extremely inefficient in allowing light to pass, and exposures based on theoretical values might be quite wrong. To remedy this situation, manufacturers test the lenses on an optical bench and calibrate them in true f-stops, or T-stops. Although most lenses have both scales printed on them, always use the T-stop scale. In general, the white scale is f-stops and the red scale is T-stops.

LUMINANCE

Measurements of the intensity of light are based on a standard candle, which was the amount of light produced by a certain type of candle. This has been replaced by the *candela* (cd). The luminous intensity of a lamp is often quoted in *candlepower.*

Light that falls on a surface is quantified in terms of *footcandles*. One footcandle (FC) is equal to the luminous flux of light from one candela falling on a surface that is 1 foot from the source. In the metric system, the unit is the *meter-candle*, or *lux*. One FC equals 10.764 lux. Lumens per square foot are the same as footcandles. Most incident-type light meters are calibrated in footcandles or lux.

Two important factors affect the illumination of a surface. The first is the inverse square law. The amount of light falling on a surface falls off drastically with fairly small movement away from the source. The inverse square law states that the intensity change is inversely proportional to the square of the distance:

$$I = \frac{1}{D^2}$$

$$\text{intensity change} = \frac{1}{\text{distance}^2}$$

Thus, doubling the distance cuts the light to one-quarter of its former intensity. In practice, the design of the lighting unit alters this ratio.

The second important factor is the angle of incidence. Common sense tells us that the amount of light decreases as the surface is tilted away from the source. In fact, it is proportional to the cosine of the angle of incidence. This is called the *cosine law.*

The luminance of a surface is measured in candles per square foot or footlamberts. A footlambert is the amount of light reflected by a diffuse surface with 100% reflectance when the surface receives 1 FC and is at right angles to the source. Candles per square foot are obtained by dividing the footlambert value by π, which compensates for the spherical nature of diffuse reflection. Spot meters are sometimes calibrated in candles per square foot.

LIGHTING RATIO

The lighting ratio is the relationship of the key light to the fill light. Table 4.3 lists many common ratios.

Table 4.3 Lighting Ratios

Exposure Difference between Key and Fill (Stops)	Ratio
2/3	1.5:1
1	2:1
1 1/3	2.5:1
1 2/3	3:1
2	4:1
2 1/3	5:1
2 2/3	6:1
3	8:1
3 1/3	10:1
3 2/3	13:1
4	16:1
5	32:1

FILM CAMERA EXPOSURE

Exposure is determined by these formulas:

$$\text{shutter speed for } 180^\circ \text{ shutter} = \frac{1}{2 \times \text{frame rate (fps)}}$$

$$\text{exposure (sec.)} = \frac{\text{shutter opening } (^\circ)}{360 \times \text{frame rate (fps)}}$$

Tables 4.4 to 4.16 cover most situations.

Table 4.4 Shutter Angle and Exposure at 24 fps

Shutter Angle (°)	Exposure
180	1/48
175	1/49
172.8	1/50
170	1/51
160	1/54
150	1/58
144	1/60

(continued)

Table 4.4 Shutter Angle and Exposure at 24 fps *(continued)*

Shutter Angle (°)	Exposure
150	1/62
130	1/66
90	1/96
80	1/108
70	1/123
60	1/144
50	1/173
40	1/216
30	1/288
20	1/432
10	1/844
5	1/1728

Table 4.5 Exposure with 180° Shutter Angle

Frame Rate (fps)	Exposure (sec.)
8	1/16
12	1/24
16	1/32
24	1/50
25	1/50
32	1/60
48	1/100
96	1/200
120	1/250

Table 4.6 Exposure Variation with Shutter Angle

180° Shutter	Exposure Change (Stops)	165° Shutter	120° Shutter
180	No change	165	120
140	–1/3	130	100
110	2/3	100	80
90	1	80	60
70	1 1/3	65	50
55	1 2/3	50	40
45	2	40	30
35	2 1/3	30	
30	2 2/3	25	
22	3	20	
18	3 1/3	15	

Table 4.7 Footage Used at Various Frame Rates (in Feet per Minute)

	Frame Rate (fps)								
Format	8	12	16	24	25	32	48	96	120
35mm film	30	45	60	90	93.75	120	80	360	450
16mm film	12	18	24	36	37.5	48	72	144	180

Table 4.8 Exposure Adjustment for High-Speed Filming

Frame Rate (fps)	Exposure Change (Stops)
24	Normal
25	Normal
30	1/3
32	1/2
38	2/3
48	1
60	1 1/3
76	1 2/3
96	2
120	2 1/3
150	2 2/3
190	3
240	3 1/3
300	3 2/3
380	4
480	4 1/3

Table 4.9 Exposure Adjustment for Low-Speed Filming

Frame Rate (fps)	Exposure Change (Stops)
6	2
7.5	1 2/3
9.5	1 1/3
12	1
15	2/3
19	1/3
24	Normal
25	Normal

Table 4.10 Incident Light (FC) at 24 or 25 fps with a 180° Shutter

ASA	1	1.2	1.4	2	2.8	4
12	50	100	200	400	800	1600
16	40	80	160	320	640	1280
19	32	64	128	256	512	1024
25	25	50	100	200	400	800
32	20	40	80	160	320	630
40	16	32	64	128	256	512
50	12.5	25	50	100	200	400
64	10	20	40	80	160	320
80	8	16	32	64	128	256
100	6	12	24	48	96	192
125	5	10	20	40	80	160
160	4	8	16	32	64	128
200	3	6	12	24	48	96
250	2.5	5	10	20	40	80
320	2	4	8	16	32	64
400	1.6	3	6	13	26	51
500	1.25	2.5	5	10	20	40
640	1	2	4	8	16	32
800	0.8	1.6	3	6	13	26
1000	0.6	1.2	2.4	5	10	19
1250	0.5	1	2	4	8	16
1600	0.4	0.8	2	3	6	13
2000	0.3	0.6	1	2	5	10
2600	0.25	0.5	1	2	4	8
3200	0.2	0.4	0.8	2	3	6
4000	0.15	0.31	0.62	1	2	5
5000	0.12	0.24	0.48	1	2	4
6400	0.1	0.2	0.4	0.8	1.6	3

T-stop					
5.6	8	11	16	22	32
3200	6400	12,800	25,600	51,200	102,400
2560	5120	10,240	20,480	40,960	81,920
2048	4096	8192	16,384	32,768	65,536
1600	3200	6400	12,800	25,600	51,200
1250	2500	5000	10,000	20,000	40,000
1024	2048	4096	8192	16,384	32,768
800	1600	3200	6400	12,800	25,600
640	1280	2560	5120	10,240	20,480
512	1024	2048	4096	8192	16,384
384	768	1536	3072	6144	12,288
320	640	1280	2560	5120	10,240
256	512	1024	2048	4096	8192
192	384	768	1536	3072	6144
160	320	640	1280	2560	5120
128	256	512	1024	2048	4096
102	205	410	819	1638	3277
80	160	320	640	1280	2560
64	128	256	512	1024	2048
51	102	205	410	819	1638
38	77	154	307	614	1229
32	64	128	256	512	1024
26	51	102	205	410	819
19	38	77	154	307	614
16	32	64	128	256	512
13	26	51	102	205	410
10	20	39	79	158	315
8	15	31	61	123	246
6	13	26	51	102	205

Table 4.11 Polaroid Film Exposure Correlations

								ASA and	
500	—32K	400	—32K	320	—32K	250	—32K	200	—32K
32	*250*	32	*500*	32		32		32	
28	*125*	28	*250*	28	*500*	28		28	
25	64	25	*125*	25	*250*	25	*500*	25	
22	*	22	64	22	*125*	22	*250*	22	*500*
20	*	20	*	20	64	20	*125*	20	*250*
17	45	17	*	17	*	17	64	17	*125*
16	*	16	45	16	*	16	*	16	64
14	*	14	*	14	45	14	*	14	*
12	32	12	*	12	*	12	45	12	*
11	28	11	32	11	*	11	*	11	45
10	25	10	28	10	32	10	*	10	*
9	22	9	25	9	28	9	32	9	*
8	20	8	22	8	25	8	28	8	32
7	17	7	20	7	22	7	25	7	28
6.3	16	6.3	17	6.3	20	6.3	22	6.3	25
5.6	14	5.6	16	5.6	17	5.6	20	5.6	22
5	12	5	14	5	16	5	17	5	20
4.4	11	4.4	12	4.4	14	4.4	16	4.4	17
4	10	4	11	4	12	4	14	4	16
3.5	9	3.5	10	3.5	11	3.5	12	3.5	14
3.1	8	3.1	9	3.1	10	3.1	11	3.1	12
2.8	7	2.8	8	2.8	9	2.8	10	2.8	11
2.5	6.3	2.5	7	2.5	8	2.5	9	2.5	10
2.2	5.6	2.2	6.3	2.2	7	2.2	8	2.2	9
2	5	2	5.6	2	6.3	2	7	2	8
1.8	4.4	1.8	5	1.8	5.6	1.8	6.3	1.8	7
1.6	4	1.6	4.4	1.6	5	1.6	5.6	1.6	6.3
1.4	3.5	1.4	4	1.4	4.4	1.4	5	1.4	5.6
1.2	3.2	1.2	3.5	1.2	4	1.2	4.4	1.2	5

Table 4.11 shows the converted T-stop for ASA 3200 Polaroid films (Types 107, 107C, and 667). To use the chart, look up the metered T-stop under the ASA of the film stock you are using. The equivalent T-stop under "32K" is the correct setting at 1/60 second on the Polaroid camera. Numbers in italics indicate shutter speed at T/64. Asterisks (*) indicate one-third stops.

Equivalent T-stop

160	—32K	100	—32K	80	—32K	64	—32K	50	—32K
32		32		32		32		32	
28		28		28		28		28	
25		25		25		25		25	
22		22		22		22		22	
20	*500*	20		20		20		20	
17	*250*	17	*500*	17		17		17	
16	*125*	16	*250*	16	*500*	16		16	
14	64	14	*125*	14	*250*	14	*500*	14	
12	*	12	64	12	*125*	12	*250*	12	*500*
11	*	11	*	11	64	11	*125*	11	*250*
10	45	10	*	10	*	10	64	10	*125*
9	*	9	45	9	*	9	*	9	64
8	*	8	*	8	45	8	*	8	*
7	32	7	*	7	*	7	45	7	*
6.3	28	6.3	32	6.3	*	6.3	*	6.3	45
5.6	25	5.6	28	5.6	32	5.6	*	5.6	*
5	22	5	25	5	28	5	32	5	*
4.4	20	4.4	22	4.4	25	4.4	28	4.4	32
4	17	4	20	4	22	4	25	4	28
3.5	16	3.5	17	3.5	20	3.5	22	3.5	25
3.1	14	3.1	16	3.1	17	3.1	20	3.1	22
2.8	12	2.8	14	2.8	16	2.8	17	2.8	20
2.5	11	2.5	12	2.5	14	2.5	16	2.5	17
2.2	10	2.2	11	2.2	12	2.2	14	2.2	16
2	9	2	10	2	11	2	12	2	14
1.8	8	1.8	9	1.8	10	1.8	11	1.8	12
1.6	7	1.6	8	1.6	9	1.6	10	1.6	11
1.4	6.3	1.4	7	1.4	8	1.4	9	1.4	10
1.2	5.6	1.2	6.3	1.2	7	1.2	8	1.2	9

Table 4.12 T-Stop Compensation for Various Frame Rates

	+4 2/3	+4 1/3	+4	+3 2/3	+3 1/3	+3	+2 2/3	+2 1/3	+2	+1 2/3	+1 1/3	+1	+2/3
FPS	**1**	**1.2**	**1.5**	**2**	**2.5**	**3**	**4**	**5**	**6**	**7.5**	**9.5**	**12**	**15**
Ft/min	3.5	**4**	**5.6**	7	8.6	11.3	14	17.3	22.5	28	36	**45**	56
			90	80	72	**64**	57	50	**45**	40	35	**32**	28
		90	80	72	**64**	57	50	**45**	40	35	**32**	28	25
	90	80	72	**64**	57	50	**45**	40	35	**32**	28	25	**22**
	80	72	**64**	57	50	**45**	40	35	**32**	28	25	**22**	20
	72	**64**	57	50	**45**	40	35	**32**	28	25	**22**	20	18
	64	57	50	**45**	40	35	**32**	28	25	**22**	20	18	**16**
	57	50	**45**	40	35	**32**	28	25	**22**	20	18	**16**	14
	50	**45**	40	35	**32**	28	25	**22**	20	18	**16**	14	13
	45	40	35	**32**	28	25	**22**	20	18	**16**	14	13	**11**
	40	35	**32**	28	25	**22**	20	18	**16**	14	13	**11**	10
	35	**32**	28	25	**22**	20	18	**16**	14	13	**11**	10	9
	32	28	25	**22**	20	18	**16**	14	13	**11**	10	9	**8**
	28	25	**22**	20	18	**16**	14	13	**11**	10	9	**8**	7
	25	**22**	20	18	**16**	14	13	**11**	10	9	**8**	7	6.3
	22	20	18	**16**	14	13	**11**	10	9	**8**	7	6.3	**5.6**
	20	18	**16**	14	13	**11**	10	9	**8**	7	6.3	**5.6**	5
	18	**16**	14	13	**11**	10	9	**8**	7	6.3	**5.6**	5	4.5
	16	14	13	**11**	10	9	**8**	7	6.3	**5.6**	5	4.5	**4**
	14	13	**11**	10	9	**8**	7	6.3	**5.6**	5	4.5	**4**	3.5
	13	**11**	10	9	**8**	7	6.3	**5.6**	5	4.5	**4**	3.5	3.2
	11	10	9	**8**	7	6.3	**5.6**	5	4.5	**4**	3.5	3.2	**2.8**
	10	9	**8**	7	6.3	**5.6**	5	4.5	**4**	3.5	3.2	**2.8**	2.5
	9	**8**	7	6.3	**5.6**	5	4.5	**4**	3.5	3.2	**2.8**	2.5	2.2
	8	7	6.3	**5.6**	5	4.5	**4**	3.5	3.2	**2.8**	2.5	2.2	**2**
	7	6.3	**5.6**	5	4.5	**4**	3.5	3.2	**2.8**	2.5	2.2	**2**	1.8
	6.3	**5.6**	5	4.5	**4**	3.5	3.2	**2.8**	2.5	2.2	**2**	1.8	1.6
	5.6	5	4.5	**4**	3.5	3.2	**2.8**	2.5	2.2	**2**	1.8	1.6	**1.4**
	5	4.5	**4**	3.5	3.2	**2.8**	2.5	2.2	**2**	1.8	1.6	**1.4**	1.3
	4.5	**4**	3.5	3.2	**2.8**	2.5	2.2	**2**	1.8	1.6	**1.4**	1.3	1.1
	4	3.5	3.2	**2.8**	2.5	2.2	**2**	1.8	1.6	**1.4**	1.3	1.1	**1**
	3.5	3.2	**2.8**	2.5	2.2	**2**	1.8	1.6	**1.4**	1.3	1.1	**1**	
	3.2	**2.8**	2.5	2.2	**2**	1.8	1.6	**1.4**	1.3	1.1	**1**		
	2.8	2.5	2.2	**2**	1.8	1.6	**1.4**	1.3	1.1	**1**			
	2.5	2.2	**2**	1.8	1.6	**1.4**	1.3	1.1	**1**				
	2.2	**2**	1.8	1.6	**1.4**	1.3	1.1	**1**					
	2	1.8	1.6	**1.4**	1.3	1.1	**1**						
	1.8	1.6	**1.4**	1.3	1.1	**1**							
	1.6	**1.4**	1.3	1.1	**1**								
	1.4	1.3	1.1	**1**									
	1.3	1.1	**1**										
	1.1	**1**											
	1												

Note: 24 fps = 90 ft/min; 1440 frames per minute; 16 frames per foot.

FPS = shutter opening / 360° exposure time

+1/3	**NORM**	**−1/3**	**−2/3**	**−1**	**−1 1/3**	**−1 2/3**	**−2**	**−2 1/3**	**−2 2/3**	**−3**	**−3 1/3**	**−3 2/3**	**−4**	**−4 1/3**
19	**24**	**30**	**38**	**48**	**60**	**76**	**96**	**120**	**150**	**192**	**240**	**300**	**384**	**484**
71	**90**	117	144	180	234	288	360	468	576	720	936	1152	1440	1872
25	**22**	20	18	**16**	14	13	**11**	10	9	**8**	7	6.3	**5.6**	5
22	20	18	**16**	14	13	**11**	10	9	**8**	7	6.3	**5.6**	5	4.5
20	18	**16**	14	13	**11**	10	9	**8**	7	6.3	**5.6**	5	4.5	4
18	**16**	14	13	**11**	10	9	**8**	7	6.3	**5.6**	5	4.5	**4**	3.5
16	14	13	**11**	10	9	**8**	7	6.3	**5.6**	5	4.5	**4**	3.5	3.2
14	13	**11**	10	9	**8**	7	6.3	**5.6**	5	4.5	**4**	3.5	3.2	2.8
13	**11**	10	9	**8**	7	6.3	**5.6**	5	4.5	**4**	3.5	3.2	**2.8**	2.5
11	10	9	**8**	7	6.3	**5.6**	5	4.5	**4**	3.5	3.2	**2.8**	2.5	2.2
10	9	**8**	7	6.3	**5.6**	5	4.5	**4**	3.5	3.2	**2.8**	2.5	2.2	2
9	**8**	7	6.3	**5.6**	5	4.5	**4**	3.5	3.2	**2.8**	2.5	2.2	**2**	1.8
8	7	6.3	**5.6**	5	4.5	**4**	3.5	3.2	**2.8**	2.5	2.2	**2**	1.8	1.6
7	6.3	**5.6**	5	4.5	**4**	3.5	3.2	**2.8**	2.5	2.2	**2**	1.8	1.6	1.4
6.3	**5.6**	5	4.5	**4**	3.5	3.2	**2.8**	2.5	2.2	**2**	1.8	1.6	**1.4**	1.3
5.6	5	4.5	**4**	3.5	3.2	**2.8**	2.5	2.2	**2**	1.8	1.6	**1.4**	1.3	1.1
5	4.5	**4**	3.5	3.2	**2.8**	2.5	2.2	**2**	1.8	1.6	**1.4**	1.3	1.1	**1**
4.5	**4**	3.5	3.2	**2.8**	2.5	2.2	**2**	1.8	1.6	**1.4**	1.3	1.1	**1**	
4	3.5	3.2	**2.8**	2.5	2.2	**2**	1.8	1.6	**1.4**	1.3	1.1	**1**		
3.5	3.2	**2.8**	2.5	2.2	**2**	1.8	1.6	**1.4**	1.3	1.1	**1**			
3.2	**2.8**	2.5	2.2	**2**	1.8	1.6	**1.4**	1.3	1.1	**1**				
2.8	2.5	2.2	**2**	1.8	1.6	**1.4**	1.3	1.1	**1**					
2.5	2.2	**2**	1.8	1.6	**1.4**	1.3	1.1	**1**						
2.2	**2**	1.8	1.6	**1.4**	1.3	1.1	**1**							
2	1.8	1.6	**1.4**	1.3	1.1	**1**								
1.8	1.6	**1.4**	1.3	1.1	**1**									
1.6	**1.4**	1.3	1.1	**1**										
1.4	1.3	1.1	**1**											
1.3	1.1	**1**												
1.1	**1**													
1														

Table 4.13 T-Stop Shutter Angle Compensation

T-stop Change	Shutter Angle (°)		
+2/3	280	200	265
+1/3	235	160	200
+1/4	200	130	180
Norm	**180**	**120**	**160**
−1/3	140	100	125
−2/3	115	80	100
−1	090	60	80
−1 1/3	070	50	65
−1 2/3	060	40	50
−2	045	30	40
−2 1/3	035	25	30
−3	020	20	25

Table 4.14 Shutter Angle Compensation

Shutter	280°	235°	172.8° 180°	144° 140°	115°
T-Stop	**45**	40	35	**32**	28
	40	**35**	**32**	28	25
	35	**32**	28	25	**22**
	32	28	25	**22**	20
	28	25	**22**	20	18
	25	22	20	18	**16**
	22	20	18	**16**	14
	20	18	**16**	14	13
	18	**16**	14	13	**11**
	16	14	13	**11**	10
	14	13	**11**	10	9
	13	**11**	10	9	**8**
	11	10	9	**8**	7
	10	9	**8**	7	6.3
	9	**8**	7	6.3	**5.6**
	8	7	6.3	**5.6**	5
	7	6.3	**5.6**	5	4.5
	6.3	**5.6**	5	4.5	**4**
	5.6	5	4.5	**4**	3.5
	5	4.5	**4**	3.5	3.2
	4.5	**4**	3.5	3.2	**2.8**
	4	3.5	3.2	**2.8**	2.5
	3.5	3.2	**2.8**	2.5	2.2
	3.2	**2.8**	2.5	2.2	**2**
	2.8	2.5	2.2	**2**	1.8
	2.5	2.2	**2**	1.8	1.6
	2.2	**2**	1.8	1.6	**1.4**

90°	70°	60°	45°	35°	22.5° 20°	15°
25	**22**	20	18	**16**	14	13
22	20	18	**16**	14	13	**11**
20	18	**16**	14	13	**11**	10
18	**16**	14	13	**11**	10	9
16	14	13	**11**	10	9	**8**
14	13	**11**	10	9	**8**	7
13	**11**	10	9	**8**	7	6.3
11	10	9	**8**	7	6.3	**5.6**
10	9	**8**	7	6.3	**5.6**	5
9	**8**	7	6.3	**5.6**	5	4.5
8	7	6.3	**5.6**	5	4.5	**4**
7	6.3	**5.6**	5	4.5	**4**	3.5
6.3	**5.6**	5	4.5	**4**	3.5	3.2
5.6	5	4.5	**4**	3.5	3.2	**2.8**
5	4.5	**4**	3.5	3.2	**2.8**	2.5
4.5	**4**	3.5	3.2	**2.8**	2.5	2.2
4	3.5	3.2	**2.8**	2.5	2.2	**2**
3.5	3.2	**2.8**	2.5	2.2	**2**	1.8
3.2	**2.8**	2.5	2.2	**2**	1.8	1.6
2.8	2.5	2.2	**2**	1.8	1.6	**1.4**
2.5	2.2	**2**	1.8	1.6	**1.4**	1.3
2.2	**2**	1.8	1.6	**1.4**	1.3	1.1
2	1.8	1.6	**1.4**	1.3	1.1	1
1.8	1.6	**1.4**	1.3	1.1	1	
1.6	**1.4**	1.3	1.1	1		
1.4	1.3	1.1	1			
1.3	1.1	1				

Table 4.15 Exposure Compensation for Various Shutter Angles and High-Speed Frame Rates

	High-Speed Frame Rate (fps)						
Shutter Angle (°)	24	30	40	48	60	70	90
280	1/31	1/39	1/51	1/62	1/77	1/90	1/116
235	1/37	1/46	1/61	1/74	1/92	1/107	1/138
180	**1/48**	**1/60**	**1/80**	**1/96**	**1/120**	**1/140**	**1/180**
175	1/49	1/62	1/82	1/99	1/123	1/144	1/185
172	**1/50**	**1/63**	**1/83**	**1/100**	**1/125**	**1/146**	**1/188**
144	**1/60**	**1/75**	**1/100**	**1/120**	**1/150**	**1/175**	**1/225**
140	1/62	1/77	1/103	1/123	1/154	1/180	1/231
115	1/75	1/94	1/125	1/150	1/188	1/219	1/282
90	1/96	1/120	1/160	1/192	1/240	1/280	1/360
70	1/123	1/154	1/206	1/247	1/309	1/360	1/463
60	1/144	1/180	1/240	1/288	1/360	1/420	1/540
45	1/192	1/240	1/320	1/384	1/480	1/560	1/720
35	1/247	1/309	1/411	1/494	1/617	1/720	1/926
22.5	1/384	1/480	1/640	1/768	1/960	1/1120	1/1440
15	1/576	1/720	1/960	1/1152	1/1440	1/1680	1/2160
10	1/864	1/1080	1/1440	1/1728	1/2160	1/2520	1/3240

Note: Use this chart if you want to make compensations by adjusting

Table 4.16 Exposure Compensation for Various Shutter Angles and Low-Speed Frame Rates

	Low-Speed Frame			
Shutter Angle (°)	**24**	**18**	**16**	**12**
280	1/31	1/23	1/21	1/15
235	1/37	1/28	1/25	1/18
180	**1/48**	**1/36**	**1/32**	**1/24**
175	1/49	1/37	1/33	1/25
172.5	**1/50**	**1/38**	**1/33**	**1/25**
140	1/62	1/46	1/41	1/31
115	1/75	1/56	1/50	1/38
90	1/96	1/72	1/64	1/48
70	1/123	1/93	1/82	1/62
60	1/144	1/108	1/96	1/72
45	1/192	1/144	1/128	1/96
35	1/247	1/185	1/165	1/123
20	1/432	1/324	1/288	1/216
15	1/576	1/432	1/384	1/288
10	1/864	1/648	1/576	1/432

96	120	150	190	200	240	300	360
1/123	1/154	1/193	1/244	1/257	1/309	1/386	1/463
1/147	1/184	1/230	1/291	1/306	1/368	1/460	1/551
1/192	**1/240**	**1/300**	**1/380**	**1/400**	**1/480**	**1/600**	**1/720**
1/197	1/247	1/309	1/391	1/411	1/494	1/617	1/741
1/200	**1/250**	**1/313**	**1/397**	**1/417**	**1/501**	**1/626**	**1/751**
1/240	1/300	1/375	1/475	1/500	1/600	1/750	1/900
1/247	1/309	1/386	1/489	1/514	1/617	1/771	1/926
1/301	1/376	1/470	1/595	1/626	1/751	1/939	1/1127
1/384	1/480	1/600	1/760	1/800	1/960	1/1200	1/1440
1/494	1/617	1/771	1/977	1/1029	1/1234	1/1543	1/1851
1/576	1/720	1/900	1/1140	1/1200	1/1440	1/1800	1/2160
1/768	1/960	1/1200	1/1520	1/1600	1/1920	1/2400	1/2880
1/987	1/1234	1/1543	1/1954	1/2057	1/2469	1/3086	1/3703
1/1536	1/1920	1/2400	1/3040	1/3200	1/3840	1/4800	1/5760
1/2304	1/2880	1/3600	1/4560	1/4800	1/5760	1/7200	1/8640
1/3456	1/4320	1/5400	1/6840	1/7200	1/8640		

exposure time on the light meter.

Rate (fps)

10	8	6	4	2	1
1/13	1/10	1/8	1/5	1/3	1/1
1/15	1/12	1/9	1/6	1/3	1/2
1/20	**1/16**	**1/12**	**1/8**	**1/4**	**1/2**
1/21	1/16	1/12	1/8	1/4	1/2
1/21	**1/17**	**1/13**	**1/8**	**1/4**	**1/2**
1/26	1/21	1/15	1/10	1/5	1/3
1/31	1/25	1/19	1/13	1/6	1/3
1/40	1/32	1/24	1/16	1/8	1/4
1/51	1/41	1/31	1/21	1/10	1/5
1/60	1/48	1/36	1/24	1/12	1/6
1/80	1/64	1/48	1/32	1/16	1/8
1/103	1/82	1/62	1/41	1/21	1/10
1/180	1/144	1/108	1/72	1/36	1/18
1/240	1/192	1/144	1/96	1/48	1/24
1/360	1/288	1/216	1/144	1/72	1/36

SECTION 5

Electrical

ELECTRICAL FORMULAS

These simple DC formulas are used in electrical calculations when working on the set:

$$\text{watts} = \text{volts} \times \text{amps}$$

$$\text{kilowatts} = \frac{\text{volts} \times \text{amps}}{1000}$$

$$\text{amps} = \frac{\text{watts}}{\text{volts}}$$

$$\text{volts} = \frac{\text{watts}}{\text{amps}}$$

$$\text{amps} = \frac{\text{volts}}{\text{ohms}}$$

You can remember the basic formula, W = V × A, as *West VirginiA.*

In DC, the higher voltage is always twice the lower: 110/220, 120/240, and so on. In AC, the relationships depend on the wiring of the generator. There are two basic types of three-phase, four-wire service: wye, or star, and delta, or triangle, service. In the wye system, the nominal voltages are 120/208, 127/220, 220/380, and 230/400. The higher voltage is 1.732 (the square root of 3) times the lower voltage. In a delta system, the higher voltage is always twice the lower voltage: 110/220, 230/460, and so on.

POWER SOURCES

Generators

Generators are available in all sizes, from portable 30-amp "put-puts" to tractor-trailer rigs capable of providing 2000 amps of service.

When ordering a generator, consider the following characteristics:

1. Capacity. Be sure to allow an extra margin of safety in calculating the total load. In most cases, it is unsafe to run a generator at full load.
2. Type of power. Gennies are available in AC, DC, or AC/DC (concurrent). It is vital to think about your needs and to specify the correct service. If you are running Brute arcs, you will need 225 amps of DC for each arc. If you are running HMIs, video, and so on, you must have AC.
3. Crystal sync. If you are using HMIs, you must order a generator that provides a constant speed governed by a synchronizing crystal. Specially modified portable gennies are available that are crystal-controlled.
4. Sound blimping. A blimped generator is usually required for sound filming.
5. Physical size. Consider where the genny will be driven and parked. Be sure that it will fit and that your feeder cable can reach it.
6. Portability. There are five types of gennies: portable, hand-carry units; portable put-puts that roll; towed units that can be hitched to a truck; piggyback units that sit behind the cab of an equipment truck; and independent units from van size to full tractor-trailer size. Consider which type will be appropriate for your needs.
7. Distance of runs. For very large exteriors, it may make more sense to rent two or three smaller gennies instead of creating monstrously long cable runs to a single large genny.
8. Fuel. Do not assume that the genny rental company will provide fuel and lubricants.
9. Compatibility of connectors/adaptors with your feeder cable.

Generator Operation

The following are some general principles of generator operation:

1. Make sure that the generator is level before beginning operation to ensure proper fuel feed.
2. Always warm up a generator for at least 10 minutes before applying a load.
3. Check to make sure that the exhaust vents are open and clear before starting the generator.
4. Check the oil, fuel, and antifreeze levels before starting the generator.

5. Periodically check all fluid levels, water and oil temperatures, and frequency of output.
6. Always run a generator for 10 minutes after the load is shut off before turning off the engine.
7. During meal breaks, disconnect the load, and reduce the generator to idle.
8. Always run a ground wire from the generator chassis to a rod stuck in the earth, a water pipe, or a fire hydrant.

Generator efficiency is reduced by high altitude and high temperature. The reduction is roughly 3.5% for every 1000 feet over 500 feet above sea level. The reduction for high temperature is roughly 2% for every 10°F above 85°.

A typical 1000-amp generator holds 150 to 175 gallons of diesel and will run for roughly 20 hours.

If you are working with foreign equipment, remember that a 50-Hz genny is 20% more efficient when run at 60-Hz.

Silicon-controlled rectifier (SCR) dimmer packs can sometimes return 125% or more on the neutral. This can fool the generator's sensors and cause the output to fluctuate widely. Allow slack in the generator capacity to prevent this, and run an oversize neutral.

When ordering a generator, be sure to clearly specify total load or load per leg.

When running concurrent (generating both AC and DC at the same time), most generators provide only single-phase power. Another idiosyncrasy of some generators is that the more DC you use, the more AC is available (up to the rated limits). If you are running concurrent but are not pulling a DC load, the AC supply will be unstable. It is helpful to run a small ghost load on DC; a 1000-watt (1K) lamp will usually suffice. Concurrent loads on a typical 1000-amp genny are as follows:

700 amps DC
200 amps single-phase 120-volt AC
100 amps 220-volt AC

These are maximums. The actual loads can be any combination of these.

Tie-ins

Another common power source is the tie-in: tapping into the power supply of a building. Tie-ins are cheap and convenient and provide reliable power, but in some areas, they are strictly illegal. It is your responsibility to know the local laws and to act appropriately. Some localities require that tie-ins be performed only by licensed electricians; others require that a fire marshal be present.

Under no circumstances should anyone perform a tie-in until he or she has been trained and checked out by a senior film electrician. Always tie in after the electric meter and after the main circuit protection (fuses or breakers).

Tie-In Safety

Everyone should know these basic safety rules for tie-ins:

1. Two people should be present at a tie-in. A very real risk of electrocution is present in any tie-in. The second person must know cardiopulmonary resuscitation (CPR) and electrical rescue techniques. If at all possible, the second person should be another film electrician.
2. Place only one hand in the box at any time. The most dangerous situation is for current to run across the chest and heart from one hand to another.
3. Stand on a rubber mat or a low wooden box, such as a half or quarter apple box. Wear rubber-sole shoes, if possible, and long insulated lineman's gloves, unless they make the operation dangerously awkward.
4. Wear safety glasses.
5. Have an ABC fire extinguisher nearby.
6. Never stick anything made of metal in the box. Metal screwdrivers should be wrapped with electrical tape down the shank.
7. If the fuse box is behind a door, lock it or block it with sandbags, or have a guard on it so that no one can swing the door open and push you into the live connectors.
8. Always tie in on the load side after the fuses or main circuit breakers.
9. Always meter the voltage of all legs, and meter the case to determine that it is not hot. Check to see if the power is AC or DC.
10. Use sash cord to tie the feeder cable up in a strain relief. Make sure that there is no pressure on the tie-in clips that might pull them loose. Put the strain relief on before you make the connections. Ensure that the metal ends are not free to swing into the box or get in your way.
11. Use pieces of rubber mat or cardboard to "card off" the hot lugs and provide insulation anywhere that the tie-in clips might contact a hot lug and the case, creating an arc.
12. Always clamp onto the neutral (white) first, then the hot legs. Always disconnect the neutral last when breaking the tie-in. If you have a case ground (green), connect it before the neutral.

13. Always use a bull-switch (disconnect and fuses) between your tie-in and the load.
14. Never leave a tie-in in place overnight.
15. Always tape all neutrals so that they cannot come loose.
16. Color-code all connections and lines.
17. Be sure that you are using connectors of the appropriate size.
18. Tape or brace the door of the fuse box so that it cannot swing closed on the connectors.
19. Put a rubber mat or show card over the open box so that no one can accidentally touch it. If necessary, cordon off the area.
20. If you feel the tie-in would not be safe or legal or if you are not trained, tested, and qualified, do not do it. The gaffer is the absolute and final authority concerning electrical safety on the set.

Determining KVA

In many industrial and commercial settings, the service is high-voltage, and a portion is stepped down by transformers for the 120-volt service. In these situations, it is not enough to look at the wire feeding the 120-volt box; you must also consider the capacity of the transformer, which is often only designed to run a few houselights and wall sockets. Transformers are rated in kilovolt amps (KVA). When you realize that a volt amp is really a watt (remember that volts times amps equals watts), the process becomes clear.

Let's take a simple single-phase example. A transformer is rated at 77 KVA. This is 77,000 watts.

$$\text{amps} = \frac{\text{KVA} \times 1000}{\text{volts}}$$

$$\frac{77 \times 1000}{120} = 640$$

We divide by the voltage and get 640 amps. Thus, we cannot exceed 640 amps per leg, even if the feed wire and the fuses are rated higher.

With two-phase, four-wire service, there is an additional factor:

$$\text{amps} = \frac{\text{KVA} \times 1000}{\text{volts} \times 2}$$

In three-phase service, given the KVA and the voltage, the amperage is found by this formula:

$$\text{amps} = \frac{\text{KVA} \times 1000}{\text{volts} \times 1.73}$$

To understand these relationships, we must recall the following:

Two-phase current = 2 x single-phase current.
Three-phase current = 1.73 x single-phase current.
The current in the neutral of a two-phase, three-wire service is 141% greater than either of the other two conductors of that circuit.

Wall Outlets

For very small setups in which only a small amount of light is needed, such as documentary and small-unit video, it is possible to plug small units into the walls. In most areas, wall convenience outlets are usually 15-amp and occasionally 20-amp circuits; the standard two- or three-prong Edison plug duplex outlet is, by convention, rated at 15 amps. If there is nothing else on the circuit, they will usually hold a 2K light (16.6 amps). Remember the following when plugging into a wall outlet:

1. Check to see what is on the circuit. Switch off anything that is not needed. The simplest technique is to station people throughout the house while someone switches each breaker on and off and labels them. It takes a few minutes, but it is worth doing.
2. Have some spare fuses handy. If the building has circuit breakers, be sure that the fuse box is not behind a locked door.
3. Never plug into a circuit that serves computers, delicate electronics, any type of medical life-support equipment, or security systems.
4. Switch the lights off whenever you can.
5. Do not assume that each room has its own circuit. It is general practice in laying out household electrical service to have circuits serve different areas to distribute the load. One circuit might serve an outlet in the hallway and in an upstairs bathroom, while an outlet a few feet away is served by an entirely different circuit. If possible, try to get the architectural plans of the building to examine the electrical layout.
6. Never bypass the fuses.

7. Let the lights burn for a few minutes after plugging. It is better that the fuses blow now than when you are shooting.

Batteries

Most types of rechargeable batteries require an 8- to 10-hour charge. Quick charging will reduce the life of any type of battery. Extremes of temperature will adversely affect the output and life of batteries. Batteries are rated in amp-hours, which are based on a hypothetical 20-hour use. For example, a battery rated at 100 amp-hours will deliver 5 amps for 20 hours.

Four types of batteries are commonly used in film and video production: lead-acid low-antimony, heavy-duty lead acid, high-antimony, and nicad batteries.

Lead-acid Low-Antimony Batteries

These are standard automobile batteries. They are not generally designed for continuous output, but they can serve adequately in many applications. It is possible to run a continuous charge off the vehicle's alternator for one or more batteries. For charging several batteries, use a diode battery splitter. For long-term use, it may be helpful to put a heavy-duty alternator in the vehicle. As a general rule, any auto battery rated at less than 60 amp-hours may pose problems. A hydrometer, used to check the charge state, is helpful if you are doing a lot of battery work.

Motorcycle batteries are more compact but still provide a substantial load capacity. Battery rigs, consisting of ten 12-volt car batteries (for a total of 120 volts) can run a few film lights for an hour or less. Even large lights, such as 10Ks and Brutes, can be run off high-amperage battery rigs, but only for very short periods of time. They can be concealed in a car trunk, on a running rig, or in other places where you cannot get power.

Heavy-Duty Lead Acid Batteries

These marine-type batteries are designed for continuous output. One of the most useful applications of battery rigs is to power work lights for night wraps when the tie-in is taken down or the producer wants to get the generator off the clock.

High-Antimony Batteries

These are the types of batteries used for industrial applications, such as forklifts. They are designed for continuous heavy-duty output. They are extremely heavy and are generally available only up to 6-volt units.

Nicads

Nickel-cadmium batteries have become the standard for powering film and video cameras and sunguns. They are available in both sealed and vented varieties, but the sealed type are nearly universal. They run at an internal pressure of 100 pounds per square inch (psi), but there is little danger of explosion. Nicads are preferable to lead-acid batteries because their output is fairly stable over the life of the charge. The disadvantage is that there is little warning of the end of the charge, which can occur suddenly.

Battery memory problems can be avoided by running a battery until it is fully discharged, although you should avoid a deep discharge, which can occur when a battery continues to operate after normal discharge. Constantly topping off a battery that is not fully discharged will reduce its capacity. Try to run a battery for its full capacity, or use a discharger to drain it fully. Avoid overdraining nicad batteries. If a memory problem occurs, discharge and recharge the battery several times. Recharge requires 8 to 10 hours. When running several batteries, label them, and keep a record of their use and recharging. Nicads, like all batteries, should not be stored in a discharged state. Protect nicads from shock and puncture, which can cause internal shorts.

Battery Tips

1. Keep batteries at moderate temperatures, neither too hot nor too cold.
2. Do not put batteries on a cold floor or damp, cold ground.
3. Never charge batteries in a case piled on top of each other; allow air to circulate.
4. Do not charge a battery for more than the recommended time (usually 15 hours or less for nicads).
5. Protect batteries from physical abuse in shipping and handling.

Inverters

If you need only a small amount of AC, inverters are available that convert 12-volt DC, such as from a car battery, to 120-volt AC at 60 Hz. Inverters are available in capacities from 500 watts to 4000 watts. They produce a "squine" wave, which is a squared-off sine wave.

AMPACITY

Ampacity is a measure of the maximum safe current-carrying capacity of a conductor. Typical ampacities for copper wire are given in Table 5.1, and power usage at various voltages is shown in Table 5.2.

Table 5.1 Typical Ampacities for Copper Cable

	Rated at 90° C	Rated at 75° C	Rated at 60° [a]
Type W, SC, SCE, E			
#0000	400	360	300
#000	350	310	260
#00	300	265	225
#0	260	230	195
#2	190	170	140
#4	140	125	105
#6	100	95	80
#8	80	70	60
Types S, SJ, SJO, SPT, ET, etc.			
#2	95		
#4	70		
#6	55		
#8	40		
#10	30		
#12	25		
#14	18		
#16	13		
#18	10		

[a] If the type of cable is not known, use these ampacities.

CALCULATING VOLTAGE DROP

Voltage drop is a function of resistance. On long cable runs, the supply voltage can be reduced enough to affect the color temperature of lights. Voltage drop can prevent HMIs, xenons, and video equipment from operating properly.

The formula for voltage drop is as follows:

$$VD = C \times R$$

$$\text{voltage drop} = \text{current (amps)} \times \text{resistance (ohms)}$$

If you call voltage drop V, you can remember this formula as VCR. The current is the total amperage of the expected load. Resistance is the resistance per foot of the cable multiplied by the total run (the distance in both directions). The resistance of standard copper conductors is shown in Table 5.3.

Table 5.2 Power Usage (A) at Various Voltages

	Voltage (V)						
Wattage (W)	12	110	115	120	208	220	440
10	0.83	0.09	0.09	0.08	0.05	0.05	0.02
25	2.08	0.23	0.22	0.21	0.12	0.11	0.06
50	4.17	0.45	0.43	0.42	0.24	0.23	0.11
60	5	0.55	0.52	0.5	0.29	0.27	0.14
70	5.8	0.64	0.61	0.58	0.34	0.32	0.16
80	6.7	0.7	0.7	0.67	0.38	0.36	0.18
90	7.5	0.8	0.8	0.75	0.43	0.41	0.2
100	8.3	0.9	0.9	0.8	0.48	0.45	0.23
150	12.5	1.4	1.3	1.3	0.7	0.68	0.34
200	17	1.8	1.7	1.7	1	0.9	0.45
250	21	2.3	2.2	2.1	1.2	1.1	0.6
300	25	2.7	2.6	2.5	1.4	1.4	0.7
450	38	4.1	3.9	3.8	2.2	2	1
500	42	5	4.3	4.2	2.4	2.3	1.1
750	63	7	6.5	6.3	3.6	3.4	1.7
1000	83	9	9	8.3	4.8	4.5	2.3
1500	125	14	13	12.5	7.2	6.8	3.4
2000	167	18	17	16.7	9.6	9.1	4.5
2500	208	23	22	21	12	11	5.7
3000	250	27	26	25	14	14	6.8
4000	333	36	35	33	19	18	9
5000	417	46	44	42	24	23	11
6000	500	55	52	50	29	27	14
7000	583	64	61	58	34	32	16
8000	667	73	70	67	39	36	18
10,000	833	91	87	83	48	46	23
12,000	1000	109	104	100	58	55	27
15,000	1250	136	130	125	72	68	34
25,000	2083	227	217	208	120	114	57
50,000	4167	455	435	417	240	227	114
75,000	6250	682	652	625	361	341	171
100,000	8333	909	870	833	481	455	227

For example, suppose we have a 500-foot run of #6 cable from the generator, which is running at 120 volts with a load of 60 amps per leg. The calculation of voltage drop is as follows:

voltage drop = 60 X (1000 X 0.000491) = 29.46

ELECTRICAL SAFETY

Safety Note: Electricity is always inherently dangerous and must never be handled by anyone other than trained and certified technicians. The information in this book is intended to foster safe and uniform practices among techni-

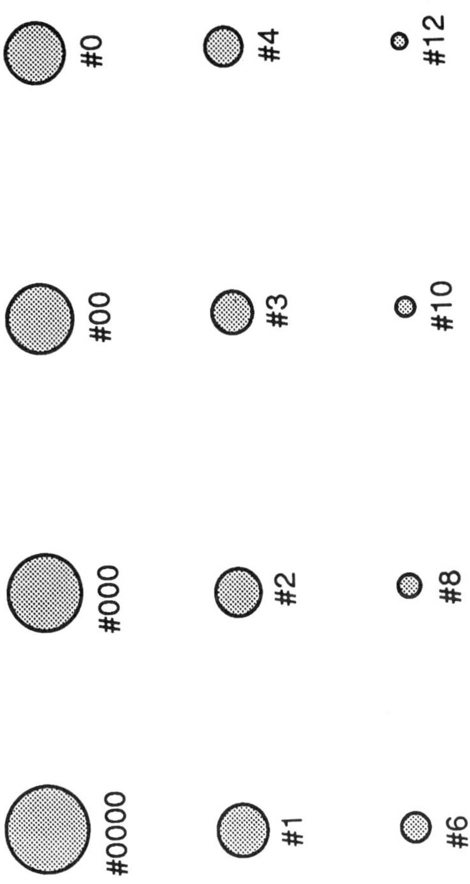

Figure 5.1 Wire sizes without insulation. (Reprinted from Blain Brown, *Motion Picture and Video Lighting*, Boston-Focal Press, 1992. With permission.)

Table 5.3 Resistance in Copper Conductors

	Resistance	
Wire Size	**Ohms/ft.**	**Ohms/1000 ft.**
#14	0.0031400	3.14
#12	0.0019800	1.98
#10	0.0012400	1.24
#8	0.0007780	0.778
#6	0.0004910	0.491
#	0.0003080	0.308
#2	0.0001940	0.194
#1	0.0001540	0.154
#0	0.0001220	0.122
#00	0.0000967	0.0967
#000	0.0000766	0.0766
#0000	0.0000608	0.0608

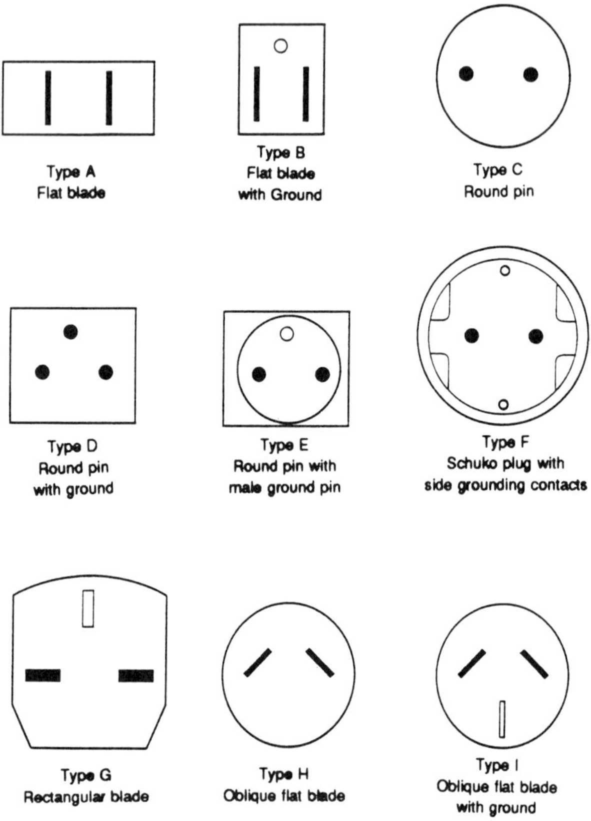

Figure 5.2 Electrical plug types.

cians and is in no way intended to replace adequate professional training and apprenticeship in the field of motion-picture and video production.

1. Ground all systems whenever possible.
2. Always tape the neutrals, and never fuse the neutral.
3. Keep distribution boxes away from water and off of wet ground.
4. Always ground HMIs with substantial wire.
5. Do not allow anyone except an electrician to plug in a light or provide power.
6. Always use a properly rated, fused disconnect (bull switch) near the power supply.
7. Check the voltage before plugging in anything.
8. Tape over any loose hot connectors or energized metal.
9. Never overload distribution equipment.

10. Make sure that the fuse is the weakest link of the chain. The capacity of any fuse should always be less than the ampacity of any part of the system.
11. Never bypass fuses.
12. Route cables sensibly, and tape them down or bag them when necessary. Use rubber mats over any cables where there is substantial traffic.
13. Never touch two lights or light stands at the same time.
14. Never assume the power is AC; check for DC.
15. Coil distribution cable in a figure-eight pattern, not in circles.

Electricity and Water

When working near water, follow these precautions:

1. Keep all stage boxes and connectors dry by wrapping them in plastic and keeping them on half apple boxes. Gaffer's tape is not resistant to water or cold; plastic electrical tape works better. Garbage bags are useful, but visqueen or heavy plastic are better.
2. Ground everything.
3. Keep HMI and xenon ballasts out of water and off of damp ground.
4. Use waterproof shoes, rubber gloves, and a waterproof suit, if necessary. Place dry rubber mats wherever someone might be working with hot items, such as HMI ballasts, distribution boxes, and so on.
5. When equipment, including cable, has been around salt water, wash it down if you can.

HMI Safety

The firing voltage on an HMI can be 13,000 volts or more. Follow these safety guidelines:

1. Always ground the ballast. The ground should be of substantial wire (at least #12 or larger) and attached to the ground metal with something that can take a large load, such as a trico, vice grips, an anderson clamp, and so on.
2. Read voltage from the ballast to a ground and from the head to a ground.
3. Never operate an HMI with the lens off. The lens filters harmful UV radiation, which can cause substantial eye and skin damage.
4. Never attempt to defeat the microswitch that prevents the unit from firing if the lens is open.
5. Do not let anyone lean on a stand or sit on a ballast.

Grounding Rules

In general, any metal object that is in some way solidly connected to the earth will serve as a suitable ground. A metal rod buried deep in the ground is the most basic and perhaps most reliable ground. Most permanently installed electrical systems are grounded. Many building codes require that the neutral and ground be bonded together at the box and that a direct ground run from the box to the earth. This ground is then continued by the continuous metal contact of the conduit or bx to the metal housing of all devices.

Cold-water pipes are a reliable ground because they have a continuous metal-to-metal circuit connected to the supply pipes, which are buried in earth. Hot water pipes are less reliable because the metal-to-metal contact may be broken at the hot water heater. Emergency sprinkler system pipes are grounded, but it is unsafe (and in most cases illegal) to ground to them. Grounded (five-wire) systems are now required by the National Electrical Code.

General guidelines include the following:

1. Always check for adequate ground with a voltage meter. Read the potential voltage between the ground and a hot source.
2. Remember that paint is an insulator. You will not get a good ground if you do not scrape down to bare metal.
3. A ground is not truly safe if it is not capable of carrying the entire load.
4. When in doubt, ground it.

DIMMERS

There are three basic types of dimmers: resistance, autotransformer, and electronic.

Resistance dimmers operate by placing a variable resistance in the power line. The excess energy is burned off as heat. Resistance dimmers are available up to 10K; they are heavy and clumsy, but cheap. The major problem with resistance dimmers is that they must be loaded to at least 80% of their capacity to operate. If you put a 5K lamp on a 10K dimmer, for example, the dimmer will only reduce the output a small amount; you will not be able to dim the light all the way. This sometimes necessitates the use of a dummy load.

Autotransformers operate as variable transformers and alter the voltage. They do not have to be loaded to capacity, and they do not generate excess heat, but they do operate only on AC. Known as *variacs* (for variable AC), they are standard equipment, particularly in the 1K and 2K sizes.

For larger applications, silicon-controlled rectifiers are used. SCRs are electronic devices that are small, quiet, and relatively inexpensive. They can be controlled remotely by dimmer boards, which means that the dimmer packs themselves can be near the lights. This saves cabling; only a small control cable must be run from the board to the dimmer packs.

SCR dimmers do not alter the voltage. They work by clipping the waveform so that the voltage heats the filament for a shorter period of time. As a result, the output of this type of dimmer cannot be read with an ordinary voltage meter. A volt-ohmmeter (VOM), which reads root mean square (RMS) voltage, must be used. There must be a load to read the output. The shorter rise time can sometimes cause filament sing and create radio frequency (RF) and audio frequency (AF) noise. The RF interference can be transmitted back along the power line and can cause problems, particularly for unbalanced, high-impedance sound systems. In most cases, with properly grounded audio systems, there should be no problem, but a portable radio can be used to test.

When using an SCR dimmer with a generator, the genny must be frequency-controlled. The loss of sync will cause flicker. Because most dimmers are voltage-regulated, raising the voltage of the generator will not increase the output. An anomaly of these systems is that the neutral load can, in some cases, be higher than the hot line.

SCR dimmers are basically theatrical equipment, so their connectors are often not compatible with the rest of the equipment. As a rule, the outputs are theatrical three-pin connectors, either 60-amp or 100-amp. It is important to order adaptors for whatever plugging system you are using.

The neutral is sometimes reversed (male instead of female). The easiest way to run into trouble with dimmer, is to forget to order feeder cable with the neutral reversed or with turnarounds (female-to-female connectors).

Control panels vary in sophistication. Some are simply sets of slider switches, one for each circuit. Others include masters and submasters and may have separate banks for X and Y scenes, making it possible to do a cue from one preset to another. The next level is soft patching, which allows electronic routing of each line to a dimming circuit. The most sophisticated panels feature computer control, timed cues, and other sophisticated control features. Most control panels will run any set of dimmers.

The effect of dimming on color temperature varies with the source, as shown in Table 5.4.

Table 5.4 Effect of Dimming on Color Output

Type of Lamp	Color Shift	CCT Direction	Degree of Shift
Incandescent/ tungsten halogen	Orange-red	Lower	Marked
Fluorescent	Not discernible	Negligible	Negligible
Metal halide	Blue	Higher	Drastic
Mercury	Not discernible	Negligible	Negligible

WIRE TYPES

A typical wire coding is as follows: 12/3 SJ 600V (UL). This indicates that the wire has three conductors of #12 wire. It is type SJ (see chart below), is rated for service up to 600 volts, and is certified by Underwriter's Laboratory. S and SJ are commonly used as cable in film and video. Wire types such as THHN, THN and THWN are prevalent as household wiring.

Code	Type
A	Asbestos—dry use only
T	Dry use only; operate at less than 140°F under full current load
F	Fixture wire—CF has cotton insulation, AF has asbestos insulation, and SF has silicone insulation
R	Rubber or neoprene
S	Appliance cord, stranded conductors, cotton between wire and insulation, rubber outer jacket—S is rough service, SJ is more flexible and is for lighter service, and SV is for light service
SP	Lamp cord
SPT	Lamp cord; plastic insulation
X	Very tough; heat- and moisture-resistant
...H	Higher load current temperatures, up to 167°F
...HH	Load current temperatures up to 194°F
...N	Nylon jacket; gas- and oil-resistant
...O	Neoprene jacket
W	Portable, hard use
...W	Wet use
UF	Underground feeder; moisture-resistant
USE	Underground service entrance cable; moisture- and heat-resistant
SC, SCE, SCT	Entertainment cable (the new code requirement for film and video use); similar to welding cable, but double-jacketed

INTERNATIONAL STANDARDS

Table 5.5 lists the prevalent video and electrical supply standards for most countries.

Table 5.5 International Video and Electrical Standards

Country	Video Standard	Frequency (H)[a]	Voltage (V)
Afghanistan	PAL	50	220/380
Algeria	SECAM(H)	50	127/220/380
Andorra	PAL	50	220
Angola		50	220/330
Antigua	NTSC	60	230
Antillies	NTSC	50/60	127/220
Argentina	PAL	50DC	240/415
Australia	PAL	50	240/415
Austria	PAL	50DC	220/380
Azores	PAL	50	110/220/380
Bahamas	NTSC	60	110/220
Bahrain	PAL	50	220
Bangladesh	PAL	50	230/400
Barbados	NTSC	50/60	110/220
Belgium	PAL	50	220/380
Bermuda	NTSC	60	115/230
Bolivia	NTSC	50/60	110/220
Botswana		50	220
Brazil	PAL-M	50/60DC	110/127/220
Bulgaria	SECAM(V)	50	220/380
Burma	NTSC	50	220/440
Burundi		50	220/380
Cambodia		50	120/208/220
Cameroon		50	127/220
Canada	NTSC	60	120/240
Canary Islands	PAL	50	110/220
Central African Republic		50	220
Chad		50	220
Chile	NTSC	50DC	220/380
China	PAL	50	220
Columbia	SECAM(V)	60	110/220
Congo	SECAM(V)	50	220
Costa Rica	NTSC	60	120/220
Curaçao and Aruba	NTSC	50/60	127/220
Cyprus		50	240/415
Czechoslovakia	SECAM(V)	50	220/380
Denmark	PAL	50DC	220/380
Dominican Republic	NTSC	60	230
Ecuador	NTSC	60	110/220
East Germany, Former	SECAM(V)	50	220

(continued)

Table 5.5 International Video and Electrical Standards *(continued)*

Country	Video Standard	Frequency (H)[a]	Voltage (V)
Egypt	SECAM(V)	50	110/220
El Salvador	NTSC	60	115/230
Ethiopia		50	127/220
Fiji	PAL	50	240/415
Finland	PAL	50	220/230
France	SECAM(V)	50	120–230
Gabon	SECAM(V)	50	220/380
Gambia		50	230
Ghana	SECAM(V)	50	220/440
Gibraltar	PAL	50	240
Greece	SECAM	50DC	127/220
Greenland	NTSC	50	220/380
Guadeloupe	SECAM(V)	50	127/220/380
Guam	NTSC	60	110/220
Guatemala	NTSC	60	110/220
Guinea		50	220/380
Guyana	SECAM(V)	50	127/220
Haiti	SECAM(V)	60	115/230
Honduras		60	110
Hong Kong	PAL	50	200/346
Hungary	SECAM(V)	50	220/380
Iceland	PAL	50	220/380
India		50DC	230/300/400
Indonesia	PAL	50	127/220
Iran	SECAM(H), PAL	50	220/380
Iraq	SECAM(H)	50	220/380
Ireland	PAL	50	220/380
Italy	PAL	50	127/220
Ivory Coast	SECAM(V)	50	220/380
Jamaica		50	110/220
Japan	NTSC	50/60	100/220
Jordan	PAL	50	220/380
Kenya	PAL	50	240/415
Kuwait	PAL	50	240/415
Lebanon	SECAM(V)	50	110/190
Leeward Islands		60	230
Lesotho		50	220
Liberia	PAL	60	120
Libya	PAL	50	127/220
Luxembourg	PAL, SECAM(V)	50	110/220
Macao		50	110/220
Madeira		50DC	220/380
Madagascar		50	110/220
Malawi		50	230/400
Malaysia	PAL	50	230/400

(continued)

Table 5.5 International Video and Electrical Standards *(continued)*

Country	Video Standard	Frequency (H)[a]	Voltage (V)
Mali		50	230/380
Malta		50	240/415
Martinique	SECAM(V)	50	220
Mauritania		50	220/380
Mauritius	SECAM(V)	50	230/400
Mexico	NTSC	60	110/220
Midway	NTSC		
Monaco	SECAM(V)	50	127/220
Morocco	SECAM(V)	50	115–220
Mozambique		50	220/380
Netherlands	PAL	50	127/220
New Caledonia	SECAM(V)	50	127–380
New Zealand	PAL	50	230/400
Nicaragua	NTSC	60	120
Niger		50	220/380
Nigeria	PAL	50	230/400
North Korea	SECAM	60	100/200
Norway	PAL	50	230
Oman	PAL	50	220
Pakistan	PAL	50	230/400
Palestine	PAL	50	220/380
Panama	NTSC	60	115/230
Paraguay		50DC	220
Peru	NTSC	60	220
Philippines		60	220
Poland	SECAM(V)	50	220/380
Portugal	PAL	50	220/380
Romania	SECAM	50	220/380
Rwanda		50	220
Saint Kitts	NTSC	60	220
Saint Pierre and Miquelon	SECAM	50	115
Samoa	NTSC	50	230
Saudi Arabia	SECAM(H)	50/60	120–415
Senegal	SECAM(V)	50	127/220
Sierra Leone	PAL	50	230/440
Singapore	PAL	50	230/400
Somalia		50	230
South Africa	PAL	50DC	230/380
South Korea	NTSC	60	100
Spain	PAL	50	127 to 380
Sri Lanka		50	230/400
Sudan	PAL	50	240
Suriname	NTSC	50/60	110/127
Sweden	PAL	50DC	127 to 380
Switzerland	PAL	50	220/380

(continued)

Table 5.5 International Video and Electrical Standards *(continued)*

Country	Video Standard	Frequency (H)[a]	Voltage (V)
Syria		50	115/200
Tahiti	SECAM(V)	60	120/240
Taiwan	NTSC	60	110–220
Tanzania	PAL	50	230
Thailand	PAL	50	220/380
Tibet		50DC	220
Togo	SECAM	50	127/220
Trinidad and Tobago	NTSC	60	115/230
Tunisia	SECAM(V)	50	115–380
Turkey	PAL	50	220/380
Uganda	PAL	50	240/415
United Kingdom	PAL	50	240/415
United States	NTSC	60	120/240
Upper Volta		50	220/380
Uruguay		50	220
USSR, Former	SECAM(V)	50	127/220
Venezuela	NTSC	50/60	120/240
Vietnam		50	120–230
Virgin Islands	NTSC	60	110
West Germany, Former	PAL	50DC	220/380
Yemen		50	220
Yugoslavia, Former	PAL	50	220/380

Note: DC means that DC power is available in addition to AC power.

Table 5.6 Knot System for Identifying Feeder Cable

No knot	Blue leg
One knot	Red leg
Two knots	Black leg
Tied together	Neutral
Tied together with two knots	Ground

Note: Knots should be tired in the tie ropes at both ends of each piece of feeder cable.

SECTION 6

Lighting

BULBS

Table 6.1 shows the bulbs required for typical lighting units, and Table 6.2 lists practical bulbs.

PHOTOMETRIC DATA

Photometric data for tungsten fresnels, HMIs, openface fixtures, soft lights, xenons, Muscolights, and miscellaneous units are presented in Tables 6.3 to 6.9.

LIGHTING FOR PROCESS PHOTOGRAPHY

Chroma key

Chroma key, also known as *blue screen* or *process photography*, is a method of producing mattes for compositing. The background can be made of a translucent blue or green backing that is backlit by either PAR 40 bulbs, evenly spaced, or flicker-free blue fluorescent lamps. It can also be a front-lit, evenly painted backdrop. A few basic principles apply in lighting for chroma key:

- The background lighting must be uniform.
- Variations in the background surface must be eliminated with fill light.
- The foreground subject should be as far away from the background as practical to prevent blue light from splashing back onto the subject.
- The incident light level at the background should match the incident light level at the subject.
- A polarizer can be used to eliminate glare from the floor.

Ultimatte

Ideal exposure levels for Ultimatte are theoretically those that provide the greatest difference between the density of the blue layer and the densities of the green and red layers. With a blue background that is lit with blue light separately from the foreground subject, it is possible to achieve RGB levels of 80 to 90 IRE units of blue with less than 10 units of green or red. "Theoretically this is a signal an Ultimatte

Table 6.1 Bulbs for Typical Lighting Units

Fixture	Bulb	Wattage (W)	Color Temperature
Inkie			
	ESS	250	2950K
	FEV	200	3200K
	BJD	200	3200K
	CCM	200	3075K
	CGP	150	3075K
	ESP	150	2900K
	ESR	100	2850K
	CEB	100	2975K
	CBX	75	2925K
	CAX	50	2875K
Pepper 100			
	FEV	200	3200K
	ESR	100	2900K
Pepper 300			
	FKW	300	3200K
	CP81	300	3200K
	M38	300	3000K
Midget			
	ESS	250	2950K
	FEV	200	3200K
	BJD	200	3200K
	CCM	200	3075K
	CGP	150	3075K
	ESP	150	2900K
	ESR	100	2850K
	CEB	100	2975K
	CBX	75	2925K
	CAX	50	2875K
Pepper 420			
	EKB	420	3200K
	FEM	400	3250K
	DYG	250	3400K
	DZM	250	3400K
	FDS	150	3400K
	EYL	100	3200K
Tweenie II			
	FRK	650	3200K
	FRL	650	3200K

Voltage (V)	Socket/Bulb
	Double-contact bayonet candelabra
120	
120	
120	
115–125	
115–120	
120	
120	
115–125	
115–125	
115–125	
	Double-contact bayonet candelabra
120	
120	
	2-pin prefocus
120	
230	
230	
	Double-contact bayonet candelabra
120	
120	
120	
115–125	
115–120	
120	
120	
115–125	
115–125	
115–125	
	2–pin prefocus
120	
120	
30	
24	
24	
12	
	2–pin prefocus
120	CP-89
220	

(continued)

Table 6.1 Bulbs for Typical Lighting Units *(continued)*

Fixture	Bulb	Wattage (W)	Color Temperature
	FRM	650	3200K
	FRG	500	3200K
	FRH	500	3200K
	FRJ	500	3200K
	FRW	300	3200K
	FSK	300	3200K
Pepper 650			
	FRK	650	3200K
	EKD	650	3400K
	DYR	650	3200K
	EKB	420	3200K
	FEM	400	3250K
	DYG	250	3400K
	DZM	250	3400K
	FDS	150	3400K
	EYL	100	3200K
1K fresnel			
	EGT	1000	3200K
	EGR	750	3200K
	EGN	500	3200K
	FKJ	1000	3200K
Pepper 500, 1K			
	EGT	1000	3200K
	EGR	750	3200K
	CP39	650	3200K
	EGN	500	3200K
	CP40	100	3200K
2K fresnel			
	CYX	2000	3200K
	CXZ	1500	3200K
	CY	1000	3200K
	FKK	2000	3200K
5K fresnel			
	DPT	5000	3200K
	ECN	5000	3200K
10K fresnel			
	DTY	10,000	3200K
	EBA	10,000	3200K
	ECP	10,000	3200K

Voltage (V)	Socket/Bulb
240	
120	
220	
240	
120	
240	
	2–pin prefocus
120	CP-89
120	
220/240	
120	
120	
30	
24	
24	
12	
	Medium bi-post
120	
120	
120	
220/240	CP-40
	Medium bi-post
120	
120	
220	
120	
220	
	Mogul bi-post
120	
120	
120	
220/240	
	Mogul bi-post
120	
120	
	Mogul bi-post
120	
120	
120	

(continued)

Table 6.1 Bulbs for Typical Lighting Units *(continued)*

Fixture	Bulb	Wattage (W)	Color Temperature
Openface Units			
600-W openface			
	DYS/DYV	600	3200K
	DYR	650	3200K
	EKD	650	3400K
	EKB	420	3200K
	DYG	250	3400K
	EYL	100	3300K
650-W openface			
	FAD	650	3200K
	FBX	650	3200K
	DWY	650	3400K
	FDA	400	3200K
	EHR	400	3000K
	EHP	300	3000K
	DXX	800	3200K
1K openface			
	DXW	1000	3200K
	FBY	1000	3200K
	BRH	1000	3350K
	DXN	1000	3400K
	FCB	600	3250K
	FGD	500	3200K
2K openface (mightie, blonde)			
	FEY	2000	3200K
	FEX	2000	3200K
	DVV	1500	3200K
	FER	1000	3200K
	EHS	1000	3100K
	DWS	1000	3400K
	DWT	1000	3000K
Skypan			
	DPT	5000	3200K
	ECN	5000	3200K
	CYX	2000	3200K
	CXZ	1500	3200K
	CYV	1000	3200K
	FKK	2000	3200K

Voltage (V)	Socket/Bulb
	2–pin prefocus
120	
220/240	
120	
120	
30	
12	
	Recessed single contact
120	
120	
120	
120	
120	
120	
230/240	
	Recessed single contact
120	
120	
120	
120	
120	
120	
	Recessed single contact
120	
240	
120	
120	
120	
120	
120	
	Mogul bi-post
120	
120	
120	
120	
120	
220/240	

(continued)

Table 6.1 Bulbs for Typical Lighting Units *(continued)*

Fixture	Bulb	Wattage (W)	Color Temperature
1K broad and nook			
	FCM	1000	3200K
	FHM	1000	3200K
	EME	800	3200K
	EMF	800	3200K
	EJG	750	3200K
	EMD	750	3200K
	FDF	500	3200K
	FDN	500	3200K
	FCL	500	3000K
	FCZ	500	3000K
	EHM	300	2950K
	EHZ	300	2950K
2K broad			
	FFW	2000	3200K
	Q1500T4/4CL	1500	3200K
	Q1500T4/4	1500	3200K
	Q1000T3/1CL	1000	3200K
	FFT	1000	3200K
650-W nook			
	DXX	800	3200K
	FAD	650	3200K
	FBX	650	3200K
	DWY	650	3400K
	FFM	420	3200K
	FDA	400	3200K
	EHR	400	3000K
	EHP	300	3000K
2K nook (Mole)			
	FEY	2000	3200K
	FEX	2000	3200K
	FER/EHS	1000	3200K
	DWT	1000	3000K
1500-W cyc strip (Mole)			
	FBD	1500	3200K
	FGT	1500	3200K
	FFT	1000	3200K

Voltage (V)	Socket/Bulb
	Recessed single contact
120	
120	Frosted
240	
240	Frosted
120	
120	Frosted
120	
120	Frosted
120	
120	Frosted
120	
120	Frosted
	Recessed single contact
120	
120	
120	Frosted
120	
120	
	Recessed single contact
230/240	
120	
120	Frosted
120	
120	
120	
120	
120	
	Recessed single contact
120	
240	
120	
120	
	Recessed single contact
120	
120	
120	

(continued)

Table 6.1 Bulbs for Typical Lighting Units *(continued)*

Fixture	Bulb	Wattage (W)	Color Temperature
1K cyc strip (Mole)			
	FCM	1000	3200K
	FHM	1000	3200K
	EME	800	3200K
	EMF	800	3200K
	EJG	750	3200K
	EMD	750	3200K
	FDF	500	3200K
	FDN	500	3200K
	FCL	500	3000K
	FCZ	500	3000K
	EHM	300	2950K
	EHZ	300	2950K
1500-W Molefar Far Cycs			
	FBD	1500	3200K
	FGT	1500	3200K
	FFT	1000	3200K
	FGV	1000	3200K
Lowell Light, Molite, and Molegator			
	EAL	500	3200K
	DXB	500	3400K
	DXC	500	3400K
	EAH	500	3400K
	BFA	375	3400K
6K overhead cluster (Coffin light)			
	1000/SBIF	1000	3050K
	DKZ/DSE	1000	3200K
	1000	1000	3050K
	1000/IF	1000	3050K
	7750/SBIF	750	3050K
2K quad light			
	EAL	500	3200K
	DXB	500	3400K
	DXC	500	3400K
	EAH	500	3400K
	BFA	375	3400K
2K scoop			
	Q2000/4CL	2000	3200K
	BWG	2000	3200K
	BWF	2000	3200K

Voltage (V)	Socket/Bulb	
	Recessed single contact	
120		
120	Frosted	
240		
240	Frosted	
120		
120	Frosted	
120		
120	Frosted	
120		
120	Frosted	
120		
120	Frosted	
	Recessed single contact	
120		
120		
120		
120		
	Medium screw base	
120	R-40	Medium flood
120	R-40	Spot
120	R-40	Flood
220/240	R-40	Flood
120	R-40	Medium flood
	Mogul screw base	
120	Frosted	
120		
120		
120	Frosted	
120	Frosted	
	Medium screw base	
120	R-40	Medium flood
120	R-40	Spot
120	R-40	Flood
220/240	R-40	Flood
120	R-40	Medium flood
	Mogul screw	
120		
120	Frosted	
120		

(continued)

Table 6.1 Bulbs for Typical Lighting Units *(continued)*

Fixture	Bulb	Wattage (W)	Color Temperature
1K scoop			
	EGJ	1000	3200K
	EGK	1000	3200K
	EGF	750	3200K
	EGG	750	3000K
	EGC	500	3200K
	EGE	500	3000K
Soft Lights[a]			
1K and larger			
	FCM	1000	3200K
	FHM	1000	3200K
	EME	800	3200K
	EMF	800	3200K
	EJG	750	3200K
	EMD	750	3200K
	FDF	500	3200K
	FDN	500	3200K
	FCL	500	3000K
	FCZ	500	3000K
	EHM	300	2950K
	EHZ	300	2950K
750-W soft light			
	EME	800	3200K
	EMF	800	3200K
	EJG	750	3200K
	EMD	750	3200K
	FDF	500	3200K
	FDN	500	3200K
	FCL	500	3000K
	FCZ	500	3000K
	EHM	300	2950K
	EHZ	300	2950K
Pepper 400 soft			
	FDA	400	3200K
FAY lights			
	FAY	650	Daylight
	FBJ	650	3400K

[a]Soft lights vary only in the number of bulbs they use.

Voltage (V)	Socket/Bulb
	Medium prefocus
120	
120	Frosted
120	
120	
120	
120	
	Recessed single contact
120	
120	Frosted
240	
240	Frosted
120	
120	Frosted
120	
120	Frosted
120	
120	Frosted
120	
120	Frosted
	Recessed single contact
240	
240	Frosted
120	
120	Frosted
120	
120	Frosted
120	
120	Frosted
120	
120	Frosted
	Recessed single contact
120	
	Ferrule contacts: PAR 36
120	Medium
120	Spot

(continued)

Table 6.1 Bulbs for Typical Lighting Units *(continued)*

Fixture	Bulb	Wattage (W)	Color Temperature
	DXK	650	3400K
	FCX	650	3200K
	FCW	650	3200K
	FGS	250	3400K
1K PAR and PAR clusters			
	FGM	1000	Daylight
	FGN	1000	Daylight
	FFN	1000	3200K
	FFP	1000	3200K
	FFR	1000	3200K
	FFS	1000	3200K
	500PAR 64/NSP	500	2800K
	500PAR 64/MFL	500	2800K
	500PAR 64/WFL	500	2800K
2K Molelipso			
	BWA	2000	3200K
1K Molelipso			
	EGJ	1000	3200K
	EGF	750	3200K
	EGG	750	3200K
Lekos			
	CP77	1000	3200K
	FEL	1000	3200K
	FKR	650	3100K
	EHG	750	3000K
	EHF	750	3200K
	EHD	500	3000K
	EHC/EHB	500	3200K
	JD500	500	2900K
	EVR	500	2900K
	Q400CL/ML	400	2900K
	EHT	250	3000K
	150 Q/CL	150	2900K
Lowell VIP Pro-light			
	GCA	250	3200K
	GCB	200	3200K
	GCC	100	3200K
	FSH	125	3200K

Voltage (V)	Socket/Bulb
120	Medium
120	Medium
120	Wide
120	Spot
	Extended mogul end prong
120	Narrow spot
120	Medium flood
120	Very narrow spot
120	Narrow spot
120	Medium flood
120	Wide flood
120	Narrow spot
120	Medium flood
120	Wide flood
	Mogul bi-post
120	
	Mogul bi-post
120	
120	
120	
220/240	Medium 2–pin
120	Medium 2–pin
220/240	
120	Medium 2–pin
120	Medium 2–pin
120	Medium 2–pin
120	Medium 2–pin
220/240	
120	Minican
120	
120	Minican
120	
	Miniature 2–pin
120	
30	
12	
120	

(continued)

Table 6.1 Bulbs for Typical Lighting Units *(continued)*

Fixture	Bulb	Wattage (W)	Color Temperature
Lowell VIP V-light			
	GDA	500	3150K
	V1–220/30	500	3150K
	V1–240/50	500	3150K
Lowell Tota-light			
	EMD	750	3200K
	EMF	800	3200K
	FWM	650	3200K
	FCZ	500	3200K
	FDN	500	3200K
	EHZ	300	2900K
Lowell Omni-light			
	EKD	650	3400K
	DYS/BHC	600	3200K
	EKB	420	3200K
	DYR/220	650	3200K
	DYR/240	650	3200K
	FTK	500	3200K
	DYG	250	3400K
	EYL	100	3200K
Lowell DP-light			
	FEL	1000	
	FEL	1000	3200K
	FEP/220	1000	3200K
	FEP/240	1000	3200K
	FKR/220	650	3200K
	FKR/240	650	3200K
	EHF	750	3200K
	EHG	750	3000K
	EHD	500	3000K
	EHC/EHB	500	3200K
Video Camera Lights			
MR-16	EYP	42	3050K
	EXN	40	3050K
	FLR	70	3350K
	EYC	75	3050K
	EXV	100	3350K

Voltage (V)	Socket/Bulb
	Recessed double contact
120	
220/230	
240/250	
	Recessed double contact
120	
240	
120	
120	
120	
120	
	2–pin prefocus
120	
120	
120	
220	
240	
120	
30	
12	
	Medium 2–pin
120	
120	
220	
240	
220	
240	
120	
120	
120	
120	
12	Rim-mount 2-pin
12	Rim-mount 2-pin
14.4	Rim-mount 2-pin
12	Rim-mount 2-pin
12	Rim-mount 2-pin

(continued)

Table 6.1 Bulbs for Typical Lighting Units *(continued)*

Fixture	Bulb	Wattage (W)	Color Temperature
MR-16	FMG	150	3300K
	ENH	250	3250K
	EXX	250	3300K
T-3	FLP	70	3350K
T-6	FKT	250	3125K

Table 6.2 Practical Bulbs

Designation of Bulb	Wattage (W)	Type of Bulb
25-W	25	Household
40-W	40	Household
60-W	60	Household
75-W	75	Household
100-W	100	Household
150-W	150	Household
200-W	200	Household
ECA	250	Photoflood
ECT	500	Photoflood
BBA (#1 flood)	250	Photoflood
EBV (#2 flood)	500	Blue photoflood
BCA (#B1 flood)	250	Blue photoflood
EBW (#B2 flood)	500	Blue Photoflood
211	75	Enlarger bulb
212	150	Enlarger bulb
213	250	Enlarger bulb
EAL	500	Reflector flood
DWD	300	Reflector flood
DWC	150	Reflector flood
BEP	300	Reflector flood
EBR	375	Reflector flood

Voltage (V)	Socket/Bulb
120	Rim-mount 2-pin
120	Rim-mount 2-pin
120	Rim-mount 2-pin
14.4	Miniature screw
120	2-pin prefocus

Size	Base	Color Temperature (K)
A-19	Medium screw	2600
A-19	Medium screw	2600
A-19	Medium screw	2600
A-19	Medium screw	2600
A-19	Medium screw	2600
A-21	Medium screw	2800
A-23	Medium screw	2800
A-23	Medium screw	3200
PS-25	Medium screw	3200
A-21	Medium screw	3400
PS-25	Medium screw	4800
A-21	Medium screw	4800
PS-25	Medium screw	4800
A-21	Medium screw	2950
A-21	Medium screw	2950
A-21	Medium screw	2950
R-40	Medium screw	3200
R-40	Medium screw	2800
R-40	Medium screw	2800
R-30	Medium screw	3400
R-30	Medium screw	3400

Table 6.3 Photometric Data: Tungsten Fresnels

Fixture	Bulb	Distance (ft.)	Beamspread (ft.)	Output (FC)
Inky	FEV			
Flood		5	4.8	90
		10	9.3	25
		15	14	10
Spot		5	0.6	780
		10	1.1	195
		15	1.7	90
Tweenie	FRK			
Flood		5	6	280
		10	11	78
		15	17	30
		20	23	18
Spot		5	1	2265
		10	1.5	660
		15	2	315
		20	3	180
Baby	EGT			
Flood		5	4.3	700
		10	8.5	180
		15	12.8	80
		20	17.1	45
		30	25.6	20
Spot		5	0.8	6320
		10	1.5	1720
		15	2.2	770
		20	3	440
		30	4.5	195
Junior	CYX			
Flood		10	9	490
		15	13	220
		20	17	130
		30	26	55
		45	40	25
Spot		10	1.6	3920
		15	2.5	1745
		20	3.4	1000
		30	5	445
		45	8	200

Table 6.3 Photometric Data: Tungsten Fresnels *(continued)*

Fixture	Bulb	Distance (ft.)	Beamspread (ft.)	Output (FC)
Senior	DPY			
Flood		10	9	950
		15	14	425
		20	19	240
		30	28	110
		50	46	40
Spot		10	2	5800
		15	3	2620
		20	4	1470
		30	5.5	655
		50	9	235
Tenner	DTY			
Flood		10	6.5	3600
		20	12	1040
		30	18	460
		40	24	260
		50	30	165
		100	49	40
Spot		10	2	16,320
		20	3.5	5280
		30	5	2465
		40	7	1390
		50	9	890
		100	17	220
Brute arc	White-flame or yellow-flame carbon			
Flood		10	5.5	10,000
		20	10.5	2650
		30	15.8	1190
		40	21	670
		50	26	430
		100	53	110
Spot		10	1	62,300
		20	1.8	19,500
		30	2.8	9000
		40	3.7	5060
		50	4.6	3240
		100	9.2	810

(continued)

Table 6.3 Photometric Data: Tungsten Fresnels *(continued)*

Fixture	Bulb	Distance (ft.)	Beamspread (ft.)	Output (FC)
Brute arc				
Flood		20	10.5	2650
		30	15.8	1190
		50	32	300
		70	45	155
		100	65	75
		140	90	38
Spot		20	1.8	19,500
		30	2.8	9000
		50	4	5000
		70	5.5	2550
		100	8	1250
		140	12	650

Table 6.4 Photometric Data: HMIs

Fixture	Distance (ft.)	Beamspread (ft.)	Output (FC)
575-W HMI fresnel			
Flood	10	6.5	300
	15	10	86
	20	12.5	64
	25	18	30
	30	21	19
Spot	10	1.5	1150
	15	2.5	780
	20	2.75	706
	25	3	325
	30	3.15	228
1200-W HMI fresnel			
Flood	10	10	490
	15	16	215
	20	18	168
	25	26	84
	30	36	54
Spot	10	1.3	7150
	15	2.5	2700
	20	3	2230

Table 6.4 Photometric Data: HMIs *(continued)*

Fixture	Distance (ft.)	Beamspread (ft.)	Output (FC)
	25	4	1000
	30	5	670
2500-W HMI fresnel			
Flood	10	9	1800
	15	19	580
	20	22	410
	25	27	240
	30	36	150
Spot	10	1.6	13,200
	15	2.3	4800
	20	3	3450
	25	4	2000
	30	4.5	1200
4K HMI fresnel			
Flood	10	8.5	2000
	15	14.5	750
	20	18	510
	25	26	300
	30	31	195
Spot	10	2	28,000
	15	3.6	10,000
	20	4.3	7150
	25	4.9	3900
	30	6	2500
6K HMI fresnel			
Flood	10	8.5	4100
	15	14	1500
	20	18	1000
	25	26	575
	30	31	370
Spot	10	2	49,000
	15	3.6	17,000
	20	4.3	12,250
	25	5	6800
	30	6	4400

(continued)

Table 6.4 Photometric Data: HMIs *(continued)*

Fixture	Distance (ft.)	Beamspread (ft.)	Output (FC)
12K HMI fresnel			
Flood	10	9	5800
	15	12	2900
	20	17	1650
	25	21	1050
	30	25	730
Spot	10	1.5	45,000
	15	2	27,000
	20	2.5	16,000
	25	3	10,500
	30	3.5	7300
18K HMI fresnel			
Flood	15	17	3240
	30	33	810
	60	67	203
	100	112	73
	150	168	32
Spot	15	2	41,500
	30	4	10,350
	60	8	2600
	100	14	935
	150	20	415

Fixture	Distance (ft.)	Output (FC)
575-W HMI PAR		
Very narrow spot	15	2000
	25	720
	35	360
Narrow spot	15	1775
	25	640
	35	325
Medium flood	15	667
	25	240
	35	125
Wide flood	15	110
	25	40
	35	20

Fixture	Distance (ft.)	Output (FC)
1200-W HMI PAR		
Very narrow spot	20	4500
	40	1125
	60	500
Narrow spot	20	3250
	40	815
	60	360
Medium flood	20	1500
	40	375
	60	165
Wide flood	20	425
	40	104
	60	47

Table 6.5 Photometric Data: Openface Fixtures

Fixture	Bulb	Distance (ft.)	Beamspread (ft.)	Output (FC)
650-W Openface	FAD			
Flood		6	8	265
		8	11	135
		10	14	85
		15	21	40
		20	22	20
Spot		6	2	2100
		8	2.6	1200
		10	4	780
		15	5	350
		20	7	190
1K openface	DWX			
Flood		6	7	450
		10	12	150
		15	19	70
		20	25	40
		25	32	25
Spot		6	1.8	3300
		10	3	1200
		15	4.5	540

(continued)

Table 6.5 Photometric Data: Openface Fixtures *(continued)*

Fixture	Bulb	Distance (ft.)	Beamspread (ft.)	Output (FC)
		20	6	304
		25	7.5	195
2K openface	FEY			
Flood		10	12	330
		15	16	145
		20	22	85
		30	32	35
		40	40	20
Spot		10	3.5	2500
		15	5	1100
		20	6.5	625
		30	9	280
		40	12	155
5K skypan	DPY			
		10	14	500
		15	20	245
		20	25	145
		30	37	65
		50	60	25
Lowell DP-light	FEL			
Flood		5		297
		10		88
		15		40
		20		23
		25		16
Spot		5		3000
		10		711
		15		307
		20		166
		25		109
Lowell Tota-light	EMD (750-W)			
		5		146
		10		41
		15		21
		20		13
		25		9

Note: Most openface lights have an oval beam. The beamspreads given here are averages.

Table 6.6 Photometric Data: Soft Lights

Fixture	Bulb	Distance (ft.)	Output (FC)
Baby soft	FCM	4	200
		6	90
		8	50
		10	30
		12	20
2K studio soft	FCM	4	295
		6	135
		8	75
		10	50
		12	35
		14	25
4K baby soft	FCM	4	1030
		6	500
		8	270
		10	180
		12	125
		14	85
		20	45
		24	30
4K studio soft	FCM	4	1440
		6	660
		8	360
		10	240
		12	165
		16	95
		20	60
		24	40
8K studio soft	FCM	4	3000
		6	1300
		8	750
		10	480
		12	325
		16	180
		20	120
		24	80

Table 6.7 Photometric Data: Xenons

Fixture	Distance (ft.)	Beamspread	Beam Angle (°)	Output (FC)
1K xenon				
Full spot	50	12"	Collimated	14,500
	100	14"	Collimated	3625
	200	18"	Collimated	900
Medium beam	50	14"	1.5	9500
	100	24"	1.5	2375
	200	36"	1.5	600
Wide beam	50	5'	10	1750
	100	10'	10	438
	200	25'	10	110
2K xenon				
Full spot	50	14"	Collimated	55,000
	100	14"	Collimated	13,750
	200	14"	Collimated	3400
Medium beam	50	14"	1.5	36,000
	100	24"	1.5	9000
	200	36"	1.5	2260
Wide beam	50	5'	10	3500
	100	10'	10	875
	200	25'	10	220
4K xenon	50	20"	Collimated	70,000
	100	20"	Collimated	17,500
	200	20"	Collimated	4500
Medium beam	50	14"	1.5	54,000
	100	24"	1.5	13,500
	200	36"	1.5	3400
Wide beam	50	5'	10	11,250
	100	10'	10	2810
	200	25'	10	700

Table 6.8 Photometric Data: Muscolights

	Beamspread	Output (FC)
Direct Throw		
	Half mile	20
	Quarter mile	80
General Flood		
	400' × 400'	20

Note: The largest effective coverage area is a quarter mile.

Table 6.9 Photometric Data: Miscellaneous Fixtures

Fixture	Bulb	Distance (ft.)	Beamspread (ft.)	Output (FC)
Maxi-brute	Nine PAR 64s			
Very narrow spot		20		10,000
		30		4500
		40		2530
		50		1620
		75		720
		100		405
		150		180
Narrow spot		20		8100
		30		3600
		40		2025
		50		1300
		75		575
		100		325
		150		145
Medium flood		20		3040
		30		1350
		40		760
		50		485
		75		215
		100		120
		150		55
Wide flood		20		1010
		30		450
		40		255
		50		160
		75		70
		100		40
		150		20
1K Molepar[a]	PAR 64			
Very narrow spot		10		5040
		20		1260
		30		560
		40		315
		50		200
		75		90
		100		50
Narrow spot		10		3600
		20		900
		30		400
		40		225
		50		145
		75		65
		100		35

(continued)

Table 6.9 Photometric Data: Miscellaneous Fixtures *(continued)*

Fixture	Bulb	Distance (ft.)	Beamspread (ft.)	Output (FC)
Medium flood		10		1350
		20		340
		30		150
		40		85
		50		55
		75		25
Wide flood		10		470
		20		120
		30		52
		40		30
		50		20
Nine-Light[b]	650-W PAR 36			
FCX—medium beam		5		8150
		10		2160
		15		960
		20		540
		30		240
		40		135
		50		85
FCW—wide beam		5		3800
		10		990
		15		440
		20		250
		30		110
		40		60
		50		40
FAY—spot		5		10,730
		10		2900
		15		1290
		20		725
		30		320
		40		180
		50		115
FBJ—spot		5		26,850
		10		7450
		15		3310
		20		1860
		30		830
		40		465
		50		300

(continued)

Table 6.9 Photometric Data: Miscellaneous Fixtures *(continued)*

Fixture	Bulb	Distance (ft.)	Beamspread (ft.)	Output (FC)
Brute arc				
Spot		20	1.8	19,500
		30	2.8	9000
		40	3.7	5060
		50	4	3240
		75	7	1440
		100	9	810
		200	19	200
Flood		20	10.5	2650
		30	15.8	1190
		40	21	670
		50	32	430
		75	40	190
		100	53	110
		200	105	30

[a]Specular intensifier can approximately double the output.
[b]All outputs given are for minimum beamspread. The output for maximum beamspread is 60% less.

should love. The problem is that the noise in the [telecine] when the blue channel has 90 units is so much greater than when the blue channel is 60 units. It turns out that reducing the exposure level of the backing results in a quieter final composite even though the Ultimatte has to do more amplification of the matte signal it creates" (Ultimatte Technical Bulletin #3).

Optimum exposure levels depend on the nature of the subject and the setup. Ultimatte needs at least 30 IRE units of separation between the background color (blue or green) and the higher of the other two colors. Ultimatte recommends exposing the blue backing to produce 50 to 60 units of blue with a maximum of 15 or 25 units of green or red. They recommend painting the background with Gothic Ultra Blue paint and lighting it with 3200K to the same level as the foreground subject.

This configuration allows you to use the same lighting for the background and the foreground subject, which has the added advantage of allowing the subject to cast shadows that will be reproduced in the final composite. This allows additional creative possibilities and makes it easier to achieve realistic effects. According to Bulletin #3, "A 1:1 lighting ratio between the foreground subject and the backing is a safe choice, even if it is not the ideal one."

When a green background can be lit separately from the foreground, it is advisable to reduce the light on the background to one stop below the light on the foreground. Ultimatte does not advise using blue light on a blue background, which they have found can produce certain transition anomalies.

Set pieces—such as tables, boxes to sit on, and so forth—that are painted blue to give the actor something to walk behind or interact with present problems. The top of the piece is almost always hotter than the shadow side. This causes problems with the composite. Lighting can help, but it may create problems of its own. One solution is to use different blue paints for the top and sides. Ultimatte recommends Gothic Ultra Blue on the top surface and Ultimatte Blue on the shadowed surfaces. Gothic Ultra has less luminance than Ultimatte Blue.

Special backings are available; they are an ideal color but are very light-absorbent, like velvet. They greatly reduce splash back and produce excellent results. They are, however, quite expensive.

Nothing will undermine the believability of a composite more quickly than a mismatch of lighting in the foreground and background. Careful attention must be paid to recreating the look, direction, and quality of the lighting in the background plate.

Color Matte Tips

- Guard against splash back.
- Block off any background screen that is not in use to minimize bounce.
- Do not use a complementary color as a backlight, although this is acceptable in chroma key.
- Ask if the director needs to see the floor, and plan accordingly.
- Do not use diffusion.
- Do not use smoke.
- Do not include the matte color in the scene.
- Avoid having anybody lie on the floor or on a table. A mirror on the floor sometimes helps.
- Use black-and-white Polaroid and a blue filter (47B) to check the uniformity of the background lighting, and meter with spot and incident meters. For viewing with the eye, a heavy orange filter is useful.

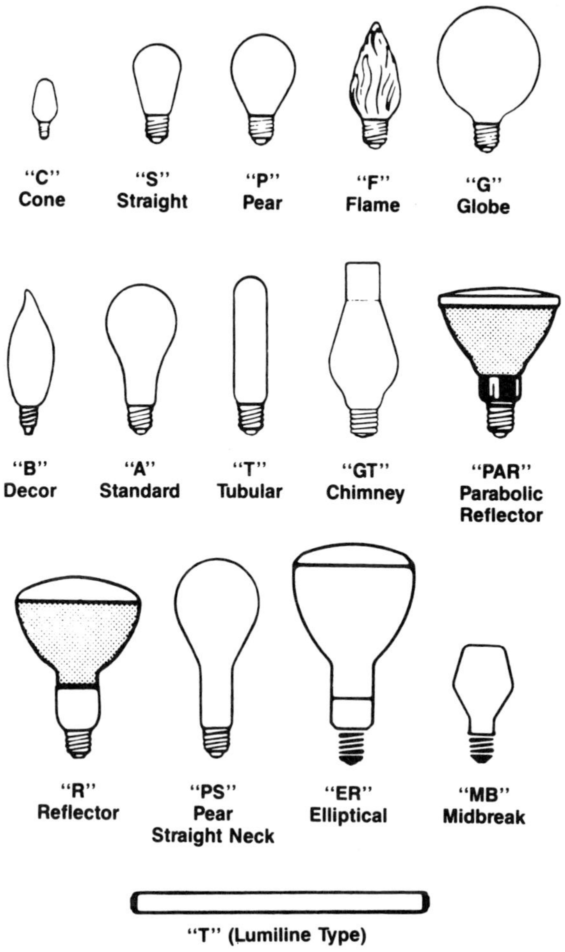

Figure 6.1 Incandescent bulb shapes (courtesy of General Electric).

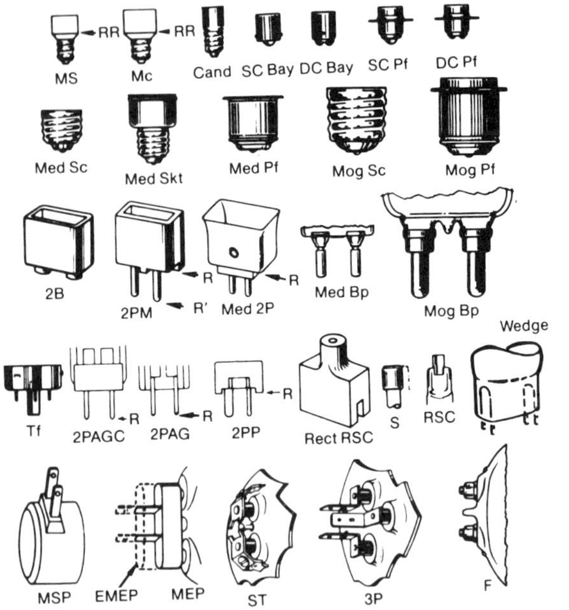

Cand — candelabra
DC Bay — double-contact bayonet candelabra
DC Pf — double-contact prefocus candelabra
EMEP — extended mogul end prong
F — ferrule contact
Mc — minican

Mog Sc — mogul screw
Mog Bp — mogul bipost
Mog Pf — mogul prefocus
MS — miniature screw (with reference shoulder) (also: Tru-Loc miniature screw)
MSP — medium side prong
Rect RSC — rectangular recessed single contact
RM2P — rim mount two pin (see Fig. 10)
RSC — recessed single contact (also: single contact recessed)
S — metal sleeve
SC Bay — single-contact bayonet candelabra

Med Sc — medium screw
Med Bp — medium bipost
Med Pf — medium prefocus
Med Skt — medium skirted
Med 2P — medium two pin
MEP — mogul end prong (also: extended mogul end prong)

SC Pf — single-contact prefocus
ST — screw terminal
TB2P — trubeam two pin (V2P*) (see Fig. 10)
Tf — trufocus (also: four pin)
TLMS — Tru-Loc miniature screw (also: miniature screw with reference shoulder)
Wedge — wedge
2B — two button
2PAG — two pin all glass (TP*)
2PAGC — two pin all glass (ceramic cover)
2PM — two pin miniature (trupin TrP*)
2PP — two pin prefocus
3P — three prong

Notes: R indicates special reference point for LCL.
(RR - at 0.531 inch diameter)
(R' indicates an obsolete reference.)
*Obsolete Designation

Figure 6.2 Incandescent bases. Courtesy of GTE-Sylvania Lighting.

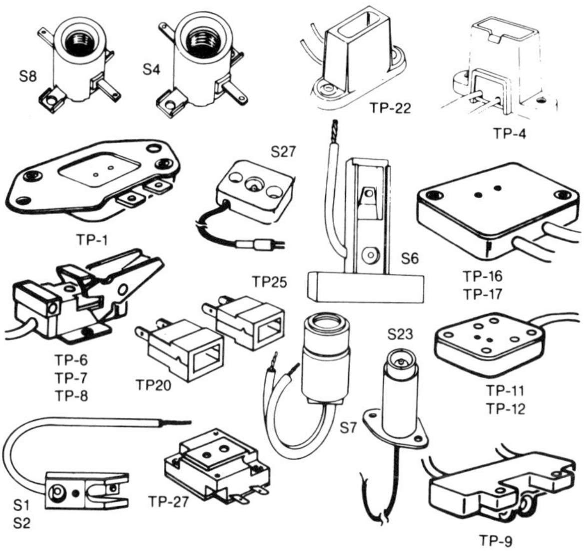

Figure 6.3 Specialized incandescent bases (courtesy of GTE-Sylvania Lighting).

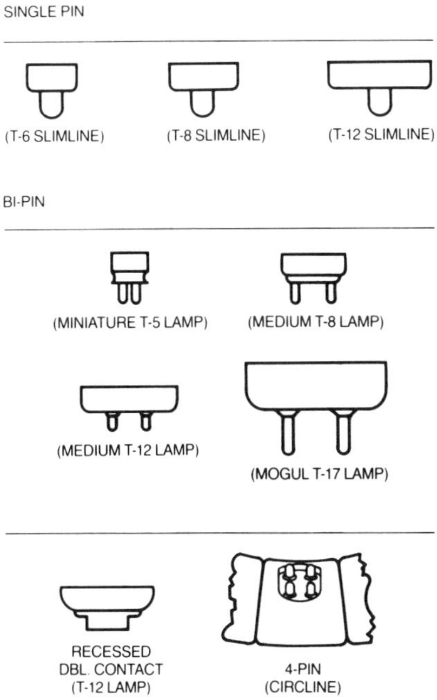

Figure 6.4 Bases for fluorescent lamps (courtesy of GTE-Sylvania Lighting).

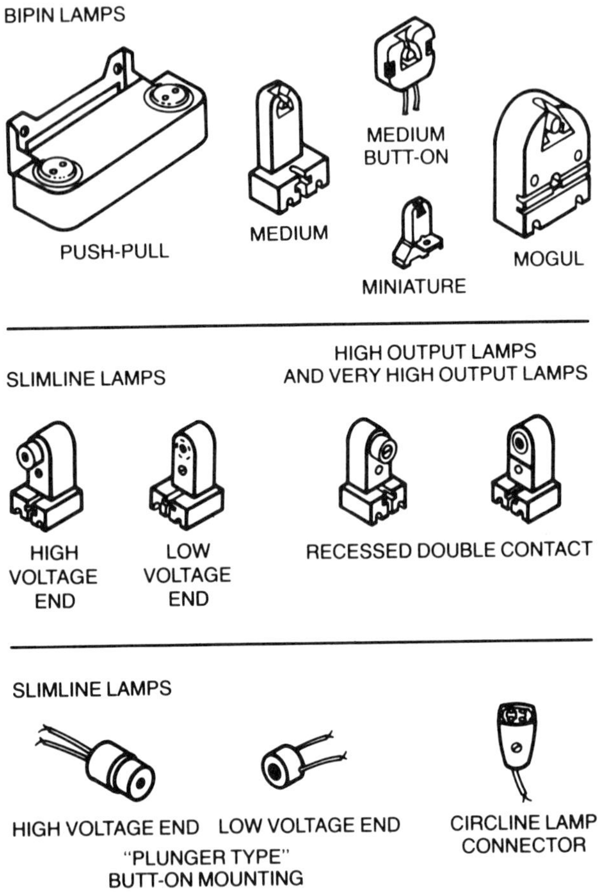

Figure 6.5 Lampholders for fluorescent lamps (courtesy of GTE-Sylvania Lighting).

SECTION 7

Raw Stock

HANDLING FILM

1. For short-term storage of film stock, a temperature of 55°F or lower is recommended. For longer than six months, the temperature should be around 0°F. Relative humidity should be 60% or less. See Table 7.2.
2. Allow raw stock to reach room temperature before opening it to avoid condensation.
3. Keep dust, hairs, and film chips out of the changing bag and the darkroom.
4. Clean magazines and film cans where dust will not fall on film handling area.
5. Place exposed film in the original black bags and place it inside the film can. Use camera tape to seal the entire can.
6. Write the film type, exposure notes, the name of production company, and other relevant data on the can.
7. Use exposed-film tape or colored tape on all cans of exposed footage.
8. Process the exposed film as soon as possible.
9. If there is a delay in processing, refrigerate or freeze the film, if possible, to avoid latent image shifts.

It is common practice to write the emulsion number, date, production name, amount of footage, mag number, camera designation (A, B, and so on), developing instructions, and ASA exposure on a piece of camera tape, which is then placed on the side of the magazine. When the roll is downloaded, this tape is then transferred to the film can. If less than the full roll is canned out, the actual footage in the can is written on the tape.

Raw stock should be protected from radiation from x-ray equipment, radioactive materials, and scanning devices. Gases and chemical vapors can also damage film. This includes mothballs, turpentine, cleaning solvents, and so forth.

WARM-UP TIMES FOR FILM

Film must be allowed to warm to room temperature before the factory seal is broken. This prevents spotting due to

Table 7.1A Motion-Picture Raw Stock: Color Films

Format	Designation	Balance	Speed (ASA)
Color Negative Films			
Eastman Kodak			
35mm	5296	Tungsten	500
	5297	Daylight	250
	5247	Tungsten	125
	5248	Tungsten	100
	5245	Daylight	50
	5293	Tungsten	200
16mm	7296	Tungsten	500
	7292	Tungsten	320
	7293	Tungsten	200
	7248	Tungsten	100
	7245	Daylight	50
Agfa			
35mm			
	XT100	Tungsten	125
	XT 320	Tungsten	320
	XTS400	Tungsten	400
16mm			
	XT100	Tungsten	125
	XT 320	Tungsten	320
	XTS400	Tungsten	400
Fugi			
35mm	F-500 (8570)	Tungsten	500
	F-250 (8550)	Tungsten	250
	F-64 (8510)	Tungsten	64
	F-250D (8560)	Daylight	250
	F-64D (8520)	Daylight	64
16mm			
	F-500 (8670)	Tungsten	500
	F-250 (8650)	Tungsten	250
	F-64 (8610)	Tungsten	64
	F-250D (8660)	Daylight	250
	F-64D (8620)	Daylight	64
Color Reversal Films			
Eastman Kodak			
35mm	7250	Tungsten	400
	7239	Daylight	160
	7240	Tungsten	125
	7251	Daylight	400

Table 7.1B Motion-Picture Raw Stock: Black-and-White Films

Size	Designation	Speed Daylight	Speed Tungsten
Black-and-White Negative Films			
Eastman Kodak			
35mm	5224 (4X)	500	400
	5222 (Double X)	250	200
	5231 (Plus X)	80	64
16mm	7224 (4X)	500	400
	7222 (Double X)	250	200
	7231 (Plus X)	80	64
Black-and-White Reveral Films			
Eastman Kodak			
16mm	7277 (4X reversal)	400	320
	7276 (Plus-X reversal)	50	40

Table 7.2 Film Storage Temperatures

Length of Storage Time	Temperature
Up to 6 months	55°F (13°C) or lower
Longer than 6 months	0°F to −10°F (−18°C– −23°C)

Note: Data courtesy of Eastman Kodak.

Table 7.3 Raw Stock Warm-up Times

Format	Warm-up Time (hr.) 25°F Rise (14°C)	100°F Rise (55°C)
8mm	1	1.5
16mm	1	1.5
35mm	3	5

Note: Data courtesy of Eastman Kodak.

condensation and unspooling due to the cold-induced looseness of the layers. Table 7.3 gives the recommended warm-up times for raw stock.

RUNNING FILM TESTS

A proper film test is the most effective way of isolating the variables of a new emulsion and understanding what you can do with it. Traditionally, a human face is used for film and video tests. The model should wear black, which will provide good contrast against a white background. Always include a gray scale and color chart in the scene for reference.

The first part of the test is key/fill balance ratios. The standard is to shoot with the fill one, two, three, and four stops lower than the key. The next part of the test is over- and underexposure. Start with the correct exposure according to your favorite metering technique. Then, in one-half-stop increments, go to three stops overexposed and three stops underexposed. Slate the steps carefully, and make sure that your camera notes are complete.

With either film or video dailies, you will want two prints. One should be a one-light print, set for a normal print on the basis of the correct first exposure of the gray scale. In this print, you will see the effect of over- and underexposure under nominal conditions and on a nominal print. For the second print, the timer or colorist should attempt to make a normal print from the negative. The printer numbers on this part of the test will be particularly instructive and will assist you in future communications with the timer.

Table 7.4 Shipping Weight of Film Cans

Format	Length of Film (ft.)	Weight
35mm	400	2lb. 3 oz.
	1000	5lb. 8 oz.
16mm	100	3.25 oz.
	400	1 lb. 1.5 oz.

SECTION 8

Gripology

This section lists basic data relating to camera support, rigging, construction, and other aspects of grip work in film and video production. Tables 8.1 to 8.16 begin on the next page.

Table 8.1 Dollies

Dolly	Width (in.)	Length (in.)	Maximum Height (in.)[a]	Minimum Height (in.)[a]	Weight
Elemack	19		56 1/4	29 1/2	250
Moviola	34 1/2	64 1/2	60 1/2	22 3/4	500
Hustler	27 1/2	51	73 (lens)	30 1/2 (lens)	420
Hybrid	27, 39	46, 54	79 (lens)	30 1/2 (lens)	420
Peewee	20, 32	43	69 (lens)	37 (lens)	280
Fisher 10	32, 26 5/8	54	63	16	420
Panther	20	39	58 1/4	31 1/2	280
Matthews western dolly	48	76			215
Matthews doorway dolly	28 1/4	51			94

[a]The term *lens* refers to the maximum or minimum height of the camera lens.

Table 8.2 Cranes

Crane	Width	Length	Maximum Height[a]	Minimum Height	Weight (lb.)
Tulip crane	35"	148"	16'6"	–24"	600
Super Nova	7'7"	20'	27'	–9'3"	28,500
Titan	7'7"	18'10"	27' (lens)	–8'	26,000
Apollo	7'7 1/2"	15'11"	19'5" (lens)	–10' 6"	17,500
Zeus	48 3/4"	7'11"	16'2" (lens)	–36"	1300
Electra II	45 1/2"	87"	14' (lens)	–20"	4000
Louma	25 1/2"	26'	31'4 1/4"	7 1/4"	990
Matthews Portable	64"	64"	16'6"	2'6"	2000
Nike	45 1/2"	87"	14' (lens)	–20"	4000
Olympian	33", 73"	7'8 1/4"	13'10"(lens)	–18"	1790
Sidewinder	38"	9'	9' (lens)	12"	1450
Shotmaker (camera car)	—	—	23' (lens)		

[a]The term *lens* refers to the maximum height of the camera lens.

Table 8.3 Overheads and Silks

Type	Nominal Size	Actual Size
Butterfly	6' × 6'	5'8" × 5'8"
Overhead	12' × 12'	11'8" × 11'8"
Overhead	20' × 20'	19'8" × 19'8"

Table 8.4 Griffolyns

Type	Designation	Surface	Thickness (Mils)
Black and white or white and white	T-55	Glossy	5
Clear	T-75	Dull	8
Black and white	T-85	Dull	10

Table 8.5 Apple Boxes

Apple Box	Dimensions (in.)
Full	12 × 8 × 20
Half	12 × 4 × 20
Quarter	12 × 2 × 20
Eighth	(pancake) 12 × 1 × 20

Table 8.6 Softwood Lumber Sizes

Nominal Size (in.)	Actual Size (in.)	Area (sq. ft.)	Board Foot ÷ Linear Foot
1 x 3	3/4 × 2 1/2	1.875	0.25
1 x 4	3/4 × 3 1/2	2.625	0.33
1 × 6	3/4 × 5 1/2	4.125	0.5
1 × 8	3/4 × 7 1/4	5.438	0.66
1 × 10	3/4 × 9 1/4	6.938	0.83
1 × 12	3/4 × 11 1/4	8.438	1
5/4 × 4	1 1/4 × 3 1/2	4.375	0.42
5/4 × 6	1 1/4 × 5 1/2	6.875	0.63
5/4 × 8	1 1/4 × 7 1/2	9.063	0.83
5/4 × 10	1 1/4 × 9 1/2	11.563	1.04
5/4 × 12	1 1/4 × 11 1/4	14.063	1.25
2 × 3	1 1/2 × 2 1/2	3.75	0.5
2 × 4	1 1/2 × 3 1/2	5.25	0.66
2 × 6	1 1/2 × 5 1/2	8.25	1
2 × 8	1 1/2 × 7 1/4	10.875	1.33
2 × 10	1 1/2 × 9 1/4	13.875	1.66
2 × 12	1 1/2 × 11 1/4	16.875	2
4 × 4	3 1/2 × 3 1/2	12.25	1.33
4 × 6	3 1/2 × 5 1/2	19.25	2
4 × 8	3 1/2 × 7 1/4	25.375	2.66
6 × 6	5 1/2 × 5 1/2	30.25	3
6 x 8	5 1/2 x 7 1/4	41.25	4

Table 8.7 Hardwood Lumber Sizes

Nominal Size (in.)	Rough Size (in.)	Actual Size (in.)
4/4	1	$^{13}/_{16}$
5/4	$1^{1}/_{4}$	$^{11}/_{16}$
6/4	$1^{1}/_{2}$	$^{15}/_{16}$
7/4	$1^{3}/_{4}$	$1^{1}/_{2}$
8/4	2	$1^{3}/_{4}$
10/4	$2^{1}/_{2}$	$2^{1}/_{4}$
12/4	3	$2^{3}/_{4}$
14/4	$3^{1}/_{2}$	$3^{1}/_{4}$
16/4	4	$3^{3}/_{4}$

Table 8.8 Hardwood Grades

Grade	Description
FAS (first and second)	The best grade; usually required for natural or stain finish
Select #1	common 66% clear wood
Select #2	common
Select #3	common

Table 8.9 Plywood Grades

Grade	Description
N	Smooth surface; "natural finish"; free of open defects
A	Smooth, paintable
B	Solid surface
C	Tight knots to $1^{1}/_{2}$"
D	Knots and knotholes to $2^{1}/_{2}$"

Table 8.10 Nail Sizes

Size	Length (in.)	Number per Pound: Common Nails	Box Nails	Finish Nails
2d	1	876	1010	1351
3d	$1^1/_4$	568	635	807
4d	$1^1/_2$	316	473	584
6d	2	181	236	309
8d	$2^1/_2$	106	145	189
10d	3	69	94	121
12d	$3^1/_4$	64	87	113
16d	$3^1/_2$	49	71	90
20d	4	31	52	62
40d	5	18		
60d	6	11		

Table 8.11 Rope Safe Working Loads (in pounds)

Diameter of Rope (in.)	Type of Rope: Manila	Sisal	Nylon	Polypropylene	Polyester	Polyethylene
$^3/_{16}$	100	75	200	150	200	150
$^1/_4$	120	90	300	250	300	250
$^5/_{16}$	200		500	400	500	350
$^3/_8$	270	200	700	500	700	500
$^1/_2$	530	400	1250	830	1200	800
$^5/_8$	880		2000	1300	1900	1050
$^3/_4$	1080	810	2800	1700	2400	1500
$^7/_8$	1540		3800	2200	3400	2100
1	1800	1350	4800	2900	4200	2500
$1^1/_8$	2400		6300	3750	5600	3300
$1^1/_4$	2700		7200	4200	6300	3700
$1^1/_2$	3700		10,200	6000	8900	5300
$1^5/_8$	4500		12,400	7300	10,800	6500
$1^3/_4$	5300		15,000	8700	12,900	7900
2	6200		17,900	10,400	15,200	9500

Table 8.12 Sash Cord

Size	Diameter (in.)
4	1/8
5	5/32
6	3/16
8	1/4
10	5/16
12	3/8

Table 8.13A Wire Rope: 7 × 19 Aircraft Cable

Diameter (in.)	Safe Load (lb.)
1/16	75
1/8	350
3/16	740
1/4	1280
5/16	1800
3/8	2400
7/16	3260
1/2	4560

Table 8.13B Wire Rope: 6 × 19 Wire Rope

Diameter (in.)	Safe Load (lb.)	Weight per Foot (lb.)	Breaking Point (lb.)
1/4	675	0.1	4800
5/16	1000	0.16	7400
3/8	1500	0.23	10,600
7/16	2000	0.31	14,400
1/2	2400	0.4	18,700
9/16	3300	0.51	23,600
5/8	4000	0.63	29,000
3/4	6000	0.9	41,400
1	10,000	1.6	56,000
1 1/8	13,000	2.03	72,800
1 1/4	16,000	2.5	112,400
1 1/2	22,000	3.6	160,000

Note: As a general rule, the safe working load of wire rope can be calculated by this formula: SWL = rope diameter^2 x 8 (tons).

Table 8.14 Chain Safe Working Loads (in pounds)

Type of Chain	Number or Size	Safe Load (lb.)
Jack chain	20	3
	18	5
	16	10
	14	16
	12	29
	10	43
	8	60
	6	88
Safety chain	00	31
	0	40
	1	58
	2	63
Steel sash chain (grip chain)	8	75
	25	95
	30	80
	35	105
	40	140
	45	175
	50	225
Welded steel chain	3/16"	520
	1/4"	900
	5/16"	1300
	3/8"	1860
Beaded chain	2	16
	6	30
	8	40
	10	45

Table 8.15 Pipe Dimensions

Nominal Size (in.)	Outside Diameter (in.)	Weight (lb./ft.)[a]
1/8	0.405	0.24
1/4	0.540	0.42
3/8	0.675	0.57
1/2	0.840	0.85
3/4	1.050	1.13
1	1.315	1.68
1 1/4	1.66	2.27
1 1/2	1.9	2.72
2	2.375	3.65
2 1/2	2.875	5.79
3	3.5	7.58
3 1/2	4	9.11
4	4.5	10.79
5	5.563	14.62
6	6.625	18.97
8	8.625	28.55

[a]Schedule 40 pipe.

SECTION 9

Video

TIME CODE

Currently, six time-code standards are in use around the world. The United States, Canada, Mexico, and Japan use the standard set by the Society of Motion Picture and Television Engineers (SMPTE). Europe and most of Asia, India, Africa, Central America, and South America use the European Broadcast Union (EBU) standard, which is based on a 50-Hz power supply and 25-fps shooting. The standards are given in Table 9.1.

In SMPTE time code, there are two further subdivisions: longitudinal and vertical interval time code. They differ in two ways: where the time code is recorded on the tape and the number of bits it requires. Longitudinal time code is recorded either on the address track or on one of the videotape's audio tracks, usually track 2. Vertical-interval time code (VITC) is recorded in the vertical interval of the video signal and has 90 bits of data, compared to longitudinal time code's 80 bits. Both types contain time-code information divided into hours, minutes, seconds, and frames. The frame is the only part that varies in different applications. Table 9.2 shows these differences.

The final video projection always runs at 29.97 fps, which is the NTSC standard, and it has time code at that

Table 9.1 Time Code Standards

Frame Rate (fps)	Standard	Most Common Uses
24	SMPTE	Film production
25	EBU 80	Film, TV, video, audio
29.97	SMPTE	Video, film production with video playback
29.97 (drop frame)	SMPTE	Video for TV broadcast
30	SMPTE	Film production for video, audio for film production
30 (drop frame)	None	Applications using a 0.1% slowdown, which converts to 29.97 fps drop frame

Table 9.2 Time Code

Frame Rate (fps)	Hours	Minutes	Seconds	Frames
24	00–23	00–59	00–59	00–23
25	00–23	00–59	00–59	00–24
29.97	00–23	00–59	00–59	00–29
30	00–23	00–59	00–59	00–29

frame rate. When transferring video from film shot at 29.97 fps, the speed of the film exactly matches the speed of the video, and the transfer is 1:1. If the camera is running at 24, 25, or 30 fps, however, there is a mismatch in running time because the film-to-tape transfer machine must run at a slightly slower rate to match the video's frame rate. A film shot at 24 fps will actually be transferred at 23.976 fps, a film shot at 25 fps will transfer at 24.975 fps, and a film shot at 30 fps will transfer at 29.97 fps. The 0.1% error is insignificant, except in the most critical applications. Only film shot at 29.97 fps will transfer with absolute timing accuracy. If the camera is run at 29.97 fps, the accompanying sync audio must also run at 29.97 fps. If the camera is run at 24, 25, or 30 fps, the time code on the audio must be recorded at 30 fps.

For time-critical applications, such as hour-long television programs that must exactly fit broadcast standards, it is necessary to compensate for the 0.1% time difference. This is accomplished by dropping the first two frame numbers of every minute. No actual frames are skipped, just the frame numbers. The final result is to adjust the time code to fit real time.

Because most professional tapes are an hour or less, the hour portion of the time code can be used to designate the tape number. This method cannot be used if there are more than 24 tapes.

Time-Code Slates

To simplify the coordination of time code and film, the smart slate was invented. The smart slate is a time-code generator that displays the code on large LEDs readable on film. Dumb slates are similar but are not time-code generators; they can only display time code generated by another source. Time-code slates are particularly valuable in filming to playback, as is common in shooting music videos. To use a slate for single- or multicamera video, place it where all of the cameras can see it. When each camera rolls, the operator zooms in on the slate for a moment, thus providing the editor with perfect synchronization for all cameras and at the same time eliminating the need for individual clapper slating.

There is one problem inherent in using the most popular playback deck (the Nagra IVS-TC) with a dumb slate. To allow for the offset in position between the time-code head and the audio head while in record mode, the Nagra shifts the time-code value. Only this shifted code is sent to the dumb slate. The result is a constant discrepancy between the code displayed on the slate and the code on the tape, which varies according to the tape speed and the time-code standard used. Some transfer systems can automatically compensate for this offset, but it is wise to mark the slate to indicate the offset.

When using a time-code slate, it is essential that the audio tape with the time code be prerolled for at least 5 seconds. In the process of syncing film to the audio, the 5-second period allows the two time-code locations to be matched and locked up. At the beginning of each take, the audio is prerolled for 5 seconds, and then the camera operator starts the camera and films the electronic slate, which records the time-code address. No extended preroll of film is needed.

VIDEO LIGHTING

Three simple rules apply for lighting video:

- Accommodate lighting ratio to the video limits of five stops brightness range.
- Avoid areas of extreme overexposure (hotspots), including specular reflections.
- Include reference black and reference white in every scene.

ADJUSTING THE GAMMA

For projects finished on video, an enormous range of image control is available, from simple adjustments of the gamma to complex Paintbox, Harry, and DaVinci image manipulations. For adjusting gamma and enlarging the image, it is generally best to do so at the time of transfer.

LOW CON PRINT FOR TRANSFER

It is difficult to shoot film that will look good in projection and will also transfer well to video. One solution is to have the film printed on special low-contrast print stock before transferring. Consultation with the lab and with the person who will do the video transfer is essential.

WAVEFORM MONITOR

On a waveform monitor, the screen is divided into 140 IEE units. A video signal ranges from 0 to 100 IEE units. The actual minimum black level is at 7.5 IEE units, and the maximum white is 100 units. During the blanking interval, the time when the scan line is moving back across the screen, the signal goes to 0 units, which is important for keeping the scan line invisible as it moves back to the other side of the screen. The sync pulse, which is a trigger that signals the beam to begin to move back across, actually dips below 0, down –40 IEE units. These blanking and sync pulses occur outside the picture area, in the so-called overscan areas.

The waveform monitor is a trace of one scan line of the picture. As this single trace moves across the screen, it records the relative brightness of the picture information. It is exactly the same as a series of spot meter readings across the set from left to right in a straight line. Totally black areas in the picture show up on the monitor as 7.5 units. Bright areas record as 90 or 100 units or more. Where the picture exceeds 100 IEE units, the video signal is overloaded. Table 9.3 relates specific signal levels in IEE units to specific exposure zones.

VECTORSCOPE

The waveform monitor tells us little about the color content and balance of a scene; for that, we need a vectorscope. The color signal of video is defined by two basic attributes: hue and saturation. A vectorscope displays these two elements in a circular display. Hue is represented by degrees of rotation from the reference point, and saturation is represented by distance from the center of the circle.

For most NTSC vectorscopes, 0° is at 3 o'clock. The six basic colors are positioned as follows:

Table 9.3 Zones and IEE Units

Zone	IEE Units
I	<7.5
II	15
III	20
IV	40
V	55
VI	80
VII	100
VIII	120

Magenta: 61°
Red: 104°
Yellow: 167°
Green: 241°
Cyan: 284°
Blue: 347°

Square brackets mark the position of each pure hue on the face of the vectorscope. These act as targets when setting up with color bars.

IRIS CONTROL

Video cameras vary in sensitivity, but in general, they run to around 100 to 125 ASA. This translates to a light level of 200 FC to achieve an f-stop f/4. Control of the iris (f-stop setting of the lens) may be at the camera or at the video engineer's station. Just as with film, the iris determines the overall exposure of the scene. Because highlight areas are so much more problematic than shadow areas, the general practice in videography is to set the exposure for the highlights and handle the shadows in another way. Most video lenses are not marked for f-stops, and reading with a light meter would be irrelevant in any case.

ELECTRONIC PUSHING

Another factor that affects overall exposure is electronic pushing. This is the electronic equivalent of forced development for film. It raises the sensitivity of the tube, allowing the camera to form an image at a lower exposure level. The boost is rated in decibels (dBs), and each 6-dB boost is the equivalent of one stop. As with film, there is a penalty to pay; in this case, it is increased electronic noise in the picture, not unlike the increased grain in pushed film.

SECTION **10**

Special Effects

COLOR-DIFFERENCE MATTES

Traveling matte is a general term for any process in which the background and foreground are photographed separately and combined after the fact, either optically or electronically. The most basic of these processes is chroma key, which works in both film and video. The foreground subject is photographed in front of an evenly illuminated blue screen. The blue is then subtracted from the scene, leaving empty space around the subject. This space then receives the background scene. It is not essential that the backing be blue; the only requirement is that none of the background color appear in the foreground subject.

Ultimatte

Ultimatte is the most widely used color-difference process in video. It is used with subjects originated on both film and video. According to Ultimatte Technical Bulletin #3, "There are several reasons why it may be advantageous to shoot Ultimatte foregrounds on film rather than video. The most obvious advantage is the possibility of non-real-time photography. Film currently offers greater flexibility than video for high speed slow motion photography or stop motion, animation and motion control photography."

As with film chroma key, blue and green are the most widely used colors, but any color that is different from that of the foreground subject may be used. Recommendations for the use of Ultimatte include the following:

- Do not use 16mm film.
- Use a pin-registered camera, such as Panaflex, Arri BL, Arri III, or Mitchell.
- Use the lowest-grain film possible. Grain introduces noise into the image.
- Do not use diffusion over the lens. Do not use heavy smoke effects.
- Always shoot a gray scale lit with neutral light (3200K or 5500K) at the beginning of each roll. Shoot the gray scale (or chip chart for video) in a place where it will not be contaminated by splash back from the background or floor.

- Whenever possible, use a polarizing filter to eliminate specular glare.
- With a video camera, avoid shooting with the lens wide open. Many video camera lenses vignette very slightly when they are wide open, which can create problems with the matte.
- In video, never compensate for low-light levels by boosting the gain. Never push film.
- See Section 6 for recommendations on lighting for chroma key and Ultimatte.

In general, these recommendations apply to all matte work.

Because matte shots generally involve extra generations in post-production, it is desirable to shoot the background plate in the highest-quality format possible. For large-scale studio productions, this often involves shooting the plates in Vistavision.

Luminance Key

Luminance key is similar in principle to chroma key, except that the difference between light and dark objects is used as the key for producing the difference matte. If the subject is primarily light-colored, then the background and all parts of the scene that you want to replace with the composited background plate should be black. The opposite is true if the subject is predominantly dark.

Luminance key is fairly simple to create, but the inherent problem is that any shadow areas in the foreground subject will become transparent to the background matte. This creates severe limitations on lighting. For a good key, the foreground objects should be about 20 to 25 IEE units above black.

Shooting Background Plates

The background scenes used in matte work and in both front and rear projection are called *background plates.*

- Background plates must be shot with a pin-registered camera.
- In video, the camera should be color-balanced for the foreground subject.
- To match the depth of focus of the foreground, shoot the background plate with the focus set at where it would be if the foreground object was actually there.
- Horizon-line height must be preplanned according to the director's intention for shooting the final composite scene. A general rule of thumb is one-third sky, two-thirds foreground. If the final plans are not known, shoot three versions: one-third sky, two-thirds fore-

ground; horizon line dead center; and two-thirds sky, one-third foreground. As a last resort, shoot the scene with a wider lens and the horizon dead center to allow for optical repositioning.

- If people or objects move in the scene, they must not get too close to the camera, as they will appear unusually large and out of perspective in the plate. At least 10 feet away from the camera is a safe distance. They should enter from the sides and not from the bottom frame line.
- Unless forced perspective is required, avoid lenses with extremely short or long focal lengths.
- Keep a process plate log sheet to record the following:
  - production name
  - scenes shot
  - scene description
  - day/night, interior/exterior
  - aperture
  - lens
  - f-stop
  - frame rate
  - distance to nearest object
  - focus distance
  - degree of tilt
  - camera height
  - filters
  - camera car speed
  - direction of shot relative to direction of camera car travel
  - sun direction
  - camera compass direction
  - weather
  - light conditions
  - time of day

Shooting Running Shots

Background plates for running shots (driving scenes) should be done from a variety of angles to give the director flexibility in the final scene. Running shot plates are generally done straight back, straight forward, 45° back on either side, 45° forward on either side, and 90° on either side.

Camera height must match the vehicle that will appear in the final composite shot. A slight downward tilt is often preferred for road shots. The camera position used to film the actors in the vehicle must be taken into account; it is usually at least shoulder height or higher.

Running shots filmed at angles other than straight forward or straight back appear to move faster. For this

Table 10.1 Compensation of Camera Car Speed for Running Shots

Speed of Camera Car for Straight Forward Shot (mph)	Speed of Camera Car for Shot 45° Forward or Backward (mph)	Speed of Camera Car for for Shot 90° to Side (mph)
70	56	40
60	48	36
50	40	30
40	32	24
30	24	18
20	16	12
10	8	6

Table 10.2 Lens Equivalents in Various Formats

	Video Tubes				Film Formats	
	1/2"	2/3"	1"	1 1/4"	35mm	16mm
Width (mm)	6.4	8.8	12.8	17.1	22.05	10.3
Height (mm)	4.8	6.6	9.6	12.8	16.03	7.5
Angle (°)	Focal Length (mm)[a]					
52	6.6	9.0	13.1	17.5	22.6	10.6
40	8.8	12.1	17.6	23.5	30.3	14.1
30	11.9	16.4	23.9	31.9	41.0	19.22
20	18.1	25.0	36.3	40.5	62.5	29.2
15	24.3	33.4	48.6	64.9	83.7	39.1
5	73.3	100.8	146.6	195.8	252.5	118.0
3	122.2	168.0	244.4	326.5	421.0	196.7

Notes: To convert a 1/2" video focal length to its equivalent 2/3" focal length, multiply by 1.375. To convert a 2/3" video focal length to its equivalent 1/2" focal length, multiply by 0.727. The equivalent focal lengths of any two formats are directly proportional to the respective image widths.

[a]Tangent of 1/2 Angle of View - 1/2 Image Size/Focal Length. Lens Angle of View = 2 x ARC TANGENT (Image Size/[2 x Focal Length])

reason, it is necessary to reduce the speed of the vehicle to create an apparent match in direction. The standard reduction is 20% for 45° shots (forward or backward) and 40% for 90° shots. Table 10.1 gives typical reductions.

Carefully plan the screen direction and perspective of the background plates; it is essential that they match the foreground. Note, for example, that there is a slight difference in perspective between different film and video formats. Consult Table 10.2 for assistance with shooting plates in different formats.

GLASS MATTE SHOTS

Glass matte shots do not require a pin-registered camera because the camera sees both the glass matte and the foreground action at the same time. However, it is essential that the camera and the glass be rigidly mounted.

The illumination level on the glass must match the background; the lighting can be natural light or copy lights at 45° on each side. It is often necessary to cover the glass matte with a black tent to prevent reflections in the glass. It may also be necessary to cover the camera and dress crew in black for the same reason.

The angle of the sun and other atmospheric conditions, as portrayed in the glass painting, must be matched at the time of shooting. Avoid atmospheric effects such as fog, dust, and rain that will not move on the glass.

A T-stop of at least T/11 to T/22 is generally needed to keep both glass and background in focus.

Panning and tilting are possible, but only on a nodal-point mount. Glass mattes are one of the few matte effects in which 16mm works as well as 35mm; indeed, the greater depth of field of 16mm is an advantage in keeping the glass and the live elements in focus.

MIRROR AND BEAMSPLITTER MIRROR SHOTS

Mirror shots, in which a partial reflector is set at 45° in front of the camera to show both foreground and background combined, are one of the oldest and simplest special-effects shots. A high-quality front-surface mirror is needed to eliminate double reflection, and as with glass shots, it is important that both scenes be illuminated to balance their exposure as seen at the image plane. As is true in all mirror shots, the focus of the reflected scene is the total distance from the focal plane to the mirror and back to the reflected subject.

REAR PROJECTION

The rear projection of static images calls for a high-intensity light source for the projector. In the past, arc-lamp projectors were used. In recent years, these have been replaced by xenon projectors. In some cases, dual-head projectors are used to increase brightness by laying identical images on top of each other.

For moving rear projection, an ordinary projector is not adequate because the movement is not pin-registered. As with still-image projection, the light source must be high-powered. In practice, rear projection equipment is highly specialized and incorporates sound blimping, reverse running, and a flat-field optical system. Synchronization between the camera and the projector can be achieved through the use of 220-volt, three-phase selsyn motors or electronic sync.

The depth of the foreground set is limited by the depth of field that will keep the projection screen in acceptable focus. Because the illumination level of the foreground must match that of the projection, this must be taken into account in planning the foreground action. Forced perspective sets may address this problem.

FRONT PROJECTION

Front projection relies on three basic elements: a 45° beamsplitter mirror between the camera and the subject, a still or motion-picture projector aimed into the beamsplitter, and a highly reflective backing behind the actors. The backing is usually made from Scotchlite, a highly reflective material manufactured by 3M.

The Scotchlite is the key to the process. Because it is as much as 1600 times more reflective than a white surface, it reflects the projected image at photographable light levels even though the projected image is quite dim in relation to the illumination on the actors. As a result, even though the projected image from the beamsplitter is falling on the actors, it is too dim to be detectable.

Scotchlite type #7610 in colorless silver is the material most commonly used. For smaller setups in which it may be necessary to have foreground lights closer to the optical axis, type #7615 and #7620 can be used. They are less reflective but higher in contrast. Scotchlite comes in rolls 2 feet wide and up to 50 yards in length. It can also be purchased in the form of ready-made screens. Scotchlite screens must be mounted flat. Uniformity can be checked with a ringlite and with high-contrast film in a still camera.

Beamsplitter mirrors are relatively inexpensive. They are commonly available from mirror dealers. Pellicle beamsplitters can also be used, but they are less stable and more easily damaged.

In setup, care must be taken that the reflecting screen is

as perpendicular as possible to the optical axis. The camera and projector must have their nodal points at exactly the same distance from the mirror, and their optical axis must align precisely. In most cases, the focal length of the camera and the projector should be the same, but some variation from this standard may be necessary to distort perspective or enlarge a portion of the projected background.

Black cloth should be used to block off unwanted reflections and stray light. The alignment of the camera and projector is critical but can be accomplished by looking through the viewfinder of the camera. Adjustments can be made until any evidence of fringe shadows disappears. Pan and tilt movements are possible only with a nodal-point mount.

Although front projection is much more tolerant of foreground light splashing on the screen than is rear projection, it is still possible for splash to degrade the image. Foreground lighting units should be 30° or more outside the optical axis. Flare from backlights can cause serious problems, however, and should be avoided. High-intensity background projectors are not necessary, but good-quality optics are important in achieving good alignment of the optical axes.

MINIATURES

Miniatures must usually be in focus from front to back, which generally calls for a small aperture. If the action of a miniature is influenced by gravity (for example, water falling, buildings toppling, and so on), the appropriate camera speed is determined by the following formula:

$$f = \sqrt{\frac{D}{d}}$$

$$\text{factor for increase of film speed} = \frac{\text{distance for real object (ft.)}}{\text{distance for miniature (ft.)}}$$

In practice, this translates to the square root of the reciprocal of the scale of the miniature. For example, if the miniature is $^{1}/_{12}$ size, then the factor is

$$\sqrt{\frac{12}{1}} = 3.5$$

In this example, the frame rate should be 3.5 x 24 = 84 fps. Table 10.3 gives various frame rates for filming miniatures.

Table 10.3 Frame Rates for Filming Miniatures

Scale of Miniature	Adjustment Factor	Adjusted Camera Speed (fps)
1/2	1.4	33
1/4	2	48
1/8	2.8	67
1/10	3.2	77
1/12	3.5	84
1/16	4	96
1/20	4.5	108
1/24	4.9	117
1/36	6	144
1/48	7	168
1/64	8	192
1/100	10	240

For an object moving independent of gravity (a moving car, a train rolling on tracks, and so on), the speed of the miniature is the result of two factors. The scale fraction is straightforward; for example, a 1/16-scale car that is supposed to be moving at 60 miles per hour (mph) must run at 1/16 of that speed, or 3.75 mph. However, compensation must be made for the fact that the camera is running at a higher frame rate. In this case, the camera runs at 96 fps (4 times normal), so the model must run at 4 times normal speed, or 15 mph.

The entire calculation can be summarized in the following formula:

$$\text{model speed (mph)} = \frac{\text{scale} \times \text{portrayed speed} \times \text{frame rate}}{\text{normal frame rate}}$$

In the preceding example, the calculation is as follows:

$$\frac{1/16 \times 60 \times 96}{24} = 15 \text{ mph}$$

The following is an alternate formula:

$$\text{portrayed speed (mph)} \times \text{scale}^2 \times 1.47 = \text{model speed (feet per second)}$$

Table 10.4 translates miles per hour into feet per second.

Table 10.4 Conversion: Miles per Hour and Feet per Second

Miles per Hour	Feet per Second
1	1
10	15
15	22
20	29
30	44
40	59
50	73
60	88
70	103
80	117
90	132
100	147

Table 10.5 Railroad Model Scales

Gauge	Scale
O	1:48
S	1:64
OO	1:75
HO	1:86
TT	1:120

Common railroad model scales are given in Table 10.5. Due to the extremely high camera speeds necessary, it is seldom practical to use models smaller than 1/24 scale.

STOP MOTION

For stop-motion filming, the camera must be rigidly mounted; if a tripod is used, it should be weighted with sandbags, strapped down, or otherwise secured. If the camera moves on a dolly or motion-control rig, its support must be solid and vibration-free. Care must be taken not to bump the camera between exposures. If the time between exposures is more than a few seconds, a capping shutter may be necessary to prevent light from leaking around the shutter mechanism.

At the end of the take, roll off several feet of film at

normal speed to ensure that the end of the stop motion section is not still in the camera body where it might be exposed to light or damaged when the film is downloaded.

DOUBLE EXPOSURE

Because with double exposure the final exposure of the film is the sum of both exposures, it is often necessary to underexpose each separate section by as much as one stop. If there is no overlap of the images and the background is black, this is not necessary.

DAY-FOR-NIGHT

Day-for-night filming has generally fallen into disuse as the advent of high-speed film and high-speed lenses has made nighttime shooting easier. In black-and-white filming, infrared film was often used to create a day-for-night effect. Filters such as Wratten #25, 29, 70, 87, 88A, and 89B were used.

In color, the effect can be achieved by a combination of underexposing one to two stops and letting the color balance shift blue, either with filtration or by shooting tungsten balance in a daylight-balance situation. It is generally best to avoid showing the sky. Also essential to a realistic day-for-night effect is the minimization of shadows. This can be obtained by shooting at noon or by shooting in open shade or with overhead silks.

MOONLIGHT EFFECT

It is a widely accepted convention that moonlight is blue. The most commonly used filter is full CTB or double blue in addition to whatever blue is used to establish the basic color balance.

WATER EFFECT

The dapple of light reflected on water can be achieved in a number of ways. Some people use broken mirrors or crumpled aluminum foil to reflect a strong directional light, usually a fresnel or a PAR. These effects tend to be somewhat stilted and artificial. The best effect is always achieved by using actual water. In a shallow pan with a black backing, water itself can be highly reflective if you use a strong enough lighting unit. It is sometimes useful to float a sheet of silvered mylar to increase the bounce.

LIGHTNING EFFECT

Because a lightning effect must be extremely powerful to be effective, it generally calls for a specially built rig. Most lightning rigs are based on carbon-arc technology. They consist of an arc ballast and a set of carbons that can be pushed together then rapidly withdrawn with a levered handle. The resulting arc produces a powerful and momentary blast of light that is very convincing.

A Brute arc can also be used by reversing the polarity of the DC so that it is "wrong" and then throwing the striking lever. The carbons will produce a brief, powerful arc but will not strike because the polarity is wrong.

Understandably, these effects can be very hard on a generator. Be sure you have plenty of headroom before attempting a lightning effect.

Hand-controlled shutters are also available for 24-inch lens units. Flashbulb rigs are sometimes used for the lightning effect. M-type or S-type flashbulbs, which have a long burn time, are most effective for this purpose. Regular flashbulbs fire very quickly and might burn while the shutter is closed. High-tech strobe-based units are also available for rental from some special-effects houses. In a pinch, an art-welder can be used.

SCRIMS AND SMOKE

Not all diffusion filters are fitted directly on the lens. Theatrical scrim and bobbinet are sometimes used to create an atmospheric haze, reduce contrast, and create a sense of distance. They can be placed at any depth in the set. For example, a white scrim placed behind the main action makes the background seem distant and hazy.

Smoke can serve the same purpose in addition to its more obvious functions. It serves as a diffusion for the lights and as a diffusion for the image reaching the lens; in both functions, it reduces contrast. Dust can serve the same purpose, and in some cases, Fuller's earth is used. Particle masks are essential when using dust and smoke.

REVERSE FILMING

With cameras that have reverse motors, such as Arri IIC, Arri III, or Mitchell, reverse filming is a simple matter of advancing the film and running the camera in reverse. With a sync sound camera that has no reverse capability, the only alternative is to run the negative backward in printing. Because this involves swapping heads for tails on the negative, it is necessary to turn the camera upside down. If finishing on video, this is unnecessary because it is simple to transfer the film backward.

SECTION 11

General Information

CARNETS

Carnets are standardized documents used to prove that you are a leaving a country with all of the equipment you brought with you. Carnets are issued by the U.S. Council for International Business. They are required in most European countries but are not accepted in South America, Africa (except South Africa), Central America, China, the Philippines, and Russia. Where they are not recognized, most governments require a cash bond or a temporary importation bond (TIB). Even when traveling without a carnet, you should always carry several copies of a detailed manifest that lists every piece of equipment and its serial number.

To purchase a carnet, contact one of the carnet offices listed in Table 11.7. They will send you application forms and instructions. They will also send a bond form. The bond is to protect against claims on the carnet and is generally 1% of a 40% valuation of the equipment (a few countries base the bond on 100% valuation). In some cases, a financial statement of the company will be accepted in lieu of a bond. Allow five working days for processing the paperwork. In an emergency, 24-hour service is available for an additional $100. The carnet form must be filled out carefully. The issuing fee is from $100 to $250.

When leaving the United States with a carnet, allow extra time for customs agents to examine every case and check the carnet. If leaving the United States with equipment of foreign manufacture, register the serial numbers and descriptions with U.S. Customs. The agent will examine the equipment and provide you with a registration form, which you must produce on reentering the United States. These forms are available from the carnet offices.

ADDITIVE COLOR CONTROL

Printer timing values are usually given on a scale of 0 to 50 for each of the color layers, normally in the sequence red, green, blue (RGB). These numbers represent the color of light in the printer, not the effect on the print. In a color negative, each color controls the amount of the complementary color in the final print. Increasing the blue will make the print more yellow. Because of this reverse effect, some labs list printer values in the complementary colors: yellow, magenta, and cyan (YMC). For timing color prints from color negatives, the changes in value are listed in Table 11.8.

Table 11.1 Latitudes of Major Cities

City	Latitude	City	Latitude
Amman	32° N	Madrid	40° N
Amsterdam	52° N	Manila	14° N
Anchorage	61° N	Melbourne	38° S
Athens	38° N	Mexico City	19° N
Auckland	37° S	Miami	26° N
Belgrade	45° N	Montreal	46° N
Berlin	53° N	Moscow	56° N
Bombay	19° N	Munich	48° N
Brussels	51° N	Nairobi	1° N
Buenos Aires	35° S	New York	41° N
Cairo	30° N	Nice	44° N
Cape Town	34° S	Oslo	60° N
Copenhagen	56° N	Paris	49° N
Dallas	33° N	Peking	40° N
Delhi	28° N	Rio de Janeiro	23° S
Dublin	52° N	Rome	42° N
Geneva	46° N	Singapore	1° N
Hamburg	54° N	Stockholm	59° N
Hong Kong	22° N	Sydney	34° S
Honolulu	21° N	Tokyo	36° N
Johannesburg	26° S	Toronto	44° N
Lisbon	39° N	Vancouver	49° N
London	52° N	Vienna	48° N
Los Angeles	34° N	Washington	39° N

Table 11.2 Hours of Daylight for Various Latitudes

	Hours of Daylight											
Latitude	Jan.	Feb.	Mar.	Apr.	May	Jun.	Jul.	Aug.	Sep.	Oct.	Nov.	Dec.
60° N	6.75	9.25	11.75	14.5	17.25	18.75	18	15.75	13	10.25	7.5	6
50° N	8.5	10.25	12	13.75	15.5	16.25	16	15.5	12.5	11.25	9	8
40° N	9.75	10.75	12	13.75	14.5	15	14.75	13.75	12.5	11.25	10	9.25
30° N	10.5	11.25	12	13	13.75	14	14	13.25	12.25	11.5	10.5	10.25
20° N	11	11.25	12	12.5	13	13.25	13.25	12.75	12.25	11.75	11.25	11
10° N	11.5	11.75	12	12.25	12.5	12.75	12.75	12.5	12.25	12	11.75	11.5
0°	12	12	12	12	12	12	12	12	12	12	12	12
10° S	12.75	12.25	12.25	12	11.75	11.25	11.5	11.75	12	12.25	12.5	12.75
20° S	13.25	12.75	12.25	11.75	11.25	11	11	11.5	12	12.5	13	13.25
30° S	14	13.25	12.25	11.5	10.5	10.25	10.5	11.25	12	13	13.75	14
40° S	14.75	13.75	12.5	11.25	10	9.25	9.75	10.75	12	13.25	14.5	15
50° S	16	15.5	12.5	10.75	9	8	8.5	10.25	12	13.75	15.5	16.25
60° S	18	15.75	13	10.25	7.5	6	6.75	9.25	11.75	14.5	17.25	18.75

Table 11.3A Conversions: Feet and Meters

Feet	Meters	Meters	Feet
1	0.3	1	3.3
5	1.5	5	16.4
10	3.0	10	32.8
20	6.1	20	65.6
30	9.1	30	98.4
40	12.2	40	131.2
50	15.2	50	164.0
60	18.3	60	196.9
70	21.3	70	229.7
80	24.4	80	262.5
90	27.4	90	295.3
100	30.5	100	328.1
200	61.0	200	656.2
300	91.4	300	984.3
400	121.9	400	1312.3
500	152.4	500	1640.4
600	182.9	600	1968.5
700	213.4	700	2296.6
800	243.8	800	2624.7
900	274.3	900	2952.8
1000	304.8	1000	3280.8

Table 11.3B Conversions: Inches and Millimeters

Inches	Millimeters	Millimeters	Inches
1	25.4	1	0.04
2	50.8	2	0.08
3	76.2	3	0.12
4	101.6	4	0.16
5	127.0	5	0.20
6	152.4	6	0.24
7	177.8	7	0.28
8	203.2	8	0.31
9	228.6	9	0.35
10	254.0	10	0.39
11	279.4	11	0.43
12	304.8	12	0.47
13	330.2	13	0.51
14	355.6	14	0.55
15	381.0	15	0.59
16	406.4	16	0.63
17	431.8	17	0.67
18	457.2	18	0.71
19	482.6	19	0.75
20	508.0	20	0.79
21	533.4	21	0.83
22	558.8	22	0.87
23	584.2	23	0.91
24	609.6	24	0.94
25	635.0	25	0.98

Table 11.3C Conversions: Inches and Decimal Inches

Inches	Decimal Inches	Inches	Decimal Inches
1/64	0.015625	33/64	0.515625
1/32	0.03125	17/32	0.53125
3/64	0.046875	35/64	0.546875
1/16	0.0625	9/16	0.5625
5/64	0.078125	37/64	0.578125
3/32	0.09375	19/32	0.59375
7/64	0.109375	39/64	0.609375
1/8	0.125	5/8	0.625
9.64	0.140625	41/64	0.640625
5/32	0.15625	21/32	0.65625
11/64	0.171875	43/64	0.671875
3/16	0.1875	11/16	0.6875
13/64	0.203125	45/64	0.703125
7/32	0.21875	23/32	0.71875
15/64	0.234375	47/64	0.734375
1/4	0.25	3/4	0.75
17/64	0.265625	49/64	0.765625
9/32	0.28125	25/32	0.78125
19/64	0.296875	51/64	0.796875
5/16	0.3125	13/16	0.8125
21/64	0.328125	53/64	0.828125
11/32	0.34375	27/32	0.84375
23/64	0.359375	55/64	0.859375
3/8	0.375	7/8	0.875
25/64	0.390625	57/64	0.890625
13/32	0.40625	29/32	0.90625
27/64	0.421875	59/64	0.921875
7/16	0.4375	15/16	0.9375
29/64	0.453125	61/64	0.953125
15/32	0.46875	31/32	0.96875
31/64	0.484375	63/64	0.984375
1/2	0.5		

Table 11.4 International Calling Codes

Nation	Code	Nation	Code
Algeria	213	Italy	39
American Samoa	684	Ivory Coast	225
Andorra	33	Japan	81
Argentina	54	Jordan	962
Aruba	297	Kenya	254
Australia	61	Korea	82
Austria	43	Kuwait	965
Bahrain	973	Liberia	231
Belgium	32	Libya	218
Belize	501	Liechtenstein	41
Bolivia	591	Luxembourg	352
Brazil	55	Malawi	265
Cameroon	237	Malaysia	60
Chile	56	Mexico	52
China	86	Monaco	33
Colombia	57	Morocco	212
Costa Rica	506	Namibia	264
Cyprus	357	Netherlands	31
Czechoslovakia	42	Netherlands Antilles	599
Denmark	45	New Caledonia	687
East Germany, former	37	New Zealand	64
Ecuador	593	Nicaragua	505
Egypt	20	Nigeria	234
El Salvador	503	Norway	47
England	44	Oman	968
Ethiopia	251	Pakistan	92
Fiji	679	Panama	507
Finland	358	Papua New Guinea	675
France	33	Paraguay	595
French Antilles	596	Peru	51
French Polynesia, Tahiti	689	Philippines	63
Gabon	241	Poland	48
Greece	30	Qatar	974
Guam	671	Romania	40
Guantanamo Bay (Cuba)	53	Saipan	670
Guatemala	502	San Marino	39
Guyana	592	Saudi Arabia	966
Haiti	509	Scotland	44
Honduras	504	Senegal	221
Hong Kong	852	Singapore	65
Hungary	36	South Africa	27
Iceland	354	Spain	34
India	91	Sri Lanka	94
Indonesia	62	Suriname	597
Iran	98	Sweden	46
Iraq	964	Switzerland	41
Ireland	353	Tahiti	689
Israel	972	Taiwan	886

(continued)

Table 11.4 International Calling Codes *(continued)*

Nation	Code	Nation	Code
Thailand	66	Uruguay	598
Tunisia	216	Vatican City	39
Turkey	90	Venezuela	58
United Arab Emirates	971	West Germany, former	49
United Kingdom (Great Britain)	44	Yemen	967
USSR, former	7		

General Dialing Instructions*
To dial an international call direct, dial the following:
1. international access code (O11)
2. country code
3. city routing code
4. local telephone number

For operator-assisted calls (person-to-person, collect, calling card calls), dial the following:
1. international access code (01)
2. country code
3. city routing code
4. local telephone number

Before the call is completed, the operator will come on the line. If you do not have the required information, dial the operator, and ask for assistance.

*For further assistance and information, dial (00) for an international operator.

Courtesy of AT&T.

Table 11.5 World Time Chart

Nation	Time Difference (Hours)	Nation	Time Difference (Hours)
American Samoa	–3	Japan	17
Andorra	9	Kenya	11
Argentina	5	Korea	17
Australia	19	Kuwait	11
Austria	9	Liberia	8
Bahamas	2	Libya	10
Bahrain	11	Liechtenstein	9
Belgium	9	Luxembourg	9
Belize	2	Malaysia[a]	15 1/2
Bolivia	4	Mexico	2
Brazil[a]	5	Monaco	9
Chile	5	Netherlands	9
Colombia	3	Netherlands Antilles	4
Costa Rica	2	New Caledonia	19
Cyprus	10	New Zealand	21
Denmark	9	Nicaragua	2
Ecuador	3	Nigeria	9
El Salvador	2	Norway	9
England	8	Panama	3
Fiji	20	Papua New Guinea	18
Finland	10	Paraguay	5
France	9	Peru	3
French Antilles	4	Philippines	16
French Polynesia	2	Portugal	8
Germany	9	Romania	10
Greece	10	Saudi Arabia	11
Guam	18	Scotland	8
Guatemala	2	Singapore	15 1/2
Guyana	5	South Africa	10
Haiti	3	Spain	9
Honduras	2	Sri Lanka	13 1/2
Hong Kong	16	Suriname	4 1/2
Indonesia[a]	15	Sweden	9
Iran	11 1/2	Switzerland	9
Iraq	11	Tahiti	–2
Ireland	8	Taiwan	16
Israel	10	Thailand	15
Italy	9	Tunisia	9
Ivory Coast	8	Turkey	10
Jamaica	2	United Arab Emirates	12

Note: To determine the time in countries listed above, add the hours indicated to Pacific standard time.

[a]This country has more than one time zone.

Courtesy of AT&T.

Table 11.6 Car Rental Companies

Company	Phone Number
Alamo	800-327-9633
Auto Europe	800-233-5555
Avis	800-331-1212
Budget	800-527-0700
Dollar	800-421-6868
Hertz	800-654-3131
National	800-328-4300
Payless	800-541-1566
Rent A Wreck	800-421-7253
Thrifty	800-331-9111

Table 11.7 Carnet Offices

Location	Phone Number	Fax Number
California (Los Angeles)	213-252-1280	213-384-0363
California (San Francisco)	415-956-3356	415-391-2716
Florida	305-562-6929	305-592-9537
Illinois	708-490-9696	708-885-8710
Maryland	301-561-0438	301-561-0974
Massachusetts	617-951-1411	617-951-1468
New York City (downtown)	212-747-1800	212-747-1948
New York City (midtown)	212-345-4480	212-944-0012
Texas	713-847-5693	713-847-0700

Table 11.8 Additive Printer Values

Printer Value	Print Value
+B	More yellow
–B	Less yellow
+G	More magenta
–G	Less magenta
+R	More cyan
–R	Less cyan
+BG	More red
+GR	More blue
+RB	More green

Table 11.9 Projection Screen Illumination

F-stop	Exposure Value	Footlamberts
f/1.5	7	4
f/2.2	8	8
f/2.5	8.5	10
f/2.8	8.75	12
f/3.2	9	16
f/4.8	10	32

Table 11.10 Script-Marking Colors and Symbols

Color or Symbol	Meaning
Red	Cast, speaking role
Yellow	Extras, non speaking
Green	Extras, atmosphere
Orange	Stunts
Blue	Special effects
Violet	Props
Pink	Animals, vehicles
Brown	Sound effects
Black box	Special equipment
Circle	Wardrobe
Asterisk	Makeup, hair
Underline	Other notes

Table 11.11 Production Strip Board Colors

Color	Meaning
Yellow	Day exterior
White	Day interior
Green	Night interior
Blue	Night exterior

Table 11.12 Sunrise and Sunset by Latitude

SUNRISE

Lat.	−55°	−50°	−45°	−40°	−35°	−30°	−20°	−10°	0°	+10°	+20°	+30°	+35°	+40°
	h m	h m	h m	h m	h m	h m	h m	h m	h m	h m	h m	h m	h m	h m
Jan. −2	3 23	3 52	4 15	4 33	4 47	5 00	5 22	5 41	5 58	6 16	6 34	6 55	7 07	7 21
2	3 27	3 56	4 18	4 36	4 50	5 03	5 25	5 43	6 00	6 17	6 36	6 56	7 08	7 22
6	3 33	4 01	4 22	4 39	4 54	5 06	5 27	5 45	6 02	6 19	6 37	6 57	7 09	7 22
10	3 39	4 06	4 27	4 43	4 57	5 09	5 30	5 48	6 04	6 20	6 37	6 57	7 09	7 22
14	3 46	4 12	4 32	4 48	5 01	5 13	5 33	5 50	6 05	6 21	6 38	6 57	7 08	7 20
18	3 53	4 18	4 37	4 52	5 05	5 16	5 35	5 52	6 07	6 22	6 38	6 56	7 07	7 19
22	4 01	4 24	4 42	4 57	5 09	5 20	5 38	5 54	6 08	6 22	6 38	6 55	7 05	7 17
26	4 10	4 31	4 48	5 02	5 13	5 23	5 40	5 55	6 09	6 23	6 37	6 53	7 03	7 14
30	4 18	4 38	4 54	5 07	5 17	5 27	5 43	5 57	6 10	6 23	6 36	6 52	7 00	7 10
Feb. 3	4 27	4 45	5 00	5 11	5 22	5 30	5 45	5 58	6 10	6 22	6 35	6 49	6 57	7 07
7	4 35	4 52	5 05	5 16	5 26	5 34	5 48	6 00	6 11	6 22	6 33	6 46	6 54	7 03
11	4 44	4 59	5 11	5 21	5 30	5 37	5 50	6 01	6 11	6 21	6 31	6 43	6 50	6 58
15	4 53	5 06	5 17	5 26	5 34	5 40	5 52	6 02	6 11	6 20	6 29	6 40	6 46	6 53
19	5 01	5 13	5 23	5 31	5 38	5 43	5 54	6 02	6 10	6 18	6 27	6 36	6 42	6 48
23	5 10	5 20	5 29	5 35	5 41	5 47	5 55	6 03	6 10	6 17	6 24	6 32	6 37	6 42
27	5 18	5 27	5 34	5 40	5 45	5 49	5 57	6 03	6 09	6 15	6 21	6 28	6 32	6 37
Mar. 3	5 27	5 34	5 40	5 45	5 49	5 52	5 58	6 04	6 09	6 13	6 18	6 24	6 27	6 31
7	5 35	5 41	5 45	5 49	5 52	5 55	6 00	6 04	6 08	6 11	6 15	6 19	6 22	6 24
11	5 43	5 47	5 50	5 53	5 56	5 58	6 01	6 04	6 07	6 09	6 12	6 15	6 16	6 18
15	5 51	5 54	5 56	5 57	5 59	6 00	6 02	6 04	6 06	6 07	6 09	6 10	6 11	6 12
19	5 59	6 00	6 01	6 02	6 02	6 03	6 04	6 04	6 05	6 05	6 05	6 05	6 05	6 05
23	6 07	6 06	6 06	6 06	6 05	6 05	6 05	6 04	6 03	6 03	6 02	6 00	6 00	5 59
27	6 15	6 13	6 11	6 10	6 09	6 08	6 06	6 04	6 02	6 00	5 58	5 56	5 54	5 52
31	6 22	6 19	6 16	6 14	6 12	6 10	6 07	6 04	6 01	5 58	5 55	5 51	5 48	5 46
Apr. 4	6 30	6 25	6 21	6 18	6 15	6 12	6 08	6 04	6 00	5 56	5 51	5 46	5 43	5 39

SUNSET

Lat.	−55°	−50°	−45°	−40°	−35°	−30°	−20°	−10°	0°	+10°	+20°	+30°	+35°	+40°
	h m	h m	h m	h m	h m	h m	h m	h m	h m	h m	h m	h m	h m	h m
Jan. −2	20 41	20 12	19 49	19 32	19 17	19 04	18 42	18 23	18 06	17 49	17 30	17 09	16 57	16 43
2	20 40	20 11	19 50	19 32	19 18	19 05	18 43	18 25	18 08	17 51	17 33	17 12	17 00	16 46
6	20 38	20 10	19 49	19 32	19 18	19 05	18 44	18 26	18 10	17 53	17 35	17 15	17 03	16 50
10	20 35	20 08	19 48	19 31	19 18	19 06	18 45	18 28	18 11	17 55	17 38	17 18	17 07	16 54
14	20 31	20 06	19 46	19 30	19 17	19 05	18 46	18 29	18 13	17 57	17 41	17 22	17 11	16 58
18	20 26	20 02	19 43	19 28	19 16	19 04	18 46	18 29	18 14	17 59	17 43	17 25	17 15	17 03
22	20 21	19 58	19 40	19 26	19 14	19 03	18 45	18 30	18 15	18 01	17 46	17 29	17 19	17 07
26	20 14	19 53	19 36	19 23	19 12	19 02	18 45	18 30	18 16	18 03	17 48	17 32	17 23	17 12
30	20 07	19 48	19 32	19 20	19 09	18 59	18 44	18 30	18 17	18 04	17 51	17 35	17 27	17 17
Feb. 3	20 00	19 42	19 27	19 16	19 06	18 57	18 42	18 29	18 17	18 06	17 53	17 39	17 31	17 21
7	19 52	19 35	19 22	19 11	19 02	18 54	18 40	18 29	18 18	18 07	17 55	17 42	17 35	17 26
11	19 43	19 28	19 16	19 07	18 58	18 51	18 39	18 28	18 18	18 08	17 57	17 46	17 39	17 31
15	19 34	19 21	19 10	19 02	18 54	18 48	18 36	18 27	18 18	18 09	17 59	17 49	17 43	17 36
19	19 25	19 13	19 04	18 56	18 50	18 44	18 34	18 25	18 17	18 09	18 01	17 52	17 46	17 40
23	19 15	19 05	18 57	18 51	18 45	18 40	18 31	18 24	18 17	18 10	18 03	17 55	17 50	17 45
27	19 06	18 57	18 50	18 45	18 40	18 36	18 28	18 22	18 16	18 10	18 04	17 58	17 54	17 49
Mar. 3	18 56	18 49	18 43	18 39	18 35	18 31	18 25	18 20	18 15	18 11	18 06	18 00	17 57	17 54
7	18 46	18 40	18 36	18 32	18 29	18 27	18 22	18 18	18 14	18 11	18 07	18 03	18 01	17 58
11	18 36	18 32	18 29	18 26	18 24	18 22	18 19	18 16	18 13	18 11	18 08	18 06	18 04	18 03
15	18 26	18 23	18 21	18 20	18 18	18 17	18 15	18 14	18 12	18 11	18 10	18 08	18 08	18 07
19	18 16	18 15	18 14	18 13	18 13	18 12	18 12	18 11	18 11	18 11	18 11	18 11	18 11	18 11
23	18 05	18 06	18 06	18 07	18 07	18 08	18 08	18 09	18 10	18 11	18 12	18 13	18 14	18 15
27	17 55	17 57	17 59	18 00	18 02	18 03	18 05	18 07	18 09	18 11	18 13	18 16	18 17	18 19
31	17 45	17 49	17 51	17 54	17 56	17 58	18 01	18 04	18 07	18 11	18 14	18 18	18 20	18 23
Apr. 4	17 35	17 40	17 44	17 47	17 50	17 53	17 58	18 02	18 06	18 10	18 15	18 20	18 24	18 27

SUNRISE

Lat.	+40°	+42°	+44°	+46°	+48°	+50°	+52°	+54°	+56°	+58°	+60°	+62°	+64°	+66°
	h m	h m	h m	h m	h m	h m	h m	h m	h m	h m	h m	h m	h m	h m
Jan. −2	7 21	7 28	7 34	7 42	7 50	7 59	8 08	8 19	8 32	8 46	9 03	9 25	9 52	10 32
2	7 22	7 28	7 35	7 42	7 50	7 59	8 08	8 19	8 31	8 45	9 02	9 22	9 49	10 26
6	7 22	7 28	7 35	7 42	7 49	7 58	8 07	8 17	8 29	8 43	8 59	9 18	9 43	10 18
10	7 22	7 27	7 34	7 41	7 48	7 56	8 05	8 15	8 26	8 39	8 55	9 13	9 36	10 07
14	7 20	7 26	7 32	7 39	7 46	7 54	8 02	8 12	8 22	8 35	8 49	9 07	9 28	9 56
18	7 19	7 24	7 30	7 36	7 43	7 50	7 58	8 07	8 18	8 29	8 43	8 59	9 19	9 44
22	7 17	7 22	7 27	7 33	7 39	7 46	7 54	8 03	8 12	8 23	8 36	8 50	9 08	9 31
26	7 14	7 19	7 24	7 29	7 35	7 42	7 49	7 57	8 06	8 16	8 27	8 41	8 57	9 17
30	7 10	7 15	7 20	7 25	7 30	7 37	7 43	7 51	7 59	8 08	8 19	8 31	8 46	9 03
Feb. 3	7 07	7 11	7 15	7 20	7 25	7 31	7 37	7 44	7 51	8 00	8 09	8 20	8 33	8 49
7	7 03	7 06	7 10	7 15	7 19	7 25	7 30	7 36	7 43	7 51	7 59	8 09	8 21	8 35
11	6 58	7 01	7 05	7 09	7 13	7 18	7 23	7 28	7 34	7 41	7 49	7 58	8 08	8 20
15	6 53	6 56	6 59	7 03	7 07	7 11	7 15	7 20	7 25	7 31	7 38	7 46	7 55	8 06
19	6 48	6 51	6 53	6 56	7 00	7 03	7 07	7 11	7 16	7 21	7 27	7 34	7 42	7 51
23	6 42	6 45	6 47	6 50	6 53	6 56	6 59	7 03	7 07	7 11	7 16	7 22	7 28	7 36
27	6 37	6 38	6 41	6 43	6 45	6 48	6 50	6 53	6 57	7 00	7 05	7 09	7 15	7 21
Mar. 3	6 31	6 32	6 34	6 36	6 37	6 39	6 42	6 44	6 47	6 50	6 53	6 57	7 01	7 06
7	6 24	6 26	6 27	6 28	6 30	6 31	6 33	6 34	6 36	6 39	6 41	6 44	6 47	6 50
11	6 18	6 19	6 20	6 21	6 22	6 23	6 24	6 25	6 26	6 28	6 29	6 31	6 33	6 35
15	6 12	6 12	6 13	6 13	6 13	6 14	6 14	6 15	6 16	6 16	6 17	6 18	6 19	6 20
19	6 05	6 05	6 05	6 05	6 05	6 05	6 05	6 05	6 05	6 05	6 05	6 05	6 05	6 05
23	5 59	5 58	5 58	5 58	5 57	5 57	5 56	5 55	5 55	5 54	5 53	5 52	5 51	5 49
27	5 52	5 52	5 51	5 50	5 49	5 48	5 47	5 45	5 44	5 42	5 41	5 39	5 36	5 34
31	5 46	5 45	5 43	5 42	5 41	5 39	5 37	5 36	5 34	5 31	5 29	5 26	5 22	5 18
Apr. 4	5 39	5 38	5 36	5 35	5 33	5 31	5 28	5 26	5 23	5 20	5 17	5 13	5 08	5 03

SUNSET

	h m	h m	h m	h m	h m	h m	h m	h m	h m	h m	h m	h m	h m	h m
Jan. −2	16 43	16 37	16 30	16 23	16 15	16 06	15 56	15 45	15 33	15 18	15 01	14 40	14 13	13 32
2	16 46	16 40	16 33	16 26	16 18	16 10	16 00	15 50	15 37	15 23	15 07	14 46	14 20	13 42
6	16 50	16 44	16 37	16 30	16 23	16 14	16 05	15 55	15 43	15 29	15 13	14 54	14 29	13 55
10	16 54	16 48	16 42	16 35	16 28	16 20	16 11	16 01	15 49	15 36	15 21	15 03	14 39	14 08
14	16 58	16 52	16 46	16 40	16 33	16 25	16 17	16 07	15 56	15 44	15 30	15 12	14 51	14 23
18	17 03	16 57	16 51	16 45	16 39	16 31	16 23	16 14	16 04	15 52	15 39	15 23	15 03	14 38
22	17 07	17 02	16 57	16 51	16 44	16 37	16 30	16 21	16 12	16 01	15 48	15 34	15 16	14 53
26	17 12	17 07	17 02	16 56	16 51	16 44	16 37	16 29	16 20	16 10	15 59	15 45	15 29	15 09
30	17 17	17 12	17 07	17 02	16 57	16 51	16 44	16 37	16 29	16 19	16 09	15 57	15 42	15 24
Feb. 3	17 21	17 17	17 13	17 08	17 03	16 58	16 52	16 45	16 37	16 29	16 19	16 08	15 55	15 40
7	17 26	17 23	17 18	17 14	17 10	17 05	16 59	16 53	16 46	16 39	16 30	16 20	16 08	15 55
11	17 31	17 28	17 24	17 20	17 16	17 11	17 06	17 01	16 55	16 48	16 41	16 32	16 22	16 09
15	17 36	17 33	17 30	17 26	17 22	17 18	17 14	17 09	17 04	16 58	16 51	16 43	16 34	16 24
19	17 40	17 38	17 35	17 32	17 29	17 25	17 21	17 17	17 12	17 07	17 02	16 55	16 47	16 38
23	17 45	17 43	17 40	17 38	17 35	17 32	17 29	17 25	17 21	17 17	17 12	17 06	17 00	16 52
27	17 49	17 48	17 46	17 43	17 41	17 39	17 36	17 33	17 30	17 26	17 22	17 18	17 12	17 06
Mar. 3	17 54	17 52	17 51	17 49	17 47	17 45	17 43	17 41	17 38	17 35	17 32	17 29	17 25	17 20
7	17 58	17 57	17 56	17 55	17 53	17 52	17 50	17 49	17 47	17 45	17 42	17 40	17 37	17 33
11	18 03	18 02	18 01	18 00	17 59	17 58	17 57	17 56	17 55	17 54	17 52	17 51	17 49	17 47
15	18 07	18 06	18 06	18 06	18 05	18 05	18 04	18 04	18 03	18 03	18 02	18 01	18 01	18 00
19	18 11	18 11	18 11	18 11	18 11	18 11	18 11	18 11	18 12	18 12	18 12	18 12	18 12	18 13
23	18 15	18 15	18 16	18 16	18 17	18 18	18 18	18 19	18 20	18 21	18 22	18 23	18 24	18 26
27	18 19	18 20	18 21	18 22	18 23	18 24	18 25	18 26	18 28	18 30	18 31	18 34	18 36	18 39
31	18 23	18 24	18 26	18 27	18 29	18 30	18 32	18 34	18 36	18 38	18 41	18 44	18 48	18 52
Apr. 4	18 27	18 29	18 30	18 32	18 34	18 36	18 39	18 41	18 44	18 47	18 51	18 55	19 00	19 05

SUNRISE

Lat.	−55°	−50°	−45°	−40°	−35°	−30°	−20°	−10°	0°	+10°	+20°	+30°	+35°	+40°
	h m	h m	h m	h m	h m	h m	h m	h m	h m	h m	h m	h m	h m	h m
Mar. 31	6 22	6 19	6 16	6 14	6 12	6 10	6 07	6 04	6 01	5 58	5 55	5 51	5 48	5 46
Apr. 4	6 30	6 25	6 21	6 18	6 15	6 12	6 08	6 04	6 00	5 56	5 51	5 46	5 43	5 39
8	6 38	6 31	6 26	6 22	6 18	6 15	6 09	6 04	5 59	5 53	5 48	5 41	5 37	5 33
12	6 45	6 38	6 31	6 26	6 21	6 17	6 10	6 04	5 57	5 51	5 44	5 37	5 32	5 27
16	6 53	6 44	6 36	6 30	6 24	6 20	6 11	6 04	5 56	5 49	5 41	5 32	5 27	5 21
20	7 01	6 50	6 41	6 34	6 28	6 22	6 12	6 04	5 56	5 47	5 38	5 28	5 22	5 15
24	7 08	6 56	6 46	6 38	6 31	6 24	6 14	6 04	5 55	5 45	5 35	5 24	5 17	5 09
28	7 16	7 02	6 51	6 42	6 34	6 27	6 15	6 04	5 54	5 44	5 33	5 20	5 13	5 04
May 2	7 23	7 08	6 56	6 46	6 37	6 29	6 16	6 05	5 54	5 42	5 30	5 16	5 08	4 59
6	7 30	7 14	7 01	6 50	6 40	6 32	6 18	6 05	5 53	5 41	5 28	5 13	5 04	4 54
10	7 38	7 20	7 05	6 54	6 43	6 35	6 19	6 06	5 53	5 40	5 26	5 10	5 01	4 50
14	7 45	7 25	7 10	6 57	6 47	6 37	6 21	6 06	5 53	5 39	5 24	5 07	4 57	4 46
18	7 51	7 31	7 14	7 01	6 50	6 40	6 22	6 07	5 53	5 38	5 23	5 05	4 54	4 42
22	7 58	7 36	7 19	7 04	6 52	6 42	6 24	6 08	5 53	5 38	5 22	5 03	4 52	4 39
26	8 04	7 40	7 22	7 08	6 55	6 44	6 25	6 09	5 53	5 38	5 21	5 01	4 50	4 36
30	8 09	7 45	7 26	7 11	6 58	6 47	6 27	6 10	5 54	5 38	5 20	5 00	4 48	4 34
June 3	8 14	7 49	7 29	7 14	7 00	6 49	6 29	6 11	5 54	5 38	5 20	4 59	4 47	4 32
7	8 18	7 52	7 32	7 16	7 02	6 51	6 30	6 12	5 55	5 38	5 20	4 58	4 46	4 31
11	8 22	7 55	7 35	7 18	7 04	6 52	6 31	6 13	5 56	5 39	5 20	4 58	4 45	4 31
15	8 24	7 57	7 37	7 20	7 06	6 54	6 33	6 14	5 57	5 39	5 20	4 58	4 45	4 30
19	8 26	7 59	7 38	7 21	7 07	6 55	6 34	6 15	5 58	5 40	5 21	4 59	4 46	4 31
23	8 27	8 00	7 39	7 22	7 08	6 56	6 34	6 16	5 58	5 41	5 22	5 00	4 47	4 32
27	8 27	8 00	7 39	7 23	7 09	6 56	6 35	6 17	5 59	5 42	5 23	5 01	4 48	4 33
July 1	8 26	8 00	7 39	7 23	7 09	6 56	6 36	6 17	6 00	5 43	5 24	5 02	4 50	4 35
5	8 24	7 58	7 38	7 22	7 08	6 56	6 36	6 18	6 01	5 44	5 25	5 04	4 51	4 37

SUNSET

Lat.	−55°	−50°	−45°	−40°	−35°	−30°	−20°	−10°	0°	+10°	+20°	+30°	+35°	+40°
	h m	h m	h m	h m	h m	h m	h m	h m	h m	h m	h m	h m	h m	h m
Mar. 31	17 45	17 49	17 51	17 54	17 56	17 58	18 01	18 04	18 07	18 11	18 14	18 18	18 20	18 23
Apr. 4	17 35	17 40	17 44	17 47	17 50	17 53	17 58	18 02	18 06	18 10	18 15	18 20	18 24	18 27
8	17 25	17 32	17 37	17 41	17 45	17 48	17 55	18 00	18 05	18 10	18 16	18 23	18 27	18 31
12	17 15	17 23	17 30	17 35	17 40	17 44	17 51	17 58	18 04	18 10	18 17	18 25	18 30	18 35
16	17 06	17 15	17 23	17 29	17 35	17 40	17 48	17 56	18 03	18 11	18 19	18 28	18 33	18 39
20	16 56	17 07	17 16	17 23	17 30	17 35	17 45	17 54	18 02	18 11	18 20	18 30	18 36	18 43
24	16 47	17 00	17 10	17 18	17 25	17 31	17 42	17 52	18 01	18 11	18 21	18 33	18 40	18 47
28	16 38	16 52	17 03	17 13	17 21	17 28	17 40	17 51	18 01	18 11	18 22	18 35	18 43	18 51
May 2	16 30	16 45	16 58	17 08	17 16	17 24	17 37	17 49	18 00	18 12	18 24	18 38	18 46	18 56
6	16 22	16 39	16 52	17 03	17 12	17 21	17 35	17 48	18 00	18 12	18 25	18 41	18 49	19 00
10	16 14	16 33	16 47	16 59	17 09	17 18	17 33	17 47	18 00	18 13	18 27	18 43	18 53	19 03
14	16 07	16 27	16 42	16 55	17 06	17 15	17 32	17 46	18 00	18 14	18 28	18 46	18 56	19 07
18	16 01	16 22	16 38	16 51	17 03	17 13	17 30	17 46	18 00	18 14	18 30	18 48	18 59	19 11
22	15 55	16 17	16 34	16 48	17 00	17 11	17 29	17 45	18 00	18 15	18 32	18 51	19 02	19 15
26	15 50	16 13	16 31	16 46	16 58	17 09	17 28	17 45	18 01	18 16	18 33	18 53	19 05	19 18
30	15 45	16 10	16 29	16 44	16 57	17 08	17 28	17 45	18 01	18 17	18 35	18 55	19 07	19 21
June 3	15 42	16 07	16 26	16 42	16 56	17 07	17 28	17 45	18 02	18 18	18 36	18 57	19 10	19 24
7	15 39	16 05	16 25	16 41	16 55	17 07	17 28	17 46	18 02	18 20	18 38	18 59	19 12	19 27
11	15 37	16 04	16 24	16 41	16 55	17 07	17 28	17 46	18 03	18 21	18 39	19 01	19 14	19 29
15	15 36	16 03	16 24	16 41	16 55	17 07	17 28	17 47	18 04	18 22	18 41	19 03	19 15	19 30
19	15 36	16 03	16 24	16 41	16 55	17 08	17 29	17 47	18 05	18 23	18 42	19 04	19 17	19 32
23	15 37	16 04	16 25	16 42	16 56	17 09	17 30	17 48	18 06	18 23	18 42	19 04	19 18	19 33
27	15 39	16 06	16 27	16 43	16 57	17 10	17 31	17 49	18 07	18 24	18 43	19 05	19 18	19 33
July 1	15 42	16 08	16 29	16 45	16 59	17 11	17 32	17 50	18 07	18 25	18 43	19 05	19 18	19 33
5	15 45	16 11	16 31	16 47	17 01	17 13	17 33	17 51	18 08	18 25	18 44	19 05	19 17	19 32

SUNRISE

Lat.		+40°	+42°	+44°	+46°	+48°	+50°	+52°	+54°	+56°	+58°	+60°	+62°	+64°	+66°
		h m	h m	h m	h m	h m	h m	h m	h m	h m	h m	h m	h m	h m	h m
Mar.	31	5 46	5 45	5 43	5 42	5 41	5 39	5 37	5 36	5 34	5 31	5 29	5 26	5 22	5 18
Apr.	4	5 39	5 38	5 36	5 35	5 33	5 31	5 28	5 26	5 23	5 20	5 17	5 13	5 08	5 03
	8	5 33	5 31	5 29	5 27	5 25	5 22	5 19	5 16	5 13	5 09	5 05	5 00	4 54	4 47
	12	5 27	5 25	5 22	5 20	5 17	5 14	5 10	5 06	5 02	4 58	4 53	4 47	4 40	4 32
	16	5 21	5 18	5 15	5 12	5 09	5 05	5 01	4 57	4 52	4 47	4 41	4 34	4 26	4 16
	20	5 15	5 12	5 09	5 05	5 01	4 57	4 53	4 48	4 42	4 36	4 29	4 21	4 12	4 01
	24	5 09	5 06	5 02	4 58	4 54	4 50	4 44	4 39	4 33	4 26	4 18	4 08	3 58	3 45
	28	5 04	5 00	4 56	4 52	4 47	4 42	4 36	4 30	4 23	4 15	4 06	3 56	3 44	3 29
May	2	4 59	4 55	4 50	4 46	4 40	4 35	4 29	4 22	4 14	4 05	3 55	3 44	3 30	3 14
	6	4 54	4 50	4 45	4 40	4 34	4 28	4 21	4 14	4 05	3 56	3 45	3 32	3 17	2 58
	10	4 50	4 45	4 40	4 34	4 28	4 22	4 14	4 06	3 57	3 47	3 35	3 20	3 03	2 42
	14	4 46	4 41	4 35	4 29	4 23	4 16	4 08	3 59	3 49	3 38	3 25	3 09	2 50	2 26
	18	4 42	4 37	4 31	4 25	4 18	4 10	4 02	3 52	3 42	3 30	3 16	2 59	2 38	2 10
	22	4 39	4 33	4 27	4 21	4 13	4 05	3 56	3 47	3 35	3 22	3 07	2 49	2 25	1 54
	26	4 36	4 30	4 24	4 17	4 09	4 01	3 52	3 41	3 29	3 16	2 59	2 39	2 14	1 38
	30	4 34	4 28	4 21	4 14	4 06	3 57	3 48	3 37	3 24	3 10	2 52	2 31	2 03	1 21
June	3	4 32	4 26	4 19	4 12	4 04	3 54	3 44	3 33	3 20	3 05	2 46	2 24	1 53	1 04
	7	4 31	4 25	4 18	4 10	4 02	3 52	3 42	3 30	3 17	3 01	2 42	2 18	1 45	0 45
	11	4 31	4 24	4 17	4 09	4 00	3 51	3 40	3 28	3 14	2 58	2 38	2 13	1 38	0 21
	15	4 30	4 24	4 16	4 08	4 00	3 50	3 39	3 27	3 13	2 56	2 36	2 10	1 33	** **
	19	4 31	4 24	4 17	4 09	4 00	3 50	3 39	3 27	3 13	2 56	2 35	2 09	1 31	** **
	23	4 32	4 25	4 18	4 10	4 01	3 51	3 40	3 28	3 14	2 57	2 36	2 10	1 31	** **
	27	4 33	4 26	4 19	4 11	4 02	3 53	3 42	3 29	3 15	2 59	2 38	2 12	1 35	** **
July	1	4 35	4 28	4 21	4 13	4 04	3 55	3 44	3 32	3 18	3 02	2 42	2 17	1 41	0 18
	5	4 37	4 30	4 23	4 15	4 07	3 58	3 47	3 35	3 22	3 06	2 47	2 22	1 49	0 46

SUNSET

		h m	h m	h m	h m	h m	h m	h m	h m	h m	h m	h m	h m	h m	h m
Mar.	31	18 23	18 24	18 26	18 27	18 29	18 30	18 32	18 34	18 36	18 38	18 41	18 44	18 48	18 52
Apr.	4	18 27	18 29	18 30	18 32	18 34	18 36	18 39	18 41	18 44	18 47	18 51	18 55	19 00	19 05
	8	18 31	18 33	18 35	18 38	18 40	18 43	18 46	18 49	18 52	18 56	19 01	19 06	19 12	19 18
	12	18 35	18 38	18 40	18 43	18 46	18 49	18 52	18 56	19 01	19 05	19 11	19 17	19 24	19 32
	16	18 39	18 42	18 45	18 48	18 52	18 55	18 59	19 04	19 09	19 14	19 20	19 28	19 36	19 46
	20	18 43	18 46	18 50	18 53	18 57	19 01	19 06	19 11	19 17	19 23	19 30	19 39	19 48	19 59
	24	18 47	18 51	18 55	18 59	19 03	19 08	19 13	19 19	19 25	19 32	19 40	19 50	20 01	20 14
	28	18 51	18 55	18 59	19 04	19 09	19 14	19 20	19 26	19 33	19 41	19 50	20 01	20 13	20 28
May	2	18 56	19 00	19 04	19 09	19 14	19 20	19 26	19 33	19 41	19 50	20 00	20 12	20 26	20 43
	6	19 00	19 04	19 09	19 14	19 20	19 26	19 33	19 41	19 49	19 59	20 10	20 23	20 39	20 58
	10	19 03	19 08	19 14	19 19	19 25	19 32	19 40	19 48	19 57	20 08	20 20	20 34	20 52	21 14
	14	19 07	19 13	19 18	19 24	19 31	19 38	19 46	19 55	20 05	20 16	20 29	20 45	21 05	21 29
	18	19 11	19 17	19 22	19 29	19 36	19 43	19 52	20 01	20 12	20 24	20 39	20 56	21 17	21 46
	22	19 15	19 20	19 27	19 33	19 41	19 49	19 58	20 08	20 19	20 32	20 48	21 06	21 30	22 03
	26	19 18	19 24	19 31	19 38	19 45	19 54	20 03	20 14	20 26	20 40	20 56	21 16	21 42	22 20
	30	19 21	19 27	19 34	19 41	19 49	19 58	20 08	20 19	20 32	20 46	21 04	21 26	21 54	22 38
June	3	19 24	19 30	19 37	19 45	19 53	20 02	20 12	20 24	20 37	20 52	21 11	21 34	22 05	22 57
	7	19 27	19 33	19 40	19 48	19 56	20 06	20 16	20 28	20 42	20 58	21 17	21 41	22 15	23 18
	11	19 29	19 35	19 43	19 51	19 59	20 09	20 19	20 31	20 45	21 02	21 22	21 47	22 23	23 48
	15	19 30	19 37	19 45	19 53	20 01	20 11	20 22	20 34	20 48	21 05	21 25	21 51	22 29	** **
	19	19 32	19 39	19 46	19 54	20 03	20 12	20 23	20 36	20 50	21 07	21 27	21 54	22 32	** **
	23	19 33	19 39	19 47	19 55	20 03	20 13	20 24	20 36	20 51	21 07	21 28	21 54	22 32	** **
	27	19 33	19 40	19 47	19 55	20 04	20 13	20 24	20 36	20 50	21 07	21 27	21 53	22 30	** **
July	1	19 33	19 39	19 47	19 54	20 03	20 12	20 23	20 35	20 49	21 05	21 25	21 50	22 25	23 41
	5	19 32	19 39	19 46	19 53	20 02	20 11	20 21	20 33	20 47	21 02	21 21	21 45	22 18	23 18

(** **) indicates Sun continuously above horizon.

SUNRISE

Lat.	−55°	−50°	−45°	−40°	−35°	−30°	−20°	−10°	0°	+10°	+20°	+30°	+35°	+40°
	h m	h m	h m	h m	h m	h m	h m	h m	h m	h m	h m	h m	h m	h m
July 1	8 26	8 00	7 39	7 23	7 09	6 56	6 36	6 17	6 00	5 43	5 24	5 02	4 50	4 35
5	8 24	7 58	7 38	7 22	7 08	6 56	6 36	6 18	6 01	5 44	5 25	5 04	4 51	4 37
9	8 21	7 56	7 37	7 21	7 08	6 56	6 36	6 18	6 02	5 45	5 27	5 06	4 54	4 39
13	8 18	7 53	7 35	7 19	7 06	6 55	6 35	6 18	6 02	5 46	5 28	5 08	4 56	4 42
17	8 13	7 50	7 32	7 17	7 05	6 54	6 35	6 18	6 03	5 47	5 30	5 10	4 58	4 45
21	8 08	7 46	7 29	7 14	7 02	6 52	6 34	6 18	6 03	5 48	5 31	5 12	5 01	4 48
25	8 02	7 41	7 25	7 11	7 00	6 50	6 33	6 17	6 03	5 48	5 33	5 15	5 04	4 52
29	7 55	7 36	7 20	7 08	6 57	6 47	6 31	6 17	6 03	5 49	5 34	5 17	5 07	4 55
Aug. 2	7 48	7 30	7 16	7 04	6 54	6 45	6 29	6 16	6 03	5 50	5 36	5 19	5 10	4 59
6	7 41	7 24	7 10	6 59	6 50	6 42	6 27	6 14	6 02	5 50	5 37	5 22	5 13	5 03
10	7 32	7 17	7 05	6 55	6 46	6 38	6 25	6 13	6 02	5 51	5 38	5 24	5 16	5 07
14	7 24	7 10	6 59	6 50	6 42	6 35	6 22	6 12	6 01	5 51	5 40	5 27	5 19	5 10
18	7 15	7 03	6 53	6 44	6 37	6 31	6 20	6 10	6 00	5 51	5 41	5 29	5 22	5 14
22	7 06	6 55	6 46	6 39	6 32	6 27	6 17	6 08	6 00	5 51	5 42	5 31	5 25	5 18
26	6 56	6 47	6 39	6 33	6 27	6 22	6 14	6 06	5 58	5 51	5 43	5 34	5 28	5 22
30	6 47	6 39	6 32	6 27	6 22	6 18	6 10	6 04	5 57	5 51	5 44	5 36	5 31	5 26
Sept. 3	6 37	6 30	6 25	6 21	6 17	6 13	6 07	6 01	5 56	5 51	5 45	5 38	5 34	5 29
7	6 27	6 22	6 18	6 14	6 11	6 08	6 03	5 59	5 55	5 50	5 46	5 40	5 37	5 33
11	6 17	6 13	6 10	6 08	6 05	6 03	6 00	5 57	5 53	5 50	5 46	5 42	5 40	5 37
15	6 07	6 05	6 03	6 01	6 00	5 58	5 56	5 54	5 52	5 50	5 47	5 44	5 43	5 41
19	5 56	5 56	5 55	5 54	5 54	5 53	5 52	5 52	5 51	5 49	5 48	5 47	5 46	5 45
23	5 46	5 47	5 47	5 48	5 48	5 48	5 49	5 49	5 49	5 49	5 49	5 49	5 49	5 48
27	5 36	5 38	5 40	5 41	5 42	5 43	5 45	5 47	5 48	5 49	5 50	5 51	5 52	5 52
Oct. 1	5 26	5 29	5 32	5 35	5 37	5 39	5 42	5 44	5 46	5 49	5 51	5 53	5 55	5 56
5	5 15	5 21	5 25	5 28	5 31	5 34	5 38	5 42	5 45	5 48	5 52	5 56	5 58	6 00

SUNSET

Lat.	−55°	−50°	−45°	−40°	−35°	−30°	−20°	−10°	0°	+10°	+20°	+30°	+35°	+40°
	h m	h m	h m	h m	h m	h m	h m	h m	h m	h m	h m	h m	h m	h m
July 1	15 42	16 08	16 29	16 45	16 59	17 11	17 32	17 50	18 07	18 25	18 43	19 05	19 18	19 33
5	15 45	16 11	16 31	16 47	17 01	17 13	17 33	17 51	18 08	18 25	18 44	19 05	19 17	19 32
9	15 49	16 14	16 34	16 50	17 03	17 15	17 35	17 52	18 09	18 25	18 43	19 04	19 17	19 31
13	15 54	16 18	16 37	16 52	17 05	17 17	17 36	17 53	18 09	18 26	18 43	19 03	19 15	19 29
17	16 00	16 23	16 41	16 55	17 08	17 19	17 38	17 54	18 10	18 25	18 42	19 02	19 13	19 27
21	16 05	16 27	16 45	16 59	17 11	17 21	17 39	17 55	18 10	18 25	18 41	19 00	19 11	19 24
25	16 12	16 32	16 49	17 02	17 13	17 23	17 41	17 56	18 10	18 24	18 40	18 58	19 08	19 21
29	16 18	16 38	16 53	17 05	17 16	17 26	17 42	17 56	18 10	18 24	18 38	18 55	19 05	19 17
Aug. 2	16 25	16 43	16 57	17 09	17 19	17 28	17 43	17 57	18 10	18 23	18 37	18 53	19 02	19 13
6	16 32	16 48	17 02	17 13	17 22	17 30	17 45	17 57	18 09	18 21	18 34	18 49	18 58	19 08
10	16 39	16 54	17 06	17 16	17 25	17 33	17 46	17 58	18 09	18 20	18 32	18 46	18 54	19 03
14	16 46	17 00	17 11	17 20	17 28	17 35	17 47	17 58	18 08	18 18	18 29	18 42	18 50	18 58
18	16 53	17 06	17 16	17 24	17 31	17 37	17 48	17 58	18 07	18 17	18 27	18 38	18 45	18 53
22	17 01	17 11	17 20	17 28	17 34	17 39	17 49	17 58	18 06	18 15	18 24	18 34	18 40	18 47
26	17 08	17 17	17 25	17 31	17 37	17 42	17 50	17 58	18 05	18 12	18 20	18 30	18 35	18 41
30	17 15	17 23	17 30	17 35	17 40	17 44	17 51	17 58	18 04	18 10	18 17	18 25	18 30	18 35
Sept. 3	17 23	17 29	17 34	17 39	17 43	17 46	17 52	17 57	18 03	18 08	18 14	18 20	18 24	18 29
7	17 30	17 35	17 39	17 42	17 45	17 48	17 53	17 57	18 01	18 05	18 10	18 15	18 19	18 22
11	17 37	17 41	17 44	17 46	17 48	17 50	17 54	17 57	18 00	18 03	18 06	18 10	18 13	18 16
15	17 45	17 47	17 48	17 50	17 51	17 52	17 55	17 56	17 58	18 00	18 03	18 05	18 07	18 09
19	17 52	17 53	17 53	17 54	17 54	17 55	17 55	17 56	17 57	17 58	17 59	18 00	18 01	18 02
23	18 00	17 59	17 58	17 58	17 57	17 57	17 56	17 56	17 56	17 55	17 55	17 55	17 56	17 56
27	18 07	18 05	18 03	18 01	18 00	17 59	17 57	17 56	17 54	17 53	17 52	17 51	17 50	17 49
Oct. 1	18 15	18 11	18 08	18 05	18 03	18 01	17 58	17 55	17 53	17 51	17 48	17 46	17 44	17 43
5	18 23	18 17	18 13	18 09	18 06	18 04	17 59	17 55	17 52	17 48	17 45	17 41	17 39	17 36

SUNRISE

Lat.	+40°	+42°	+44°	+46°	+48°	+50°	+52°	+54°	+56°	+58°	+60°	+62°	+64°	+66°
	h m	h m	h m	h m	h m	h m	h m	h m	h m	h m	h m	h m	h m	h m
July 1	4 35	4 28	4 21	4 13	4 04	3 55	3 44	3 32	3 18	3 02	2 42	2 17	1 41	0 18
5	4 37	4 30	4 23	4 15	4 07	3 58	3 47	3 35	3 22	3 06	2 47	2 22	1 49	0 46
9	4 39	4 33	4 26	4 18	4 10	4 01	3 51	3 40	3 26	3 11	2 53	2 30	1 59	1 07
13	4 42	4 36	4 29	4 22	4 14	4 05	3 55	3 44	3 32	3 17	3 00	2 38	2 09	1 26
17	4 45	4 39	4 33	4 26	4 18	4 10	4 00	3 50	3 38	3 24	3 07	2 47	2 21	1 44
21	4 48	4 43	4 36	4 30	4 22	4 14	4 05	3 55	3 44	3 31	3 15	2 57	2 33	2 01
25	4 52	4 46	4 40	4 34	4 27	4 19	4 11	4 02	3 51	3 39	3 24	3 07	2 46	2 17
29	4 55	4 50	4 45	4 39	4 32	4 25	4 17	4 08	3 58	3 47	3 33	3 18	2 58	2 33
Aug. 2	4 59	4 54	4 49	4 43	4 37	4 30	4 23	4 15	4 05	3 55	3 43	3 28	3 11	2 49
6	5 03	4 58	4 53	4 48	4 42	4 36	4 29	4 22	4 13	4 03	3 52	3 39	3 23	3 04
10	5 07	5 02	4 58	4 53	4 48	4 42	4 36	4 29	4 21	4 12	4 02	3 50	3 36	3 19
14	5 10	5 07	5 02	4 58	4 53	4 48	4 42	4 36	4 29	4 21	4 11	4 01	3 48	3 33
18	5 14	5 11	5 07	5 03	4 59	4 54	4 49	4 43	4 36	4 29	4 21	4 12	4 01	3 48
22	5 18	5 15	5 12	5 08	5 04	5 00	4 55	4 50	4 44	4 38	4 31	4 22	4 13	4 01
26	5 22	5 19	5 16	5 13	5 10	5 06	5 02	4 57	4 52	4 47	4 40	4 33	4 25	4 15
30	5 26	5 23	5 21	5 18	5 15	5 12	5 08	5 04	5 00	4 55	4 50	4 44	4 37	4 28
Sept. 3	5 29	5 27	5 25	5 23	5 20	5 18	5 15	5 11	5 08	5 04	4 59	4 54	4 48	4 41
7	5 33	5 32	5 30	5 28	5 26	5 24	5 21	5 19	5 16	5 12	5 09	5 05	5 00	4 54
11	5 37	5 36	5 34	5 33	5 31	5 30	5 28	5 26	5 23	5 21	5 18	5 15	5 11	5 07
15	5 41	5 40	5 39	5 38	5 37	5 36	5 34	5 33	5 31	5 29	5 28	5 25	5 23	5 20
19	5 45	5 44	5 43	5 43	5 42	5 42	5 41	5 40	5 39	5 38	5 37	5 36	5 34	5 32
23	5 48	5 48	5 48	5 48	5 48	5 48	5 47	5 47	5 47	5 47	5 46	5 46	5 45	5 45
27	5 52	5 52	5 53	5 53	5 53	5 54	5 54	5 54	5 55	5 55	5 56	5 56	5 57	5 58
Oct. 1	5 56	5 57	5 57	5 58	5 59	6 00	6 01	6 02	6 03	6 04	6 05	6 07	6 08	6 10
5	6 00	6 01	6 02	6 03	6 05	6 06	6 07	6 09	6 11	6 13	6 15	6 17	6 20	6 23

SUNSET

Lat.	+40°	+42°	+44°	+46°	+48°	+50°	+52°	+54°	+56°	+58°	+60°	+62°	+64°	+66°
	h m	h m	h m	h m	h m	h m	h m	h m	h m	h m	h m	h m	h m	h m
July 1	19 33	19 39	19 47	19 54	20 03	20 12	20 23	20 35	20 49	21 05	21 25	21 50	22 25	23 41
5	19 32	19 39	19 46	19 53	20 02	20 11	20 21	20 33	20 47	21 02	21 21	21 45	22 18	23 18
9	19 31	19 37	19 44	19 51	20 00	20 09	20 19	20 30	20 43	20 58	21 17	21 39	22 10	22 59
13	19 29	19 35	19 42	19 49	19 57	20 06	20 15	20 26	20 39	20 53	21 11	21 32	22 00	22 42
17	19 27	19 33	19 39	19 46	19 54	20 02	20 11	20 22	20 34	20 47	21 04	21 23	21 49	22 25
21	19 24	19 30	19 36	19 42	19 50	19 58	20 06	20 16	20 28	20 41	20 56	21 14	21 37	22 09
25	19 21	19 26	19 32	19 38	19 45	19 53	20 01	20 10	20 21	20 33	20 47	21 04	21 25	21 52
29	19 17	19 22	19 28	19 33	19 40	19 47	19 55	20 04	20 14	20 25	20 38	20 53	21 12	21 36
Aug. 2	19 13	19 18	19 23	19 28	19 34	19 41	19 48	19 56	20 06	20 16	20 28	20 42	20 59	21 21
6	19 08	19 13	19 18	19 23	19 28	19 35	19 41	19 49	19 57	20 07	20 18	20 31	20 46	21 05
10	19 03	19 08	19 12	19 17	19 22	19 28	19 34	19 41	19 48	19 57	20 07	20 19	20 32	20 49
14	18 58	19 02	19 06	19 10	19 15	19 20	19 26	19 32	19 39	19 47	19 56	20 06	20 19	20 33
18	18 53	18 56	19 00	19 04	19 08	19 13	19 18	19 24	19 30	19 37	19 45	19 54	20 05	20 18
22	18 47	18 50	18 53	18 57	19 01	19 05	19 09	19 14	19 20	19 26	19 33	19 41	19 51	20 02
26	18 41	18 44	18 47	18 50	18 53	18 57	19 01	19 05	19 10	19 15	19 22	19 29	19 37	19 46
30	18 35	18 37	18 40	18 42	18 45	18 48	18 52	18 56	19 00	19 04	19 10	19 16	19 23	19 31
Sept. 3	18 29	18 31	18 33	18 35	18 37	18 40	18 43	18 46	18 49	18 53	18 58	19 03	19 09	19 15
7	18 22	18 24	18 25	18 27	18 29	18 31	18 34	18 36	18 39	18 42	18 46	18 50	18 54	19 00
11	18 16	18 17	18 18	18 19	18 21	18 23	18 24	18 26	18 28	18 31	18 34	18 37	18 40	18 44
15	18 09	18 10	18 11	18 12	18 13	18 14	18 15	18 16	18 18	18 20	18 21	18 24	18 26	18 29
19	18 02	18 03	18 03	18 04	18 04	18 05	18 06	18 06	18 07	18 08	18 09	18 10	18 12	18 13
23	17 56	17 56	17 56	17 56	17 56	17 56	17 56	17 56	17 57	17 57	17 57	17 57	17 58	17 58
27	17 49	17 49	17 48	17 48	17 48	17 47	17 47	17 47	17 46	17 45	17 45	17 44	17 44	17 43
Oct. 1	17 43	17 42	17 41	17 40	17 40	17 39	17 38	17 37	17 35	17 34	17 33	17 31	17 29	17 27
5	17 36	17 35	17 34	17 33	17 31	17 30	17 28	17 27	17 25	17 23	17 21	17 18	17 15	17 12

SUNRISE

Lat.	−55°	−50°	−45°	−40°	−35°	−30°	−20°	−10°	0°	+10°	+20°	+30°	+35°	+40°
	h m	h m	h m	h m	h m	h m	h m	h m	h m	h m	h m	h m	h m	h m
Oct. 1	5 26	5 29	5 32	5 35	5 37	5 39	5 42	5 44	5 46	5 49	5 51	5 53	5 55	5 56
5	5 15	5 21	5 25	5 28	5 31	5 34	5 38	5 42	5 45	5 48	5 52	5 56	5 58	6 00
9	5 05	5 12	5 17	5 22	5 26	5 29	5 35	5 39	5 44	5 48	5 53	5 58	6 01	6 04
13	4 55	5 04	5 10	5 16	5 20	5 24	5 31	5 37	5 43	5 48	5 54	6 00	6 04	6 08
17	4 46	4 55	5 03	5 10	5 15	5 20	5 28	5 35	5 42	5 49	5 55	6 03	6 07	6 12
21	4 36	4 47	4 56	5 04	5 10	5 16	5 25	5 34	5 41	5 49	5 57	6 06	6 11	6 17
25	4 27	4 39	4 50	4 58	5 05	5 12	5 23	5 32	5 41	5 49	5 58	6 09	6 14	6 21
29	4 18	4 32	4 43	4 53	5 01	5 08	5 20	5 31	5 40	5 50	6 00	6 12	6 18	6 26
Nov. 2	4 09	4 25	4 38	4 48	4 57	5 05	5 18	5 29	5 40	5 51	6 02	6 15	6 22	6 30
6	4 01	4 18	4 32	4 43	4 53	5 02	5 16	5 29	5 40	5 52	6 04	6 18	6 26	6 35
10	3 53	4 12	4 27	4 39	4 50	4 59	5 14	5 28	5 40	5 53	6 06	6 21	6 29	6 39
14	3 45	4 06	4 22	4 36	4 47	4 56	5 13	5 28	5 41	5 54	6 08	6 24	6 33	6 44
18	3 39	4 01	4 18	4 32	4 44	4 55	5 12	5 27	5 42	5 56	6 11	6 27	6 37	6 48
22	3 33	3 56	4 15	4 30	4 42	4 53	5 12	5 28	5 43	5 57	6 13	6 31	6 41	6 53
26	3 27	3 52	4 12	4 27	4 41	4 52	5 11	5 28	5 44	5 59	6 15	6 34	6 45	6 57
30	3 23	3 49	4 10	4 26	4 40	4 51	5 12	5 29	5 45	6 01	6 18	6 37	6 49	7 02
Dec. 4	3 19	3 47	4 08	4 25	4 39	4 51	5 12	5 30	5 47	6 03	6 21	6 41	6 52	7 05
8	3 17	3 46	4 07	4 24	4 39	4 52	5 13	5 31	5 48	6 05	6 23	6 44	6 55	7 09
12	3 16	3 45	4 07	4 25	4 40	4 52	5 14	5 33	5 50	6 07	6 25	6 46	6 58	7 12
16	3 15	3 45	4 08	4 26	4 41	4 54	5 16	5 34	5 52	6 09	6 28	6 49	7 01	7 15
20	3 16	3 46	4 09	4 27	4 42	4 55	5 17	5 36	5 54	6 11	6 30	6 51	7 04	7 18
24	3 18	3 48	4 11	4 29	4 44	4 57	5 19	5 38	5 56	6 13	6 32	6 53	7 05	7 20
28	3 22	3 51	4 14	4 32	4 47	5 00	5 21	5 40	5 58	6 15	6 34	6 55	7 07	7 21
32	3 26	3 55	4 17	4 35	4 49	5 02	5 24	5 43	6 00	6 17	6 35	6 56	7 08	7 22
36	3 31	3 59	4 21	4 38	4 53	5 05	5 26	5 45	6 02	6 18	6 36	6 57	7 09	7 22

SUNSET

	h m	h m	h m	h m	h m	h m	h m	h m	h m	h m	h m	h m	h m	h m
Oct. 1	18 15	18 11	18 08	18 05	18 03	18 01	17 58	17 55	17 53	17 51	17 48	17 46	17 44	17 43
5	18 23	18 17	18 13	18 09	18 06	18 04	17 59	17 55	17 52	17 48	17 45	17 41	17 39	17 36
9	18 30	18 24	18 18	18 13	18 09	18 06	18 00	17 55	17 51	17 46	17 41	17 36	17 33	17 30
13	18 38	18 30	18 23	18 18	18 13	18 09	18 01	17 55	17 50	17 44	17 38	17 32	17 28	17 24
17	18 46	18 36	18 28	18 22	18 16	18 11	18 03	17 55	17 49	17 42	17 35	17 27	17 23	17 18
21	18 55	18 43	18 34	18 26	18 20	18 14	18 04	17 56	17 48	17 40	17 32	17 23	17 18	17 12
25	19 03	18 50	18 39	18 31	18 23	18 17	18 06	17 56	17 47	17 39	17 30	17 19	17 13	17 07
29	19 11	18 57	18 45	18 35	18 27	18 20	18 08	17 57	17 47	17 37	17 27	17 16	17 09	17 01
Nov. 2	19 20	19 03	18 50	18 40	18 31	18 23	18 10	17 58	17 47	17 36	17 25	17 12	17 05	16 57
6	19 28	19 10	18 56	18 45	18 35	18 26	18 12	17 59	17 47	17 36	17 23	17 09	17 01	16 52
10	19 37	19 17	19 02	18 49	18 39	18 29	18 14	18 00	17 47	17 35	17 22	17 07	16 58	16 48
14	19 45	19 24	19 07	18 54	18 43	18 33	18 16	18 01	17 48	17 35	17 21	17 04	16 55	16 45
18	19 53	19 30	19 13	18 59	18 47	18 36	18 18	18 03	17 49	17 35	17 20	17 03	16 53	16 42
22	20 01	19 37	19 18	19 03	18 51	18 40	18 21	18 05	17 50	17 35	17 19	17 01	16 51	16 39
26	20 08	19 43	19 23	19 08	18 54	18 43	18 23	18 07	17 51	17 35	17 19	17 00	16 49	16 37
30	20 15	19 49	19 28	19 12	18 58	18 46	18 26	18 09	17 52	17 36	17 19	17 00	16 49	16 36
Dec. 4	20 22	19 54	19 33	19 16	19 02	18 49	18 29	18 11	17 54	17 37	17 20	17 00	16 48	16 35
8	20 27	19 59	19 37	19 20	19 05	18 52	18 31	18 13	17 56	17 39	17 21	17 00	16 48	16 35
12	20 32	20 03	19 41	19 23	19 08	18 55	18 34	18 15	17 57	17 40	17 22	17 01	16 49	16 35
16	20 36	20 06	19 44	19 26	19 11	18 58	18 36	18 17	17 59	17 42	17 24	17 02	16 50	16 36
20	20 39	20 09	19 46	19 28	19 13	19 00	18 38	18 19	18 01	17 44	17 25	17 04	16 52	16 37
24	20 41	20 11	19 48	19 30	19 15	19 02	18 40	18 21	18 03	17 46	17 27	17 06	16 54	16 40
28	20 41	20 12	19 49	19 31	19 16	19 04	18 42	18 23	18 05	17 48	17 30	17 09	16 56	16 42
32	20 41	20 12	19 50	19 32	19 17	19 05	18 43	18 24	18 07	17 50	17 32	17 11	16 59	16 45
36	20 39	20 11	19 49	19 32	19 18	19 05	18 44	18 26	18 09	17 52	17 35	17 14	17 02	16 49

SUNRISE

Lat.	+40°	+42°	+44°	+46°	+48°	+50°	+52°	+54°	+56°	+58°	+60°	+62°	+64°	+66°
	h m	h m	h m	h m	h m	h m	h m	h m	h m	h m	h m	h m	h m	h m
Oct. 1	5 56	5 57	5 57	5 58	5 59	6 00	6 01	6 02	6 03	6 04	6 05	6 07	6 08	6 10
5	6 00	6 01	6 02	6 03	6 05	6 06	6 07	6 09	6 11	6 13	6 15	6 17	6 20	6 23
9	6 04	6 06	6 07	6 09	6 10	6 12	6 14	6 16	6 19	6 21	6 24	6 28	6 32	6 36
13	6 08	6 10	6 12	6 14	6 16	6 18	6 21	6 24	6 27	6 30	6 34	6 39	6 43	6 49
17	6 12	6 15	6 17	6 19	6 22	6 25	6 28	6 31	6 35	6 39	6 44	6 49	6 55	7 03
21	6 17	6 19	6 22	6 25	6 28	6 31	6 35	6 39	6 44	6 48	6 54	7 00	7 08	7 16
25	6 21	6 24	6 27	6 30	6 34	6 38	6 42	6 47	6 52	6 58	7 04	7 12	7 20	7 30
29	6 26	6 29	6 32	6 36	6 40	6 45	6 49	6 55	7 00	7 07	7 14	7 23	7 33	7 44
Nov. 2	6 30	6 34	6 38	6 42	6 46	6 51	6 57	7 02	7 09	7 16	7 25	7 34	7 45	7 59
6	6 35	6 39	6 43	6 48	6 52	6 58	7 04	7 10	7 17	7 26	7 35	7 46	7 58	8 13
10	6 39	6 44	6 48	6 53	6 59	7 04	7 11	7 18	7 26	7 35	7 45	7 57	8 11	8 28
14	6 44	6 49	6 54	6 59	7 05	7 11	7 18	7 26	7 34	7 44	7 55	8 08	8 24	8 43
18	6 48	6 53	6 59	7 04	7 11	7 17	7 25	7 33	7 43	7 53	8 05	8 20	8 37	8 58
22	6 53	6 58	7 04	7 10	7 16	7 24	7 32	7 40	7 50	8 02	8 15	8 31	8 49	9 14
26	6 57	7 03	7 09	7 15	7 22	7 30	7 38	7 47	7 58	8 10	8 24	8 41	9 02	9 29
30	7 02	7 07	7 13	7 20	7 27	7 35	7 44	7 54	8 05	8 18	8 33	8 51	9 13	9 43
Dec. 4	7 05	7 11	7 18	7 25	7 32	7 41	7 50	8 00	8 12	8 25	8 41	9 00	9 24	9 57
8	7 09	7 15	7 22	7 29	7 37	7 45	7 55	8 05	8 17	8 31	8 48	9 08	9 34	10 10
12	7 12	7 19	7 25	7 33	7 41	7 49	7 59	8 10	8 22	8 37	8 54	9 14	9 41	10 21
16	7 15	7 22	7 28	7 36	7 44	7 53	8 03	8 14	8 26	8 41	8 58	9 20	9 48	10 29
20	7 18	7 24	7 31	7 38	7 46	7 55	8 05	8 16	8 29	8 44	9 01	9 23	9 52	10 34
24	7 20	7 26	7 33	7 40	7 48	7 57	8 07	8 18	8 31	8 46	9 03	9 25	9 53	10 36
28	7 21	7 27	7 34	7 42	7 50	7 58	8 08	8 19	8 32	8 46	9 04	9 25	9 53	10 34
32	7 22	7 28	7 35	7 42	7 50	7 59	8 08	8 19	8 31	8 46	9 02	9 23	9 50	10 28
36	7 22	7 28	7 35	7 42	7 50	7 58	8 07	8 18	8 30	8 44	9 00	9 20	9 45	10 20

SUNSET

Lat.	+40°	+42°	+44°	+46°	+48°	+50°	+52°	+54°	+56°	+58°	+60°	+62°	+64°	+66°
	h m	h m	h m	h m	h m	h m	h m	h m	h m	h m	h m	h m	h m	h m
Oct. 1	17 43	17 42	17 41	17 40	17 40	17 39	17 38	17 37	17 35	17 34	17 33	17 31	17 29	17 27
5	17 36	17 35	17 34	17 33	17 31	17 30	17 28	17 27	17 25	17 23	17 21	17 18	17 15	17 12
9	17 30	17 28	17 27	17 25	17 23	17 22	17 19	17 17	17 15	17 12	17 09	17 05	17 02	16 57
13	17 24	17 22	17 20	17 18	17 16	17 13	17 11	17 08	17 05	17 01	16 57	16 53	16 48	16 42
17	17 18	17 16	17 13	17 11	17 08	17 05	17 02	16 58	16 55	16 50	16 46	16 40	16 34	16 27
21	17 12	17 09	17 07	17 04	17 01	16 57	16 53	16 49	16 45	16 40	16 34	16 28	16 20	16 12
25	17 07	17 04	17 00	16 57	16 53	16 50	16 45	16 41	16 35	16 30	16 23	16 16	16 07	15 57
29	17 01	16 58	16 55	16 51	16 47	16 42	16 37	16 32	16 26	16 20	16 12	16 04	15 54	15 42
Nov. 2	16 57	16 53	16 49	16 45	16 40	16 35	16 30	16 24	16 17	16 10	16 02	15 52	15 41	15 27
6	16 52	16 48	16 44	16 39	16 34	16 29	16 23	16 16	16 09	16 01	15 52	15 41	15 28	15 13
10	16 48	16 44	16 39	16 34	16 29	16 23	16 16	16 09	16 01	15 52	15 42	15 30	15 16	14 59
14	16 45	16 40	16 35	16 30	16 24	16 17	16 10	16 03	15 54	15 44	15 33	15 20	15 04	14 45
18	16 42	16 37	16 31	16 25	16 19	16 12	16 05	15 57	15 47	15 37	15 24	15 10	14 53	14 31
22	16 39	16 34	16 28	16 22	16 15	16 08	16 00	15 51	15 41	15 30	15 17	15 01	14 42	14 18
26	16 37	16 31	16 26	16 19	16 12	16 05	15 56	15 47	15 36	15 24	15 10	14 53	14 32	14 05
30	16 36	16 30	16 24	16 17	16 10	16 02	15 53	15 43	15 32	15 19	15 04	14 46	14 24	13 54
Dec. 4	16 35	16 29	16 22	16 15	16 08	16 00	15 50	15 40	15 29	15 15	14 59	14 40	14 16	13 43
8	16 35	16 28	16 22	16 15	16 07	15 58	15 49	15 38	15 26	15 12	14 56	14 36	14 10	13 34
12	16 35	16 29	16 22	16 15	16 07	15 58	15 48	15 37	15 25	15 11	14 54	14 33	14 06	13 27
16	16 36	16 30	16 23	16 15	16 07	15 59	15 49	15 38	15 25	15 10	14 53	14 32	14 04	13 22
20	16 37	16 31	16 24	16 17	16 09	16 00	15 50	15 39	15 26	15 11	14 54	14 32	14 04	13 21
24	16 40	16 33	16 26	16 19	16 11	16 02	15 52	15 41	15 28	15 14	14 56	14 34	14 06	13 24
28	16 42	16 36	16 29	16 22	16 14	16 05	15 55	15 44	15 32	15 17	15 00	14 38	14 11	13 30
32	16 45	16 39	16 32	16 25	16 17	16 09	15 59	15 48	15 36	15 22	15 05	14 44	14 18	13 39
36	16 49	16 43	16 36	16 29	16 21	16 13	16 04	15 53	15 41	15 27	15 11	14 51	14 26	13 51

Table 11.13 The Seven Great Lies

1. Don't go by that monitor.
2. Don't worry. We can fix it in post.
3. It'll only be a half day.
4. It's a simple shot. I know exactly what I want.
5. Work with me this time, and when we get one with a real budget . . .
6. It won't look that way on film.
7. I mailed the check this morning.

SECTION 12

Checklists

This section contains typical checklists of tools, expendables, and supplies for the camera, electrical, grip, and production departments. Tables 12.1 to 12.17 begin on the next page.

Table 12.1 Tools for the Director of Photography, Lighting Director and Gaffer

1. Incident meter
2. Spot meter
3. Color temperature meter
4. Gel books
5. HMI sync charts
6. 18% gray card
7. Gray scale
8. Color chart
9. Viewing filters
10. Compass
11. Flashlight
12. Sun charts or sun indicator

Table 12.2 Electrician's Tools

1. Cutting tool (mat knife, razor knife, etc.)
2. Wooden clothespins
3. Work gloves
4. Crescent wrench (6")
5. Flashlight
6. Volt-ohmmeter (both AC and DC)
7. Continuity tester
8. Amprobe (clip-on current tester)
9. Slotted screwdriver (shank wrapped with electrical tape)
10. Slip-joint pliers (6")
11. Gaffer's tape
12. Marking pens
13. Vise grips
14. Channel-lock pliers
15. Phillips screwdrivers (#1, #2)
16. Set of hex wrenches
17. Fuse puller
18. Heavy-duty cube taps
19. Current taps
20. Three-to-two's (grounded-to-ungrounded Edison adaptors)
21. Electrical tape (black)

(continued)

Table 12.2 Electrician's Tools *(continued)*

22. Colored plastic marking tape (red, blue, yellow, white, green)
23. Spare fuses (household, stage box, barrel fuses)
24. Heavy-duty staple gun and staples
25. Tape measure
26. Wire nuts
27. Zip cord

Table 12.3 Grip Tools

1. Cutting tool (mat knife, razor knife, etc.)
2. Hammer
3. Tape measure (25')
4. Slip-joint pliers (6")
5. Channel-lock pliers
6. Work gloves
7. Slotted screwdrivers (1/4", 3/16", 1/8")
8. Phillips screwdrivers (#1, #2)
9. Flashlight
10. Heavy-duty staple gun (T-50)
11. Portable drill and drywall screws (1", 1 1/2", 2 1/2")
12. Drill bits
13. Saw (a folding tree saw plus a circular saw for big jobs)
14. Bubble level
15. Torpedo level
16. 4' level
17. Crescent wrenches (6", 8")
18. Vise grips
19. Chain vise grips
20. Motorcycle straps (ratchet straps)
21. Set of socket wrenches
22. Set of hex wrenches
23. Small pry bar
24. S-hooks
25. Speed square
26. WD-40 or silicone spray

(continued)

Table 12.3 Grip Tools *(continued)*

27. Marking pens
28. Chalk for marking the floor
29. Squeegee and spray bottle for applying gel to windows
30. Bailing wire
31. Washers, including fender washers
32. Hack saw
33. Small c-clamps
34. Camera wedges
35. Chalk line
36. Side cutters (dykes)
37. Jig saw
38. Nails (#16, #8)
39. Sunglasses to watch cloud movements
40. 3/8"-16 bolts of various lengths (camera tie downs)
41. Baby power for dolly track
42. Automatic tape gun with transfer tape

Table 12.4 Camera Assistant's Tools

1. Cloth or fiberglass measuring tape (50')
2. Metal tape measure or folding carpenter's rule
3. Flashlight
4. Swiss army knife
5. Depth-of-field, footage, and hyperfocal distance charts or calculator
6. White china marker
7. Felt-tip marking pen (Sharpie Fine Point)
8. Dry-erase marker for slate
9. Powder puff to erase slate
10. Camera tape (1" white)
11. Exposed-film tape or red or black 1" camera tape
12. Colored marking tapes for focus marks on floor
13. White matte graphic arts tape (3/16") for calibrating lenses
14. Ultra-fine-point pens in several colors for focus marks on lens tape

(continued)

Table 12.4 Camera Assistant's Tools *(continued)*

15. Magnifier with light to examine film for scratches
16. Changing bag
17. Slate
18. Mini slate (insert slate)
19. Bulb blower brush
20. Lens tissue
21. Lens cleaning fluid
22. Scissors
23. Environmentally safe canned air
24. Orangewood sticks
25. Tweezers
26. Camel hair lens brush
27. Magazine cleaning brush
28. Forceps
29. Hirschman clamp
30. Set of jeweler's screwdrivers
31. Set of metric and English hex wrenches ($^{1}/_{32}$" to $^{3}/_{16}$")
32. Phillips screwdrivers (#1 and #2)
33. Slotted screwdrivers ($^{1}/_{4}$", $^{3}/_{16}$", and $^{1}/_{8}$")
34. Needle-nose pliers
35. Slip-joint pliers (6")
36. Crescent wrench (6")
37. Small vise grips
38. File
39. Tweezers
40. Wire strippers
41. Transfer tape (snot tape) for applying gels and diffusion to rear of lens
42. Space blanket to protect camera from sun / rain
43. Camera lubricants
44. Oil dropper or syringe
45. Bubble level
46. Camera wedges
47. $^{3}/_{8}$"-16 bolts of various lengths (camera tie downs)
48. Inspection mirrors
49. Two 1" c-clamps

(continued)

Table 12.4 Camera Assistant's Tools *(continued)*

50. Compass
51. Volt-ohmmeter
52. Camera reports
53. Five-pin-to-four-pin battery cable adaptor
54. Gray card (18%) and ten-step gray scale
55. Color reference chart (Macbeth, Kodak, etc.)
56. Focus chart
57. WD-40, CRC 5-56, CRC 2-26 or silicone spray
58. Circle template for cutting gels
59. Magazine brake for Mitchell magazines
60. Kitchen lid looseners for sticky filter rings
61. Large carabiner
62. Crocus cloth for cleaning contacts
63. Chamois for eyepiece
64. Small piece of black cloth and large rubber band to block eyepiece
65. Ballpoint pen
66. Soldering iron and solder

Table 12.5 Camera Assistant's Checkout

Lay out the cases for easy access and counting.
Check the invoice, the order, and the actual equipment to be sure that everything is present.

Camera Body, Motors, and Batteries
Mount camera on head.
Inspect interior for damage, film chips, etc.
Clear the mirror, and inspect the aperture, removing it from camera, if possible. Clean the aperture and replace.
Check operation of variable shutter, if available.
Attach battery or power supply; check all batteries and power cables.
Inch camera by hand.
Run motor; check speed and noise level.

Lenses
Inspect lenses for scratches.
Hold lenses up to light; operate aperture.

(continued)

Table 12.5 Camera Assistant's Checkout *(continued)*

Operate focus; check for smooth operation and slop.

Set diopter to your eye by adjusting for sharpest focus of ground glass.

Check lenses:

- Mount lens.
- Focus on a distant object. (For zoom, go to maximum zoom.)
- See if lens indicates infinity.
- Check if lens focuses past infinity.
- Go from minimum to maximum zoom; check whether lens tracks correctly.
- Check that zoom holds focus during zoom.
- Focus on test chart; compare measured distance to eye focus.
- If necessary, apply graphic arts tape to focus ring and mark lens again.
- If possible, shoot a film test of each lens at minimum, maximum, and midrange T-stops.

Magazine and Accessories

Put short roll of film in each magazine and run; check for scratches, oil spots, ripped perforations, emulsion buildup, etc.

Attach video tap, and check operation.

Test tripods and heads for smooth operation and positive locking.

Check spreader for smooth operation.

Attach matte box, follow focus, etc., and check operation.

Inspect all filters.

Review checklist for accessories: changing bag, slate, camera reports, etc.

Lock all cases, and if necessary, mark with colored tape for A and B cameras, first and second unit, etc.

Table 12.6 Camera Department Expendables

1. Film stock
2. Environmentally safe canned air (one can for every 2 days)
3. Camera tape (white, red, black, yellow))
4. Empty cans, bags, and cores (400', 1000')
5. Camera reports, film stock reports
6. Eyepiece covers (chamois)
7. Dry-erase markers for slate
8. Powder puff for erasing slate
9. Felt-tip markers
10. White china marker pencils
11. Lens tissue
12. Lens fluid

Table 12.7 Electrical Department Expendables

1. Clothespins
2. Gaffer's tape (white, gray, and black)
3. Matte black photo paper tape (1", 2")
4. J-Lar 2" clear tape
5. Black wrap or Cinefoil
6. Three-to-two electrical grounding adaptors
7. Heavy-duty cube taps
8. Bailing wire
9. Zip cord (18/2, 16/2)
10. Quick taps (clip-on male and female two-blade electrical connectors)
11. Streaks n' Tips (black, white, brown)
12. Practical bulbs.

Table 12.8 Grip Department Expendables

1. Show card (black and white)
2. Sash cord (#8, #10)
3. Two 4' x 8' bead board
4. Two 4' x 8' foam core (black on one side, white on the other)
5. Duvetyn (roll)
6. Bundle of battens
7. Two 2" x 12" x 14' clear planks (dolly boards)
8. Two 1" x 12" x 12' clear planks
9. Two 2" x 4" x 10' lumber
10. Two 4' x 8' x 3/4" birch plywood for dolly
11. Two 4' x 8' x 3/4" AC plywood
12. One 4' x 4' x 3/4" AC plywood
13. Grip chain
14. Shiny gold card
15. Matte gold card
16. Shiny silver card
17. Matte silver card
18. Trick line (#4 mason line)
19. Railroad chalk (yellow and white)
20. Armature wire (various sizes)
21. Hemp rope (3/4")
22. T-50 staples (5/16", 1/2", 9/16")
23. Drywall screws (3/4", 1", 1 1/4", 1 5/8", 2", 2 1/2", 3")
24. Nails (6D box nails, 8D box nails, 8D scaffold nails, 16D scaffold nails, 16D common nails)
25. Baby powder
26. WD-40, CRC 5-56, or silicone spray.
27. Transfer tape for automatic tape gun
28. 4' x 4' carpet
29. Gaffer's tape
30. Dulling spray
31. Hemp rope

Note: The amounts listed are standard orders. Some jobs may require more.

Table 12.9 Car Mount Equipment

1. Tilt plate (leveling camera mount)
2. Hostess tray and/or hood mount
3. Ratchet straps
4. Gutter clips
5. Ball level
6. Suction cups (Super Grips)
7. Assorted speed rail
8. Speed rail connectors (Kee Klamps)
9. Gaffer's tape
10. Black paper tape (1", 2")
11. Duvetyn for tenting and blacking out windows
12. S-hooks
13. Sash cord (#8, #10)
14. Nuts and bolts (3/8" x 16, assorted lengths)
15. Bailing wire
16. Grip chain
17. Washers (flat, lock and fender, to fit 3/8" bolt)
18. Grip arms (standard and short arm)
19. Grip heads
20. Mafer clamps
21. Pieces of rubber mat
22. Bungee cord
23. Mag clip

Table 12.10 Standard Gel Kit

1. White diffusion (216)
2. Opal Tough Frost
3. Hampshire Frost
4. Full 85
5. CTO (full, half, quarter, eighth)
6. CTB (full, half, third, quarter, eighth)
7. Minusgreen (full, half, quarter)
8. Plusgreen (full, half, quarter)
9. Plusgreen 50
10. Fluorofilter (rolls and 4' sleeves)
11. 1000H Velum
12. Tough spun
13. Half tough spun
14. Tracing paper
15. Neutral-density gel: 0.3, 0.6, 0.9

Note: This is a standard order in addition to the gaffer's order.

Table 12.11 Standard Prop Kit

1. Paper towels
2. Garbage bags
3. First-aid kit
4. Dulling spray
5. Double-sided tape
6. Black matte spray paint
7. White matte spray paint
8. Spray adhesive
9. Cyano-acrylate glue
10. Rubber cement
11. WD-40 or CRC 5-56
12. Aluminum foil
13. Extra ponchos or rain coats
14. Ice chest
15. Fire extinguishers
16. Director's chairs
17. Bullhorn
18. Walkie-talkies, extra batteries, and chargers
19. Clip-on scoop lights with 200-W bulbs
20. Household extension cords
21. Insect repellent (or Avon Skin-So-Soft™)
22. Window cleaner
23. Plexiglas™ cleaner
24. Brass cleaner
25. Portable iron and ironing board
26. Parking signs
27. Sign markers
28. Push broom
29. Kitchen broom
30. Garage broom
31. Road cones
32. Lawn rake
33. Garden rake
34. Pickax
35. Square-nose shovel
36. Round-nose shovel
37. Water hose
38. Plastic buckets
39. Sledgehammer
40. Hot-glue gun
41. Come-along (hand hoist)

(continued)

Table 12.11 Standard Prop Kit (continued)

42. Jumper cables
43. Rubber mat
44. Visqueen (heavy plastic in rolls)
45. Monofilament line
46. Hot Set tape
47. Roll of corrugated cardboard to protect walls and floors

Table 12.12 Assistant Director's Kit

1. Production checkbook
2. Production contact sheet
3. Purchase orders
4. Insurance forms
5. Time cards and W-4 forms
6. Talent contracts or releases
7. Expense envelopes
8. Expense vouchers
9. Production reports
10. Property releases
11. Phone books
12. Change for phones and parking meters
13. Maps, directions to location
14. Strip board or storyboard
15. Schedule
16. Script and the day's sides

Table 12.13 Camera Order List

Camera Magazines
200'
400'
1000'
Long throat

Lenses
Primes
Zooms
Other lenses

Film
Low-speed
High-speed
Retaining rings
Adaptor rings
Varicon
Front mirror
Half silver mirror
Low-angle prism

Macros
Innovision
Snorkle
Dyna lens
Stabilizer
Gyros

Filters
#85
81A
81B
81C
81D
81EF
80B Polarizer

Neutral-Density
ND 0.3
ND 0.6
ND 0.9
85 ND 0.3
85 ND 0.6
85 ND 0.9

Double Fogs
Full
Half DF
Quarter DF
Eighth DF

Low-Contrast
Half LC
Quarter LC
Eighth LC

Diffusion
Black
White
1/8
1/4
1/2
1
2
(regular/close ratio)

Other
Black net
Black dot
White net
Mitchell diffuser
Star filter
Fog #1
Fog #2
Proxar #1
Proxar #2
Proxar #3
Grads
Sepia
Corals
(light/regular/heavy)
Optical flat
Enhancer

Accessories
Motors
High-speed motor
Y-cable
Lens light
Barney
French flag
Exterior eye piece
Bridge plate
Follow focus
Follow focus extension
Follow focus handle
Matte box (6x6)
Matte box (4x4)

(continued)

Table 12.13 Camera Order List *(continued)*

Matte box (3x3)
Rods

Batteries
Belt battery
Power supply

Accessories
Speed control
Crystal control
Zoom control
Zoom motor
Shoulder pad
Hand grip
Sync check

Mounts
Geared head
Fluid head
Bridge plate
Geared wedge
Underslung head
Baby legs
Sawed-off legs
Standard legs
Spreader
Pearson rig
Crane
Car mount
Camera car
Remote head
Wheelchair
Skateboard

Video
Video tap
Monitor
3/4" deck"
VHS deck
Tapes
Watchman

Miscellaneous
Changing bag
Clapstick
Insert slate
Time-code slate
Gray scale
Color chart

Expendables
Cans
Bags
Dust-off
Camera tape
Red camera tape
Black camera tape
Dry-erase marker
Powder puff
Colored pens
China markers
Camera reports
Camera lube
Chamois
Eyepiece covers
Lens tissue
Stocking (black/white)
AA batteries
AAA batteries
C batteries
D batteries
Fine-point markers

Dollies
Z-bar
Ubangi
Riser
Leveling head
Seat extension
Side boards
Jib arm
Straight track
Short track
Curved track
Bogey wheels
Ramps
Dance floor
Doorway dolly
Western dolly
Briefcase dolly

Table 12.14 Lighting Order List

Arcs
carbons
rectifier
lubricants
dousing bucket
hats

HMIs
18K HMI
12K HMI
6K HMI
4K HMI
2.5K HMI
1.2K HMI
575K HMI
1.2K HMI PAR
2.5K HMI PAR
4K HMI PAR
(extra header cable for all HMIs)

Tungstens
10K big eye
Tenner
10K baby
5K studio
5K baby
2K
2K baby
1K
Baby-baby
Tweenie
Inkie
100-W Pepper
Skypans
  Bulbs
  Skirts
Mighties
Mickies
Totas
Lowel kit
Stick-ups
Gator light

Xenons
1K xenon
2K xenon
4K xenon
7K xenon
PAR narrow
PAR medium
PAR wide

Soft Lights
1K zip/eggcrate
2K zip/eggcrate
1K soft/eggcrate
2K soft/eggcrate
4K soft/eggcrate
8K soft/eggcrate
1K cone
2K cone

Clusters
Nine-light
  3200K or FAY bulbs
Five-light
  3200K or FAY bulbs
Maxi-brute
Wendy
Dino
Musco
Mini-Musco

Specialized Lights
Xenon sungun
Tungsten sungun
HMI sungun
Batteries
Space lights
Bay lights
Chicken coop

Lekos
4 x 5 leko
6 x 8 leko
6 x 12 leko
6 x 16 leko

(continued)

Table 12.14 Lighting Order List *(continued)*

6 × 22 leko
TMP adaptors
Three-pin > Hubble
Molelipso
Inky focal spot
1K focal spot
Super trooper
Pan Arri 1200 HMI 75' header

Fluorescents
Kino-flo
High-output fluorescent tubes
Fluorescent rigs
Tubes

Stands
Cinevator
Crankovator
Senior stand
Junior stand
Baby stand
Beefy baby stand
Triple riser baby
Reflector stand
Low rollers
High boys

Accessories
Frequency meter
Walkie-talkie w/mike
Empty hampers
Western dolly
Doorway dolly
Furniture dolly
Taco cart
Rubber mat
Tarpaulin
Visqueen

Distribution
#1 tricos, four-wire
#2 tricos, four-wire
#3 tricos, four-wire
4/0 bare wire tie-in
2/0 bare wire tie-in
#2 bare wire tie-in
#6 bare wire tie-in
100-amp 3-phase breaker
Anderson clamps
Stage boxes/spider boxes three- wire/four-wire
Combo boxes
301-1/2
Hollywood box
Three-fers
Camlok tees
Camlok siamese
Adaptors
#0000
#00
#2 (four-wire)
#1
#4
#6
Bull switch or deuce board
100-amp extension
60 amp extension
4-way > Hub
4-way short>Hub
4-way > SP
4-way short>SP
Singles (12/3)
Polish adaptor

Power Source
Generator (AC/DC) (crystal)
6500-W (crystal) w/fuel can
Car batteries
Inverter

Dimmers
750 variac

(continued)

Table 12.14 Lighting Order List *(continued)*

2K variac
5K dimmer
10K dimmer
6K dimmer
12K dimmer
Dimmer board
Dimmer pacs

Grip Equipment
2K riser
1k offset arm
2K offset
1K sidearm
2K sidearm
Mafers
1K pigeon
2K pigeon
Turtle
Suspension ceiling clamp
Time square clamp
Set claw
Bazooka
Crowder clamp
1K pipe clamps
2K pipe clamps
Comet boom

Diffusion
216
Opal
Tough spun
Half tough spun
Velum (1000H)
Tracing paper
Grid cloth
Soft frost
Hampshire frost
Bleached muslin
Unbleached muslin
Sailcloth
ND 0.3
ND 0.6
ND 0.9

Gels
85
CTO
Half CTO
Quarter CTO
Eighth CTO
CTB
Half blue
Third blue
Quarter blue
Eighth blue
Y-1
MT2
MTY
UV filter
Minusgreen
Half minusgreen
Quarter minusgreen
Plusgreen
Half plusgreen
Quarter plusgreen
Fluorofilter
Straw
Theatrical gel
Other gel
White Plexiglas
Black Plexiglas
3/8" glass
Mirror
Front mirror

Expendables
Clothespins
Gaffer's tape
2" photo black tape
1" photo black tape
Double-stick tape
3M #928 snot tape
#10 sash
#8 sash
Trick line
J-Lar tape

(continued)

Table 12.14 Lighting Order List *(continued)*

Bailing wire	15-amp male plug
Cinefoil	15-amp female plug
Streaks n' Tips	Inkie sockets
Dulling spray	**Practical Bulbs**
Matte silver card	ECT—500W
Shiny silver card	ECA—250W
Matte gold card	EBV—500W, 3400K
Shiny gold card	EAL—500W, 3200K
Black flock paper	BBA—250W, 3400K
Showcard	BCA—250W, 4800K
4 x 8 foam core	EBW—500W, 4800K
4 x 8 b/w foam core	R-40 reflector bulb
30 x 40 foam core	R-20 reflector bulb
Bead board	Household bulbs
Chinese lanterns	200-W
Porcelain sockets	150-W
Zip cord (18/2)	100-W
Zip cord (16/2)	75-W
Male quick taps	60-W
Female quick taps	25-W
Add-A-Taps	Candelabra bulbs
Three-to-two adaptors	Fairy lights
Cube taps	MR 16/TP-40

Table 12.15 Grip Order List

Stands	2K pigeon
C-stands	Turtle
Hi-hi c-stand	Bazooka
Mini c-stand	Comet boom
Extra arms	Putty knife/stud
Short arms/heads	**Rags**
High-boys	6 x 6 frame
Lo-boys	6 x 6 solid
Combo heads	6 x 6 single
Combo stands	6 x 6 double
2K offset arm	6 x 6 silk
1K offset arm	6 x 6 quarter silk
2K sidearm	6 x 6 griffolyn
1K sidearm	
1K pigeon	

(continued)

Table 12.15 Grip Order List *(continued)*

12 x 12 frame
12 x 12 solid
12 x 12 single
12 x 12 double
12 x 12 silk
12 x 12 quarter silk
12 x 12 griffolyn
20 x 20 frame
20 x 20 solid
20 x 20 single
20 x 20 double
20 x 20 silk
20 x 20 griffolyn
3–5' pole cat
5–9' pole cat
9–15' pole cat
2 x 4 wall spreader
2 x 6 wall spreader

Support
1 1/4" pipe
Cheesboro R.A.
Cheesboro swivel
Speedrail
Right-angle connector
In-line connector
Sandbags
Sound blankets
Rubber mat
Umbrella
Spring clip, small
Spring clip, large
Tarpaulin

Clips and clamps
Mafers
Mafer joiner
Mafer mount plate
Mafer gooseneck
Mafer gobo head
Crowder hanger
Set claw
1K pipe clamps
2K pipe clamps
Scissor clip
Flex arm
Gaffer grip
4" c-clamp
4" stud c-clamp
4" 2K c-clamp
6" c-clamp
6" stud c-clamp
6" 2K c-clamp
8" c-clamp
8" stud c-clamp
8" 2k c-clamp
12" bar clamp
18" bar clamp
24" bar clamp
36" bar clamp
Scaffold arm
Double header
Triple header
Trombone
Times Square clamp
Frisco pin
2K riser
1K grid clamps
2K grid clamp

Parallels
6' steel parallels
6' aluminum parallesl
Parallel tops
Stack pins
Casters
Jack riser
Hand rail
Safety braces
12 x 18 single
12 x 18 double
12 x 18 solid
12 x 18 silk
12 x 18 white bobbinet
12 x 18 quarter silk

(continued)

Table 12.15 Grip Order List *(continued)*

18 x 24 double
18 x 24 solid
18 x 24 silk
18 x 24 white bobbinet
18 x 24 quarter silk
24 x 30 single
24 x 30 double
24 x 30 solid
24 x 30 silk
24 x 30 white bobbinet
24 x 30 quarter silk
24 x 36 single
24 x 36 double
24 x 36 solid
24 x 36 silk
24 x 36 white bobbinet
24 x 36 quarter silk
30 x 36 single
30 x 36 double
30 x 36 solid
30 x 36 silk
30 x 36 white bobbinet
30 x 36 quarter silk
4 x 4 single
4 x 4 double
4 x 4 solid
4 x 4 silk
4 x 4 white bobbinet
4 x 4 quarter silk
18 x 48 solid
24 x 72 solid
25 x 48 solid
Dots and fingers
Cuckaloris

Frames
12 x 24 open frame
18 x 24 open frame
24 x 30 open frame
24 x 36 open frame
4 x 4 open frame
Reflector boards
Math boards

Dolly
10' track
5' track
3' track
Curved track
Ramp track
Offset arm
Head adaptor
Starter track
Z-bar
Ubangi plate
3" riser
6" riser
9" riser
15" riser
Bogey wheels
Jib arm
Seat extension

Sticks
Baby legs
Sawed-off legs
Standard legs
Spreaders

Heads
Geared head
Fluid head
Underslung head
Extension plate
Mitchell plate
Bridge plates
Geared wedge
Shoulder pad
Western dolly

(continued)

Table 12.15 Grip Order List *(continued)*

Doorway dolly
Tube dolly
Briefcase dolly
Taco cart
Car rig
Suction cup
Double suction cup
Molefan
Shovel
Broom
Come-along

Expendables
#8 sash
#10 sash
Trick line
Hemp rope
Pulleys
Block and fall
Gaffer's tape
Paper tape
Double-stick tape
4' x 8' foam core
4' x 8' b/w foam core
30" x 40" foam core
Bead board
Show cards
Seamless
Nails
Screws
Eye hooks
Bailing wire
Grip chain
Heavy chain
Wire rope
Sponge
Squeegee
ATG tape

Duvetyn (rolls)
Black bobbinet
White bobbinet
4' ladder
6' ladder
8' ladder
10' ladder
12' ladder
14' ladder
16' ladder
20' extension
30' extension
A-frame ladder
Scissor lift
Manlift
Crane

Apple box
Full box
Half apple box
Quarter apple box
Pancake
Step-ups
Wedges
Donuts

Lumber
4' x 8' plywood
Batten
2" x 4"
2" x 6"
2" x 10"
2" x 12"

Table 12.16 Location Scout Form

Date of Scout	For scenes:
Name of Location	
Interior	**Exterior**
Address	
Contact	
Phone	
Home phone	
FAX	
Owner	
Manager	
Superintendent	
Local police phone	Police required?
Local police contact	
Who opens the location? Has key?	
Sound problems	Permit required?
Floor condition	Permit from
Elevator	Town clerk
Freight elevator	Film office
Elevator hours	Film office contact
Operator cost	Community restrictions
Staging areas	
Seating areas	
Toilets	
Kitchen	
Heat or AC working?	
Extra lights needed?	
Travel Time	From:
Public transportation	
Highway restrictions	
Public phone	
Parking	

(continued)

Parking cost

Truck parking

Access

Loading Dock/Ramp

Address of freight entrance

Supervisor

Width and height of doors

Building dollies and ladders available?

Who has them?

Nearby Restaurants

Phones Number of seats

Hours Contact

Delivery?

Electricity in Building

Type of service

Amperage

Location

Distance

Locked?

Who has key?

House electrician

Phone

Other available power

Draw map with windows, doors, ramps, stairs, etc.

Layout of Area

Compass Directions

Draw directions and map on back

Table 12.17 Travel Checklist for Distant Locations

1. Passport
2. Driver's license
3. Visa, if necessary
4. Health documents
5. Credit cards
6. Cash
7. Spare keys
8. Poncho or raincoat
9. Flashlight
10. Watch
11. Swiss army knife
12. Marking pen
13. Writing pen
14. Notebook
15. Toothbrush, toothpaste, razors, etc.
16. Comb, mirror, lip balm, soap, etc.
17. Insect repellent (or Avon Skin-So-Soft™)
18. Disposable towelettes
19. Personal first-aid kit with aspirin, prescription drugs, skin cream, etc.
20. Motion-sickness medicine
21. Diarrhea medicine
22. Sewing kit
23. Transformer/AC adaptors for razors, etc.
24. Work gloves, safety glasses, earplugs, hats, etc.
25. Sunglasses
26. Sunscreen
27. Doorstop/camera wedge
28. Personal camera and film
29. Luggage cart
30. Small location bag or belt bag
31. Rain gear, wet weather boots
32. Pocket hand-warmer
33. Colored gaffer tape for marking items
34. Phrase book or foreign language dictionary
35. Business cards
36. Traveler's checks

(continued)

Table 12.17 Travel Checklist for Distant Locations *(continued)*

37.	Important phone numbers, address book, calendar, etc.
38.	Pocket compass
39.	Maps, guidebooks
40.	Luggage ID tags
41.	Travel alarm clock
42.	Personal laundry supplies

Index

Addendum to Table 1.1

35mm Cameras

Cinema Products CM35 (Feathercam)

Silent	No [?]
Shutter Angle (°)	180
Speed (fps)	24/25 crystal, 4-48 variable
Power (V)	24
Lens Mount	Interchangeble BNCR, Nikon, Arri PL, Arri B
Registration	2-pin.
Size of Magazine (ft.)	500
Weight (lb.)	10
Note	

Eclair Cameflex

Silent	No
Shutter Angle (°)	40-200
Speed (fps)	40 (max.)
Power (V)	6/8 DC, 12/24 DC
Lens Mount	CA-mount
Size of Magazine (ft.)	200, 400, 1000

Ultracam

Silent	Yes
Shutter Angle (°)	175
Speed (fps)	8, 12, 16, 18, 20, 24, 25, 30, 32
Power (V)	28
Lens Mount	SBNCR
Registration	2-pin
Size of Magazine (ft.)	500, 1000
Weight (lb.)	31
Note	Both standard 16mm and Super 16. Swingover reflex viewfinder operates from either side. Integral 80 bit timecode.

VistaVision 35

Silent	No [?]
Shutter Angle (°)	Variable from 55 to 172.8, stops at 108 and 144
Speed (fps)	5-72 crystal
Power (V)	24
Lens Mount	BNC
Registration	3-pin
Size of Magazine (ft.)	400, 1000
Weight (lb.)	
Note	Vistatavision 8-perf format format. Can use Arriflex matte box and front accessories.

Wilcam W-7 VistaVision Highspeed

Silent	[?]
Shutter Angle (°)	180
Speed (fps)	200
Power (V)	[?]
Lens Mount	BNCR
Registration	3 dual pins
Size of Magazine (ft.)	1000
Weight (lb.)	110
Note	8-perf VistaVision format

Wilcam W-9 VistaVision Highspeed

Silent	[?]
Shutter Angle (°)	180
Speed (fps)	Max 100
Power (V)	[?]
Lens Mount	BNCR
Registration	3 dual pins
Size of Magazine (ft.)	1000
Weight (lb.)	37
Note	

Wilcam W-11 VistaVision Sound Speed

Silent	Yes
Shutter Angle (°)	144
Speed (fps)	24, 25, 30 crystal
Power (V)	36
Lens Mount	BNCR
Registration	3 dual pins
Size of Magazine (ft.)	1000
Weight (lb.)	60
Note	8-perf VistaVision format

16mm Cameras

Arriflex SR II

Silent	Yes
Shutter Angle (°)	180 (Super 16 is 172.8)
Speed (fps)	24, 25, 30 crystal, 5–75 with speed control
Power (V)	12
Lens Mount	Arri B
Registration	Pin registered compensating link
Size of Magazine (ft.)	400
Weight (lb.)	11
Note	Both standard 16mm and Super 16 available. Swingover reflex viewfinder operates from either side.

Arriflex SR II Highspeed

Silent	Yes
Shutter Angle (°)	180 (Super 16 is 172.8)
Speed (fps)	24, 25, 30 crystal, 10–150 with speed control
Power (V)	12
Lens Mount	Arri B
Registration	Pin registered compensating link
Size of Magazine (ft.)	400
Weight (lb.)	11
Note	Both standard 16mm and Super 16 available. Swingover reflex viewfinder operates from either side.

Auricon

Silent	Yes
Shutter Angle (°)	175
Speed (fps)	24
Power (V)	115 AC
Lens Mount	C-mount
Size of Magazine (ft.)	100, 400, 600
Note	Sound on film; nonreflex

Mitchell 16 Pro, HS & HSC

Silent	No
Shutter Angle (°)	Pro 0-235, HS & HSC 0-140
Speed (fps)	48-128
Power (V)	24 DC and 110 AC motors available
Lens Mount	Mitchell, C-mount adapter available
Registration	Dual claw pull-down
Size of Magazine (ft.)	400, 1200
Weight (lb.)	
Note	SSR and DSR sound recording models available with speeds from 16 to 64 fps